THE NEW ANALECTS
CONFUCIUS
RECONSTRUCTED

A Modern Reader

THE NEW ANALECTS
CONFUCIUS
RECONSTRUCTED
A Modern Reader

COMPILED BY QIAN NING
TRANSLATED BY TONY BLISHEN

Better Link Press

Contents

PREFACE: Reconstructing a Classic   9

Chinese/English glossary of significant terms   19

INNER SECTION: The Sayings of Kongzi   21

CHAPTER 1 CORE   22
1. *Ren* as the core   22
    (1) What *Ren* is   22
    (2) What *Ren* is not   23
    (3) How *Ren* is achieved   24
    (4) The *Ren* of those that possess *Ren*   26
2. The forms of *Ren*   29
    (1) *Ren* starts with Filial Piety   29
    (2) Fraternal Piety as affection   32
    (3) Integrity is the norm   32
3. Transformation to Propriety   33
    (1) Propriety based upon *Ren*   33
    (2) The basis for governing the state   33
    (3) The relationship between rulers and their ministers   34
    (4) The nature of Propriety   35
    (5) The inheritance of Propriety   36

CHAPTER 2 PATHWAY   38
1. The path to *Ren*   38
    (1) Study   38
    (2) Self-cultivation   43
    (3) Fulfillment   49

2. The path of the Gentleman 52
   (1) Gentlemanly standards 52
   (2) Gentlemen and rogues 60

CHAPTER 3 PRACTICE 65
1. Ruling the nation through government 65
   (1) Governing with Humanity 65
   (2) The rule of Virtue 66
   (3) The nation built on Integrity 69
   (4) Strengthening the nation through teaching 70
   (5) Setting an example 72
   (6) Forthright advice to the ruler 73
   (7) Give priority to the correction of titles 74
   (8) Raise the upright and select the worthy 76
   (9) More haste less speed 77
   (10) Other 77
2. Personal conduct and conduct in society 79
   (1) Honor and Riches 79
   (2) Fame 81
   (3) On being a Scholar 83
   (4) On being an official 84
   (5) Respect for teachers 86
   (6) On friendship 87
   (7) Knowledge of people 90
   (8) Behaving with Integrity 93
   (9) Love of Virtue 95
   (10) Prudence in speech 97
   (11) Leisure 99

CHAPTER 4 CASES 101
1. Evaluation of disciples 101
   (1) Yan Yuan 101
   (2) Zilu 105
   (3) Zigong 109
   (4) Other disciples 111

2. On music and poetry   118
    (1) On poetry   119
    (2) On music   122
3. Analysis of cases   124
4. A discussion of the politics of the time   125
    (1) The rule of Ji Kangzi   125
    (2) The politics of the state of Lu   128
    (3) The decline of ceremony and music   131
    (4) The vassal states   132
    (5) Mocked by the hermits   137
5. Praise and Criticism   140
    (1) Contemporaries   140
    (2) Historical personages   146

CHAPTER 5   CONSIDERATION   154
1. The Mandate of Heaven   154
2. Demons and spirits   156
3. The Master speaks of himself   158
4. Time flows like water   161

OUTER SECTION: The Remarks of the Disciples   163

CHAPTER 6 EVALUATION   164
1. During life   164
2. After death   164
3. Doctrine   166

CHAPTER 7 REMINISCENCE   168
1. Geniality   168
2. Behavior and bearing   168
    (1) At court   168
    (2) In the country   170
3. Food, dress, housing and travel   171
    (1) Dress   171

(2) Food   172

(3) Housing   173

(4) Travel   174

4. Teaching by example in word and action   174

5. The twists and turns of life   175

CHAPTER 8 EXPOSITION   177

1. Principal ideas   177

(1) Filial and Fraternal Piety   177

(2) Propriety   178

2. Study and self-cultivation   179

(1) Study   179

(2) Self-cultivation   180

3. The Gentleman and the man of principle   182

(1) Gentleman   182

(2) The man of principle   183

4. Politics and government   184

5. The path of friendship   186

6. The disciples   186

7. The mirror of history   189

Compiler's Postscript   193

Translator's Postscript   194

Analects Original Text   196

Index of Personalities   267

PREFACE
RECONSTRUCTING A CLASSIC

I. The Achilles heel of Confucianism

Confucius (551 – 479 BC, hereafter referred to by his Chinese name of Kongzi) symbolises oriental civilisation and represents the peak of traditional Chinese thought and culture. He is, perhaps, the most famous Chinese of all and his reputation a household word. For all his fame however, the *Analects*, the Confucian classic which best embody his thinking, baffle the Chinese reader. The contents of the 20 sections (*pian*) of the *Analects* are out of order, their arrangement is unsystematic and sentences are scattered haphazardly within sections. Were it not for the arduous sorting and scrupulous interpretation of generations of commentators, where could we now find so much of its profundity of utterance and meaning?

As western scholars reverently study the *Analects*, what they read is merely a disordered collection of moralistic exhortations, urging people to be "good." The exhortations smack of mediocrity and the phraseology is incoherent. On this point, those two great incisive German philosophers Kant and Hegel were representative. Kant did not believe that Kongzi was a philosopher and regarded the *Analects* as "mere moral dogma drawn up for the emperor" (*Physical Geography*); Hegel held a similarly low view of Kongzi and believed him to be just "a man with a certain amount of practical and worldly wisdom," his theories were a kind of "moral philosophy" without "a trace of analytical thought, just a few virtuous and oft repeated moral lectures" (*Lectures on the History of Philosophy*). All in all, therefore, western scholars have been left with two impressions of the *Analects*, that they lack profundity and that they are illogical[1].

Why should this be so? Here, the Achilles heel of Confucianism is visible—the reason that the most important Confucian canon, the *Analects*, are such a mess is because that they are in no sense a mature work but an unsorted collection of lecture notes.

II. The Analects: *An unsorted collection of lecture notes*

There are two levels of meaning within the statement that the *Analects* are an unsorted collection of lecture notes. First, that the *Analects* were not personally compiled and revised by Kongzi and secondly that the *Analects* as we know them now have been assembled from various lecture notes made by different disciples of Kongzi at different times.

To take the first meaning. A characteristic of the teaching technique of Kongzi was to "describe but not inscribe" (*shu er bu zuo*) in other words, not to write anything down. That he wrote nothing down did not mean that he did not formulate his theories. Everything that he taught, as well as the normal questions and answers with his disciples, was carefully noted down by the disciples themselves for transmission to later generations. There should have been an opportunity to revise and correct his disciples' notes since in his old age he corrected the *Shijing* (*Classic of Poetry*) and the *Shangshu* (*Book of Documents*)

---

[1] The views of Hegel and Kant were probably based upon the 17th century translations into latin. Later western scholars with direct access to texts in Chinese may have taken a different view.

and edited the *Chunqiu* (*Spring and Autumn Annals*). Why was it that he failed to carry out a final revision of his own work? The fact that he did not must be due to some occurrence that prevented him from doing so. One may conjecture that it was possibly due to the early death of his favorite disciple Yan Yuan, the one with the deepest understanding of his teachings and upon whom he placed all his hopes for the transmission of his doctrines. Unfortunately, Yan Yuan's early death changed everything. He had not the time to arrange his lecture notes so that Kongzi could look them over and most importantly of all there was none amongst all the other disciples who matched him in his understanding of the subtlety and profundity of his master's teachings. Kongzi was already 70 years of age and the blow was considerable, in his grief it would have been difficult to find the strength to arrange and correct his discourses by himself. The pain and anguish in Kongzi's grief-struck cry on the death of Yan Yuan "Heaven has bereaved me! Heaven has bereaved me!" is something that no outsider can appreciate.

To take the second meaning. The *Analects* as we know them now are a combination of the lecture notes taken by a great number of disciples at different times. Yan Yuan's early death prevented the transmission of a "standard edition" of the *Analects* corrected by Kongzi himself. In order to pass on his thinking, later generations of the Confucian school compiled the notes taken by the disciples at different times and on different occasions into the edition of the *Analects* that we have now. Obviously, this compilation lacked deep thought and has caused some confusion of arrangement within the *Analects* themselves. There are the records of early disciples and the recollections of later disciples; remarks by Kongzi are mixed up with the speech of disciples as in the first section known as "To study section" (Xue Er) which contains 16 sayings, seven of which are actually the remarks of disciples; in the "Zizhang (a disciple) section," the principal characters in the question and answer sessions are a later generation of disciples such as Zizhang himself, Zixia, and Ziyou. In addition there are phrases such as "Honeyed words and fine appearance" (*qiao yan ling se*) and "The Gentleman is broad in his study of the cultivated" (*bo xue yu wen*) which are repeated in different sections and constitute evidence of less than careful editing.

There were two main routes for the transmission of the *Analects*: by word of mouth from teacher to pupil and through texts discovered hidden in the walls of the Kong family residence. Following the burning of the books, including the category that contained the *Analects*, by the first emperor Qin Shihuang (259 – 210 BC) the text was on the point of extinction. By the Han dynasty only two orally transmitted copies, known respectively as the *Lu Analects* and the *Qi Analects*, survived, one in the state of Lu and the other in the state of Qi. Subsequently Zhang Yu, imperial tutor to the emperor Han Cheng (51 – 7 BC) combined them into one volume called the *Analects of Marquis Zhang* (*Zhang hou lun*). However, during the reign of the emperor Han Jing (188 – 141 BC) a cache of pre-Qin texts was miraculously discovered hidden by the family in the perimeter wall of the Kong residence. The cache included a copy of the *Analects*, subsequently known as the *Analects in Ancient Form* (*gu lun yu*). These *Analects* consisted of 21 sections and are said to have differed in their ordering compared with the Lu and Qi texts and to have "differed by more than 640 characters in the text" (Huan Tan, 23 – 50, *New Discourses*). Unfortunately the *Analects in Ancient Form* did not survive and the *Analects* that we read today are actually those edited by Zhang Yu in the first century BC. Although various versions of the *Analects* often differ in sections and text they are similar in basic content. This suggests that the contents of the *Analects*, as a record of the lecture notes of the disciples of Kongzi, are reliable.

After the Western Han dynasty the *Analects* became a classic which no one dared alter or abridge. Whether or not the text was coherent or the meaning consistent it was only possible to write commentaries and to seek truth from the inner meaning of the text. The internal logic and profundity of thinking of the *Analects* was submerged beneath the oceans of post-Han commentary.

III. *Deconstructing the* Analects

Since Kongzi himself did not edit his *Analects*, why can we not re-edit them today? For two thousand years nobody has dared, or even dared to think of doing so, but why not?

In this context "re-editing" is not the tidying up of sections, the checking of words and phrases or the interpretation of doctrine but deconstruction, taking all the sections of the *Analects* to pieces, rebuilding them and using the process of deconstruction to discover a new internal significance.

The *Analects* require deconstructing: a systematic dismantling followed by a reconstruction that displays the text's original sense, significance and logic.

The current text of the *Analects* is like a ball of hemp and it is difficult to work out where the main thread starts. Nevertheless, the *Analects* are not without a thread and the thread that has to be found first within that ball of hemp is *Ren* (仁)—Humanity.

Ren lies at the core of the teaching of Kongzi and is the starting point for the logic of his thinking. In the *Analects*, all that he strives for is to explain and expound to his disciples the inner meaning of *Ren*, the form in which it appears, the shape that it takes, the path by which it is sought, the way in which it is practiced, its practical examples and the heavenly mandate that decrees that "All beneath Heaven conforms to *Ren.*"

Astonishingly, once the *Analects* are reconstructed in this way, they take on a completely new appearance without the addition or subtraction of a single character.

IV. The new-look Analects

What do the new-look *Analects* look like?

First, the *Analects* are now divided into "inner" and "outer" sections. The inner section consists of what Kongzi himself said and the outer of what his disciples said. Thus the inner section only contains those passages beginning "The Master said…." What the disciples said, together with other accounts are relegated to the outer section.

The inner section has five chapters entitled Core, Pathway, Practice, Cases and Consideration.

The Core chapter seeks to establish what *Ren* is and is not, starting from the basis of its definition. What is its inner meaning? How can it be achieved? Thereafter it discusses the different forms *Ren* takes within different social relationships— Filial Piety, Fraternal Piety and Integrity as well as its transmuted outward manifestation—Propriety, as it becomes the rule that regulates social intercourse. Finally, from the many kinds of humane conduct it seeks to demonstrate all the different qualities of *Ren*.

The Pathway chapter describes three routes to the attainment of *Ren*—study, cultivation and practice. The humane (*Ren*) man is the superior man or Gentleman and the chapter points out the path that a Gentleman should follow in speech and behavior. The man that lacks Humanity is the Lesser man or rogue and the chapter describes the criteria that distinguish the Gentleman from the Lesser man.

The chapter on Practice discusses the practical implementation of *Ren* in the fields of government and society. It considers, first, how *Ren* should be incorporated in government and sets out an overall scheme of measures for rule—humane government, the rule of Virtue, the nation built on Fidelity, strengthening the nation through teaching as well as right speech, correct nomenclature and the selection of worth. It goes on to discuss the role of *Ren* in social relationships, and how to deal with riches, prestige and celebrity. It covers the conduct of life, the making of friends, knowledge of people as well as love of Virtue, care in speech and solitary living.

Using the case study method and on the basis of the conversations of the disciples and analysis of cases, the Cases chapter discusses practical government and the quality of individuals and examines history so as to expose the deeper layers of *Ren* in order to encourage the disciples towards a more concrete and deeper comprehension of the quality of *Ren*.

The Consideration chapter examines *Ren* in detail in the context of the "Mandate of Heaven" and discusses the philosophical topics of gods and demons, life and death and time. *Ren* has its roots in human nature and is in accord with heavenly law, and "nature and heavenly law" is one of the profoundest components of Confucianism.

The three chapters of the outer section are Evaluation, Reminiscence, and Exposition.

Evaluation: This consists of evaluations of Kongzi by his contemporaries and the defenses of his lofty image mounted by his disciples after his death as well as descriptions of their understanding of his profound thought.

Reminiscence: The disciples' memories of Kongzi, including the way he appeared and talked, his behavior and living habits and the way he taught.

Exposition: The further development by the disciples of

some of the major theories of Kongzi, such as Filial and Fraternal Piety, self-cultivation, the role of the Gentleman, government and friendship.

Without the loss or addition of a single character the reconstructed *Analects* display an appearance that is utterly different from that of the past—the arguments are fresh, the themes coherent, the ideas clearly differentiated and the exposition lucid. This is the first time that both the logic and profundity of Confucian theory has sprung so directly from the text.

V. Make the Analects *a new classic that everybody can understand*

The aim of reconstructing the *Analects* is to make them a logical and profound new classic that is intelligible to all, from East or West, without the need for elaborate notes.

In point of fact, the schemata of Kongzi's thinking is perfectly clear: *Ren* is "love of mankind"—treating others well. In a society where relationships differ from person to person, *Ren* takes different forms and manifests itself as Filial Piety, the Fraternal Piety and Integrity. *Ren* can be transmuted outwardly into Propriety and cause interpersonal relations to be governed by etiquette. Nevertheless, *Ren* has its source in the heart and is inherent in man's original nature. If an individual aspires to reach the state of *Ren*, the path lies through study, self-cultivation and practice. Those that achieve *Ren* are then "Gentlemen" and those that do not are "Lesser men." In practice Kongzi further elucidates, by way of concrete example, how the humane should rule, how they should conduct themselves in society and how they should deal with some of life's problems.

The final reflections of Kongzi concerned the relationship

between *Ren* and the "heavenly law." *Ren* is implemented in this world through the efforts of man but it is even more the Mandate of Heaven.

Kongzi amply describes his theories of *Ren* in the field of political ethics and demonstrates a deep knowledge of human nature but his views on the relationship between *Ren* and the heavenly law are fragmentary and undeveloped. The disciple Zigong once said: "What the Master wrote may be read and assimilated but what he said of human nature and the heavenly law may not be read or assimilated" (Gongye Chang section). He also frequently lamented "Not to reach the level of the Master, that is because there are no stairs to heaven" (Zizhang section). Intelligent as Zigong was he lacked understanding of Kongzi's thinking in his old age. Even less was it the case with the other disciples. Yan Yuan was probably the only one at the time who did understand. His sense and understanding of Kongzi's theories was clearly unusual. He said of Kongzi's teaching "As you gaze up, its height is vast, it is impenetrable, it seems in front but is suddenly behind" (Zihan section). There are places of mystery both in its height and in its depth. It is clear that in his consideration of *Ren* in his later years, Kongzi did not just stop at political ethics but ascended the heights of philosophical analysis. It is a matter of real regret for the *Analects* that because of the early death of Yan Yuan it was impossible to make a detailed record of the aged Kongzi's thinking on human nature and the heavenly law, and that it was even less possible to pass it on. The Kongzi that we see in the *Analects* today resembles a mountain range from whose cloud covered peaks flashes flicker through the mist.

2,500 years ago when Kongzi and his disciples were travelling in the state of Wei, they passed through a small town called Yi. The guardian official of the town insisted on meeting Kongzi and said to the disciples afterwards: "Why are you so disheartened? The world has lacked principle for a long time but your master will be a bell that calls to the people of the world." This nameless guardian was indeed prophetic. In the more than 2,000 years that have ensued Kongzi and his doctrines have been first neglected and abandoned and his works later burned and prohibited, but in the end he gradually achieved understanding and acceptance and eventually veneration and admiration.

Today, 2,500 years later, we seem to have seen the wheel of history turn full circle. Kongzi was abandoned and neglected once more when the May the 4th New Culture movement of 1919 dethroned him and the storms of the Cultural Revolution of 1966 again saw his works burned and prohibited. Today there is now a gradual understanding and acceptance and perhaps Kongzi may once more be a spiritual force that calls to the world.

Kongzi once said: "Can my teaching be implemented? That is a matter of fate; can my teaching be abandoned? That is a matter of fate." (Xian Wen section) Behind the rise and fall of an ideology stand the demands of a specific era. Whether or not fate determines that they should rise or fall, or mankind flourishes or is destroyed the teachings of Kongzi contain some of the most basic demands of human nature and it is these demands that will make the teachings of Kongzi eternal.

20 Nov 2011

CHINESE/ENGLISH GLOSSARY OF SIGNIFICANT TERMS

In classical Chinese, the language of the time of Kongzi, words were not used quite so loosely or profusely as they are in modern English. They were too precious to be wasted. In addition, there is a certain hierarchy of meaning amongst words which are used to represent qualities and concepts such as virtue and integrity, to name but two. To the modern English reader these words are on much the same level. In classical Chinese they were not. They had very specific meanings and a philosophical ranking of their own, particularly in the *Analects* where *Dao*, the Grand principle, stands at the top followed by Humanity (*Ren*) with its subsidiary manifestations, Filial piety (*Xiao*), Fraternal piety (*Ti*), Integrity (*Xin*) and so on.

These terms are set out below. When they occur in the text they are capitalised in order to help the reader embrace the particular philosophical logic of the *Analects*.

仁 *Ren* Humanity
恕 *Shu* Thoughtfulness
忠 *Zhong* Loyalty
孝 *Xiao* Filial Piety
悌 *Ti* Fraternal Piety
信 *Xin* Integrity
礼 *Li* Propriety, with its derivative manifestations rite or ceremony (according to context)
德 *De* Virtue
义 *Yi* Righteousness
圣 *Sheng* A state of sageness approaching divinity

道 *Dao* Grand Principle
天命 *Tianming* Mandate of Heaven
君子 *Junzi* Gentleman
小人 *Xiaoren* Lesser man or rogue
士 *Shi* Scholar
大同 *Datong* Great Community

INNER SECTION:
THE SAYINGS OF KONGZI

CHAPTER 1 CORE

1. *Ren* as the core

The Chinese character *Ren* (仁, Humanity) is a combined ideogram that comprises the components for "man" and "two," hence "two people," that is, the relationship between one person and another.

Ren is at the core of the exposition of the theories of the *Analects* which include its definition and meaning and the way in which the concrete demands of *Ren* may be met.

(1) What *Ren* is

1.1 Fan Chi asked about *Ren*. The Master said: "Love others." (Yan Yuan 22)
Comment This is the most precise and accurate summary of *Ren* that Kongzi made. The essence of *Ren* lies in the relationship of one person with another, that is, to treat others well and, in your heart, to regard them as friends.

1.2 The Master said: "Oh Zeng Can! My thinking has one essential, which is consistent throughout." Zeng Can replied: "True." The Master left and the disciples asked: "What did he say?" Zeng Can said: "The Master said his thinking has one essential which consists of Loyalty (*Zhong*, 忠) and Thoughtfulness (*Shu*,恕). That is all." (Li Ren 15)
Comment This is a developed interpretation of *Ren* by Kongzi. *Ren* is at the core of his thinking and its sense is Loyalty and Thoughtfulness.

1.3 The Master said: "Can one love and not feel concern? Can one be Loyal and yet not admonish?" (Xian Wen 7)

Comment From love springs anxiety and concern; and from concern springs sincerity and the ability to speak straightforwardly.

1.4 Zigong asked: "Is there a single word which may be acted upon throughout life?" The Master replied: "It is Thoughtfulness! Do not do to others that which you would not wish done to you." (Duke Ling of Wei 24)

Comment This is Kongzi's best explanation of *Shu*. In general, Loyalty is a quality that one demands of oneself but *Shu* is more an attitude that one adopts towards others.

(2) What *Ren* is not

1.5 The Master said: "Honeyed words and a fine appearance, where is the *Ren* in that!" (Xue Er 3)

Comment There is naturally no *Ren* in something that is not genuinely heartfelt.

1.6 The Master said: "Honeyed words and a fine appearance, where is the *Ren* in that!" (Yang Huo 17)

Comment This saying appears twice in the *Analects*, and demonstrates that Kongzi definitely said it and possibly that he said it several times on different occasions.

1.7 "Aggression, boasting, hatred and desire, were they not to exist would that then be *Ren?*" The Master said: "That would be difficult, whether it would be *Ren*, I do not know." (Xian Wen 1)

Comment This is a question from the disciple Yuan Xian. Aggression, boasting, hatred and desire are all defects of human nature, but Kongzi did not believe that if they were overcome, a state of *Ren* had been attained. *Ren* must not only restrain the evil in men's hearts but must, even more, develop the virtue in human nature.

(3) How *Ren* is achieved

1.8 The Master said: "Is *Ren* distant? If I desire it, it is there." (Shu Er 30)

Comment *Ren*, which springs from the heart and is deeply rooted in the original nature of mankind, is an instinctive human requirement. *Ren* is manifested by self and like self-cultivation relies on the strength of the inner spirit for achievement.

1.9 Yan Yuan asked about *Ren*. The Master said: "To control oneself and act with Propriety, that is *Ren*. Once self is controlled and Propriety is practiced then, all beneath heaven returns to *Ren*. *Ren* is of the self, how can it be obtained from others?" Yan Yuan said: "May I enquire as to its contents?" The Master said: "Do not look at that which is improper, do not listen to that which is improper, do not speak of that which is improper and do not act improperly." Yan Yuan said: "Though I am dull I shall act as you say!" (Yan Yuan 1)

Comment Here, Kongzi points out the basic requirements for the achievement of *Ren*, that it should spring from the heart and overcome the ever-expanding desires within us. He also points out that this is the fundamental path towards the world-wide realization of *Ren*. At the same time, Kongzi relates *Ren* to the concept of Propriety, giving *Ren* a concrete external form.

1.10 Zhonggong asked about *Ren*. The Master said: "Go forth as if to meet a great guest, cause people to conduct themselves as if they were preparing a great sacrifice. Do not do to others that which you would not wish done to you. Have no hatred at court, have no hatred at home." Zhonggong said: "Though I am dull I shall act as you say!" (Yan Yuan 2)

Comment What is described here is the inner meaning of *Ren*—Loyalty and Thoughtfulness. In dealing with people one should give them the respect that is due to a guest and be as careful as one would be in the handling of serious matters, this is Loyalty. "Do not do to others that which you would not wish done to you" and "Have no hatred" describe Thoughtfulness. To implement Loyalty and Thoughtfulness is to attain *Ren*.

1.11 Fan Chi asked about *Ren*. The Master said: "Honor at home, respect in affairs, Loyalty to others, even amongst barbarians, this is not to be abandoned." (Zilu 19)

Comment Fan Chi seems to have liked asking questions and asked about *Ren* a number of times. Kongzi's reply describes Loyalty and emphasizes the universal values of *Ren* beyond the borders of the state.

1.12 Zigong asked about putting *Ren* into practice. The Master said: "To do good work the craftsman must first sharpen his tools. Living within the state, work with the virtuous amongst its officials, befriend those Scholars who possess *Ren*." (Duke Ling of Wei 10)

Comment Kongzi means that to attain *Ren* one must first practice it, and that if one intends to practice it one must associate with those who possess it.

1.13 Zizhang asked Kongzi about *Ren*. Kongzi said: "To practice these five beneath heaven, that is *Ren*." Zizhang enquired and the Master said: "Respect, magnanimity, Integrity, diligence, and compassion. Respect brings no insult, magnanimity secures support, Integrity brings appointment, diligence brings speedy achievement and compassion bestows the ability to lead others." (Yang Huo 6)

Comment Kongzi has concretized the explanation of *Ren*: Of the five qualities, respect and Integrity fall within the scope of Loyalty, and magnanimity and compassion within the scope of Thoughtfulness. Diligence in this passage and the need to avoid bluster in the passage below are also the requirements of a Gentleman.

1.14 The Master said: "Strength, resolve, simplicity, and plainness of speech all approach *Ren*." (Zilu 27)

Comment These are all qualities of *Ren*. Kongzi's emphasis on plainness of speech complements his antipathy towards "Honeyed words and a fine appearance."

(4) The *Ren* of those that possess *Ren*

1.15 The Master said: "Only those that possess *Ren* can love others or hate others." (Li Ren 3)

Comment *Ren* distinguishes between love and hate, not only is there "love" there is also "hate." But who is to be hated? Of course, it is those who do not practice *Ren*.

1.16 The Master said: "If one puts one's will into *Ren* there can be no evil." (Li Ren 4)

Comment There is both good and evil in human nature and with it the ability to do good and to do evil. To practice

Ren is to cultivate good and suppress evil.

1.17 The Master said: "Those that know are not baffled, those that possess *Ren* are not anxious and those that have courage are not frightened." (Zihan 29)

Comment How can those that possess *Ren* be without anxiety? It is because *Ren* is a state of joy and fulfillment.

1.18 The Master said: "The virtuous must exercise speech but those that talk do not necessarily exercise Virtue. Those that possess *Ren* must possess courage; but the courageous do not necessarily possess *Ren*." (Xian Wen 4)

Comment Virtue is to speech as *Ren* is to courage, the former contains the latter but the latter does not necessarily contain the former. Virtue is greater than speech and *Ren* greater than courage.

1.19 The Master said: "Scholars of will and those that possess *Ren* do not seek life at the expense of *Ren* but sacrifice themselves for the sake of *Ren*." (Duke Ling of Wei 9)

Comment Those that possess *Ren* regard it as greater than their own lives.

1.20 (Fan Chi) asked about *Ren*. Kongzi said: "*Ren* is to be at the forefront of difficulty but at the rear of advantage, that may be spoken of as *Ren*." (Yong Ye 22)

Comment In *Ren*, Loyalty and Thoughtfulness may be manifested as "others first, self last," the difficult kept to oneself and the good allowed to others.

1.21 Sima Niu asked about *Ren*. The Master said: "*Ren* is to be slow to speak." Sima Niu then said: "To be slow to speak may be called *Ren*?" The Master said: "It is difficult to accomplish, but can speech be without caution?" (Yan Yuan 3)

Comment Kongzi clearly did not like the bombastic. Prudent speech is always emphasized as one of the qualities of those that possess *Ren*.

1.22 The Master said: "Those that do not possess *Ren* cannot exist long in poverty nor can they exist long in joy. Those that possess *Ren* are content in it and the wise benefit from it." (Li Ren 2)

Comment The reason that those who possess *Ren* remain content in poverty and are not engrossed by joy is that by its nature *Ren* makes people both wise and happy.

1.23 Zigong said: "Were one to bestow benefit upon the people so as to help all, how would that be? Might it be called *Ren*?" The Master said: "That would be more than *Ren*, it would be divine! Yao and Shun feared they were defective in this respect! *Ren* is to wish to stand oneself yet to help others to stand as well, to wish to attain oneself yet to help others attain as well. To come close to an understanding of others may be called the way of *Ren*." (Yong Ye 30)

Comment This discusses the relationship and distinctions between *Ren* and *Sheng* (the state of sageness approaching divinity). *Ren* is a state attained through study and *Sheng* is the successful implementation of *Ren* amongst the people and throughout society. In his old age Kongzi lamented of his life: "As to *Ren* and *Sheng*, how can I take credit?" (Shu Er section) He may have been modest in not regarding himself as possessed of *Ren* but it may be true that he did not attain *Sheng*.

2. The forms of *Ren*

Ren takes different forms in different types of social relationships: With parents it is Filial Piety, between brothers it is Fraternal Piety and with others it is Integrity. Filial Piety is the basis since the relationship between parents and children, established at birth, is the most basic social relationship of all.

(1) *Ren* starts with Filial Piety

(Filial Piety as the basis)

1.24 Zai Wo asked: "Three years mourning is a long time! If a Gentleman does not perform ceremonies for three years, the ceremonies will collapse; if he does not practice music for three years, music will be abandoned. For the old grain to be exhausted and the new grain to reach market and for the fire-drill to need replacing a year is enough." The Master said: "Would you be easy in your mind eating new rice and wearing brocade?" Zai Wo said: "I would." The Master said: "That being so, then do it! When the Gentleman observes mourning he eats but tastes nothing, takes no joy in music, lives in leisure but feels no comfort and so does not do as you would. Since you now feel as you do, then do it!" Zai Wo withdrew. The Master said: "Zai Wo is without *Ren!* A child does not leave the embrace of its mother and father until the age of three. Three years of mourning is observed everywhere. Did not Zai Wo receive three years of love from his mother and father?" (Yang Huo 21)

Comment Filial Piety is one of mankind's most basic feelings, essentially it is a repayment of the love received from a parent. The "love for others" of *Ren* starts with the love between parents and children.

1.25 Meng Yizi asked about Filial Piety. The Master said: "Do not violate Propriety." Fan Chi was once driving Kongzi and Kongzi told him: "Meng Yizi once asked me about Filial Piety and I told him: 'Do not violate Propriety.'" Fan Chi said: "What does that mean?" The Master said: "While they are alive serve one's parents with Propriety; after they are dead bury them with Propriety and sacrifice to them with Propriety." (Wei Zheng 5)

Comment Kongzi explains Filial Piety as "Do not violate Propriety" and emphasizes the demands of Propriety. In fact, there is a sense of "respect" here as well.

(While parents are alive)

1.26 Ziyou asked about Filial Piety. The Master said: "What is called Filial Piety today is just the keeping of parents. Dogs and horses are kept, and if there is no respect, where lies the difference?" (Wei Zheng 7)

Comment Filial Piety is based on *Ren*; viewed as a kind of "love for others" it would be more accurate to describe it as "loving respect."

1.27 Zixia asked about Filial Piety. The Master said: "It is not easy to always maintain a smiling countenance towards one's mother and father. Can just helping with their affairs and letting them eat first be regarded as Filial Piety?" (Wei Zheng 8)

Comment Without the qualities of love and respect, care and maintenance cannot be true Filial Piety.

1.28 The Master said: "Serving one's parents resembles offering humble advice. When they are unwilling, maintain respect and do not disobey, feel anxiety but do not hate." (Li Ren 18)

Comment Discussing Filial Piety is easy in principle but difficult in practice. This quotation forms part of life's wisdom and discusses what to do when encountering a concrete problem, rather like the guides to "How children should advise parents."

1.29 Meng Wubo asked about Filial Piety. The Master said: "Feel anxiety for the sickness of parents." (Wei Zheng 6)
Comment Filial Piety is concern for parents, most importantly concern for their health. Some traditional commentaries have interpreted this quotation as meaning that filial children should not allow their parents to worry about the illness of their children, which seems inappropriate.

1.30 The Master said: "One must know the age of parents, both for joy and for dread." (Li Ren 21)

1.31 The Master said: "Do not travel far while parents live, should you travel let your whereabouts be known." (Li Ren 19)
Comment Not to cause parents anxiety is to show concern at a psychological level. It also constitutes Filial Piety.

(After the death of parents)
1.32 The Master said: "While the father lives observe the son's aspirations; when the father is dead observe his conduct. If, after three years, he continues to follow in his father's footsteps, that is Filial Piety." (Xue Er 11)
Comment That the son should take on the aspirations of the father is a kind of Filial Piety. What Kongzi says here is very probably aimed at the families of the nobility and officials who used the concept of Filial Piety to make a

judgment on whether or not the son who was to succeed them had the necessary wisdom.

1.33 The Master said: "If, after three years, a son continues to follow in his father's footsteps, that is Filial Piety." (Li Ren 20)
Comment This sentence appears twice in the *Analects*.

(2) Fraternal Piety as affection

1.34 The Master said: "The young observe Filial Piety at home and Fraternal Piety outside, possessed of Integrity and caution in speech, they become close to *Ren* through universal love. If there is effort to spare they use it to acquire wisdom." (Xue Er 6)
Comment Filial Piety is love of parents and Fraternal Piety is the affection between elder and younger brothers. To pursue the analogy it is "All within the four seas are brothers." (Yan Yuan 5) The path to *Ren* starts with Filial Piety and runs through Fraternal Piety and from thence to universal love.

(3) Integrity is the norm

1.35 The Master said: "I do not know how it is possible to be a person and yet lack Integrity! If the shafts of carriages and carts lack joints how can they run?" (Wei Zheng 22)
Comment In society, and in the relationship between one person and another "sincerity" is a particular quality displayed by *Ren*. Sincerity is the norm upon which people should be treated.

3. Transformation to Propriety

The transformation of *Ren* into Propriety is a basic principle of government and the "contract" that exists between a ruler and his ministers. It is embodied in rites and ceremonies and forms the norm that governs the different relationships within society.

(1) Propriety based upon *Ren*

1.36 The Master said: "If man is without *Ren* what then of ceremony? If man is without *Ren* what then of music?" (Ba Yi 3)

Comment *Ren* is the foundation of ceremony and music. It is the core, and ceremony and music are its external forms. Without it, ceremony and music lose their intrinsic significance.

(2) The basis for governing the state

1.37 The Master said: "Is it possible to use Propriety to govern the state with principle? Where is the difficulty in that? If Propriety cannot be used to govern the state with principle, how can one speak of the application of Propriety?" (Li Ren 13)

Comment To govern through Propriety is to govern with *Ren*.

1.38 The Master said: "Respect without Propriety is to no avail, caution without Propriety is timidity, boldness without Propriety is sharpness of tongue. If the ruler is careful to bestow affection then the people will glory in *Ren*. If old friends are not abandoned then the people will not be heartless." (Taibo 2)

Comment Merely to aspire to *Ren* but without the constraint of Propriety makes good governance difficult. However, when a state is governed with Propriety, *Ren* arises of itself.

1.39 The Master said: "If those above take pleasure in Propriety then the people may be led with ease." (Xian Wen 41)

Comment On the one hand, governing the state through Propriety makes demands of those who govern, on the other its purpose is to render the people more easily controlled.

1.40 Zigong wished to abandon the practice of presenting a lamb for sacrifice on the 1st of each month. The Master said: "Give it! You may pity the lamb but I treasure the ceremony." (Ba Yi 17)

Comment What Kongzi and Zigong are discussing here is not the fate of a lamb or the survival or abolition of a particular rite of sacrifice but the major significance of ceremony to the state.

(3) The relationship between rulers and their ministers

1.41 Duke Ding of Lu asked: "How may rulers use their ministers and ministers serve their rulers?" The Master replied: "Rulers employ their ministers with Propriety and ministers serve their rulers with Loyalty." (Ba Yi 19)

Comment Under the monarchical political system, the first problem encountered in government is that of the relationship between ruler and minister. Propriety acts as a form of restraint on both parties and in reality is a kind of contract.

1.42 The Master said: "To serve a ruler to the utmost with Propriety, some may regard that as flattery." (Ba Yi 18)

Comment Propriety is the test which determines whether it is flattery or not.

(4) The nature of Propriety

1.43 Lin Fang asked about the basis of Propriety. The Master said: "That is a significant question! So far as ceremony is concerned frugality is better than extravagance; so far as funeral arrangements are concerned true grief is better than elaborate obsequies." (Ba Yi 4)

Comment Propriety is an external manifestation the internal nature of which is *Ren*—love of mankind. External show and the gradations of etiquette are not the basis of Propriety, true feeling of the heart is more important.

1.44 The Master said: "Extravagance shows a lack respect, frugality is simplicity. I would rather simplicity than lack of respect." (Shu Er 36)

Comment Propriety is concerned with a person's internal attitude, not with external form.

1.45 The Master said: "To wear a ceremonial hat made from hemp is in accordance with Propriety. Now, they are all made from silk and are simpler, I follow the many. Ministers once knelt in the lower hall to make obeisance, that is in accordance with Propriety. Now they make obeisance in the upper hall, that is overbearing. I do not follow the many and still kneel in the lower hall." (Zihan 3)

Comment Kongzi realized that the system of ceremonies changed and developed with the times, but one can see from his choices what it was in Propriety that he considered important.

(5) The inheritance of Propriety

1.46 The Master said: "The Zhou dynasty inherited the systems of two previous dynasties, such a proliferation of documents! I follow the Zhou." (Ba Yi 14)

Comment The Zhou dynasty was the ideal society to which Kongzi aspired. In Kongzi's view the perfection of the Zhou lay in its rich systems of ceremony and music which fully exemplified the concept of *Ren*.

1.47 Zizhang asked: "Can one know ten dynasties hence?" The Master said: "The Yin dynasty succeeded to the ceremonial system of the Xia dynasty and its losses and gains may be known; the Zhou dynasty succeeded to the systems of the Yin and its losses and gains may be known. That which succeeds to the Zhou, though it may be 100 generations hence, is also to be known." (Wei Zheng 23)

Comment Kongzi knew that the system of ceremonies would move with the times but he clearly did not consider that there could be any basic change to human nature.

1.48 The Master said: "I can speak of the ceremonies of the Xia dynasty but not of those of the state of Qi for lack of evidence; I can speak of the ceremonies of the Yin dynasty but not of those of the state of Song for lack of evidence. This is because of the lack of documents. Were they adequate, then I could provide the evidence." (Ba Yi 9)

Comment Kongzi displayed considerable confidence in his own knowledge of historical systems of ceremony. In fact, this is one of the skills that the Confucian school displayed in looking after itself. The fact that Kongzi had a profound knowledge of the essential meaning of ceremony that was beyond the ordinary is also important.

1.49 Kongzi visited the Temple of Ancestors and asked about everything. Somebody said: "Who says that this son of somebody from Zou knows Propriety? He visited the Temple of Ancestors and had to ask about everything." The Master heard and said: "That is Propriety." (Ba Yi 15)
Comment Kongzi's enthusiasm for Propriety is almost crazy and has the specialist's thirst for detail.

1.50 Kongzi visited the Temple of Ancestors and asked about everything. (Xiang Dang 21)
Comment The same as the first sentence of the previous quotation. Another example of a remark having been recorded twice.

CHAPTER 2 PATHWAY

1. The path to *Ren*

There are three paths that the individual aspirant to *Ren* takes: study, self-cultivation and practice. Study for the attainment of knowledge; self-cultivation for the nurture of character; practice is to experience enlightenment in the reality of life itself. The three paths have but one aim, to reach the realm of *Ren*.

(1) Study

(The aim of study)

2.1 The Master said: "If I hear of the Grand Principal at dawn, I will willingly die at dusk." (Li Ren 8)

Comment One studies to acquire knowledge in order to comprehend the Grand Principle that stands behind knowledge. Heaven has its principle. Man has its principle, which is *Ren*. The ultimate aim of study is the comprehension of *Ren*.

2.2 The Master said: "At fifteen I had the will to learn, at thirty I stood upon my own feet, at forty nothing disconcerted me, at fifty I knew the will of heaven, at sixty I was open to argument and at seventy whatever I desired was within bounds." (Wei Zheng 4)

Comment Kongzi is discussing the different stages that he and everybody else experiences throughout a lifetime of study. Study, or the knowledge that is studied, is in itself a process of the "comprehension of the Grand Principle." What then, after that? It is the realm of "whatever I desired was within bounds."

2.3 The Master said: "Given a few more years, I would study the *Book of Changes* from the age of fifty and would be without great fault." (Shu Er 17)

Comment One studies the *Book of Changes* to know the will of heaven and also to be "without fault."

(The pleasures of study)

2.4 The Master said: "To study and to put into practice is not that also a pleasure? When friends come from afar is that not also a joy? Not to feel resentment when misunderstood is not that the act of a Gentleman?" (Xue Er 1)

Comment This is the opening quotation of the *Analects*, it discusses the joys of study and the pleasures of a Gentleman. Whatever the circumstances, a Gentleman has his own pleasures. There is pleasure in study, and in friendship there is the pleasure that friends bring with them; and even when ignored a Gentleman cannot be robbed of his joy.

2.5 The Master said: "To like it is better than to know it, to take pleasure in it is better than to like it." (Yong Ye 20)

Comment Study should be a pleasure. In every situation, those who study the best are those who obtain the most pleasure from it.

(The need for study)

2.6 The Master said: "Those who understand from birth are at the top; those who understand after study are next; those who study out of perplexity follow; those who are perplexed but do not study are, like many of the people, at the bottom." (Jishi 9)

Comment Kongzi believed that people differed in

intellectual ability and that study was the only path to the improvement of intellect. "Those who understand from birth" belong to the category of genius and are very few in number, with most people the distinction is between those who study and those who do not.

2.7 The Master said: "I am not one of those who understood all from birth. I like the past and seek out the knowledgeable." (Shu Er 20)
Comment Unlike those prophets who liked to proclaim that they had received the "divine word," Kongzi did not describe himself as a genius. He counted himself amongst those who "liked to study," a point that he made many times.

2.8 The Master said: "In any village of ten families there is bound to be someone with my qualities of Loyalty and Integrity but not with my love of study." (Gongye Chang 28)
Comment This quotation seems to be a continuation of the previous one. Kongzi believed that apart from his love of study, he had no other outstanding attributes.

2.9 The Master said: "In the past I have not eaten all day and not slept all night, my thoughts in turmoil, all to no advantage, it would have been better to study." (Duke Ling of Wei 31)
Comment The majority of people do not "understand from birth" and can only "understand after study," consequently it is better to use the time spent in wild speculation to study hard.

2.10 The Master said: "There are those who knowing nothing yet can create, I am not one of them. Enquire widely, choose the best and follow it. Observe widely and note it. This is wisdom of the second order." (Shu Er 28)

Comment Kongzi believed that he was one of those who "understood after study" and that the crux of learning was wide enquiry and broad observation.

(Methods of study)

2.11 The Master said: "Zilu! Let me teach you about knowledge. Knowing is knowing and not knowing is not knowing, that is knowledge." (Wei Zheng 17)

Comment True understanding is to know, after study, what you know and what you do not know. The normal interpretation of this quotation, that it sets out the attitude of honesty that should be adopted towards study, is not necessarily comprehensive. One studies in order to perceive the boundary that lies between the "known" and the "unknown," that is true wisdom. This is true of the individual and true of mankind.

2.12 The Master said: "Revise the old to know the new and become a master." (Wei Zheng 11)

Comment This applies to the acquisition of knowledge and to the study of history.

2.13 The Master said: "Study without thought is futile, thought without study is dubious." (Wei Zheng 15)

Comment "Study" is to realize "*Ren*." "Without thought" is naturally to study without getting anywhere; while "without study" is obviously senseless.

2.14 The Master said: "Do not explain before they struggle to understand, do not enlighten until they struggle for words. Do not persevere with those who cannot deduce four corners from the existence of one." (Shu Er 8)

Comment This is about the techniques of teaching. For all that Kongzi believed in "education without discrimination," it seems that he could not endure stupid students.

2.15 The Master said: "Do I possess knowledge? I do not. If a rustic seeks my help, I am empty of knowledge, but I can infer the middle from the ends." (Zihan 8)

Comment "Establishing the center of a problem from its ends" was Kongzi's method of study and his doctrinal methodology. True understanding only comes from exploring a concept or object from more than one angle. This is true when Kongzi discusses Loyalty and Thoughtfulness or describes Gentlemen and rogues.

2.16 The Master said: "In study fear not to achieve and fear to lose." (Taibo 17)

Comment The attitude of mind to be adopted towards study.

2.17 The Master said: "I can still see the words that are missing from the histories. Like a man who has lent his horse to somebody who has ridden it off. The words existed originally but are now lost." (Duke Ling of Wei 26)

Comment There are many differing interpretations of the significance of this quotation and historically it has been difficult to achieve logical consistency. This new explanation may serve for the time being.

2.18 The Master said: "Strike down heterodoxy, make it harmless." (Wei Zheng 16)

Comment Historically speaking, Kongzi held firmly to a

belief in absolute truth and was no advocate of "diversity," consequently, in his eyes, there could be nothing better than attacking heterodoxy.

2.19 The Master said: "In the past they studied for themselves, now they study to look good in the eyes of others." (Xian Wen 24)

Comment Study is for self-improvement and not for self-display. The alienation of learning seems to have existed since ancient times.

2.20 The Master said: "Zilu, have you heard of the Six Words and Six Ill Consequences?" "No." "Sit and I will tell you: to love *Ren* but not study has the ill consequence of stupidity; to love knowledge but not learning has the ill consequence of lack of restraint; to love Integrity but not study has the ill consequence of confusion; to love frankness but not study has the ill consequence of injurious speech; to love courage but not study, has the ill consequence of disorder; to love strength but not study has the ill consequence of wild arrogance." (Yang Huo 8)

Comment Study is the necessary route to the achievement of *Ren*. Despite aspiring to *Ren* unwillingness to study brings with it a whole body's worth of ills.

(2) Self-cultivation

(Self-cultivation to achieve *Ren*)

2.21 The Master said: "I have not met those who love *Ren* nor those who hate those who are without *Ren*. Naturally, there are none better than those who love *Ren;* those who hate the absence of *Ren* have *Ren* of themselves and that prevents those without *Ren* imposing upon them. Will there come a day when effort may be devoted to *Ren*? I have not met those who lack this effort. Such people may exist, but I have not met them." (Li Ren 6)

Comment Although *Ren* has its origin in the heart, it does not grow naturally and requires nurture. This is the significance of self-cultivation.

2.22 The Master said: "Meet the worthy and emulate them, meet the unworthy and examine oneself." (Li Ren 17)

Comment Learning from the example of others is one of the methods of self-cultivation. There are good examples and bad examples, when one comes to learn one must distinguish between the routes of emulation and self examination.

2.23 The Master said: "Where there are three together, one must be my teacher. Choose that which has virtue and follow it and improve on that which lacks virtue." (Shu Er 22)

Comment When there is no good example to hand, there is always a bad model. Evil or defective people have a role to play in self-cultivation, this is an important view of Kongzi's.

(Correction of fault)

2.24 The Master said: "Failure to correct a fault is in itself a fault." (Duke Ling of Wei 30)

Comment Another means of self-cultivation is the correction of fault. As Kongzi saw it, man was not a sage, was certainly imperfect and was not only filled with defects but was continuously in error. So that the process of self-cultivation was also a continuous process of error correction. A fault that may be corrected is not a fault.

2.25 The Master said: "The faults of man differ from group to group. Through the examination of fault one may know whether there is *Ren* or not." (Li Ren 7)

Comment In society man is not an isolated individual but an individual who lives in complicated collective relationships. The mistakes of a single person are also often the mistakes of a group. Individual "correction of error" sometimes has an impact on the collective and is no easy matter.

2.26 The Master said: "What I fear is that Virtue may not be nurtured, that learning may not be pursued, that Righteousness may not be sought out and that evil may not be corrected." (Shu Er 3)

Comment Man has many faults but the four above are probably the major ones, the most crucial is, of course, "that evil may not be corrected."

2.27 The Master said: "The people of the past had three defects, today they are different. In the past madness was merely wild, now it is licentious; in the past the proud were merely aloof now they are arrogant; in the past a fool was merely stupid, now he is crafty." (Yang Huo 16)

Comment The faults of man move with the times and become worse and worse. Extrapolating on this basis, mankind's aspiration to *Ren* is a task that will become more and more difficult.

2.28 The Master said: "I do not understand how there can be people who are arrogant and not upright, ignorant and dishonest, and loquacious and untrustworthy." (Taibo 16)

Comment These are common faults which were present

in the past and proliferate in the present. From this we can see the difficulty of correcting faults.

2.29 The Master said: "Can one fail to accept advice that conforms with principle? But it is the proper correction of fault that is to be valued. Can one not be happy at respectful praise? But it is examination that is to be valued. To be happy without examination, to accept advice but not to correct faults properly, there is nothing that I can do with this kind of person!" (Zihan 24)

Comment Outwardly, it is easy to accept criticism, but in reality it is very difficult to mend one's ways. In the same way, it is easy to listen to praise but difficult to distinguish the truth from the falsehood.

2.30 The Master said: "Enough! I have never met anybody who, having seen his own faults, could then conduct self-examination." (Gongye Chang 27)

Comment It is difficult for someone to recognize their own faults, it is even more difficult to admit to them and to be willing to conduct self-criticism; to genuinely correct those faults after self-criticism is to pile difficulty upon difficulty.

2.31 The Master said: "There are very few who, having once been restrained by Propriety, continue in error!" (Li Ren 23)

Comment For those who wish to cease making mistakes or to make fewer mistakes, probably the only solution is to subject oneself to the "restraints of Propriety."

(Strengthen morality and clarify confusion)
2.32 Fan Chi was walking with the Master on the platform of

sacrifices for rain and said: "Dare I ask about strengthening morality, eliminating evil and clarifying confusion?" The Master said: "Excellent! Only to ask for reward after having performed the task, is that not to strengthen morality? To criticize one's own bad habits but not the faults of others, is that not to eliminate evil? In a moment of anger to forget one's safety and to involve one's relatives, is that not confusion?" (Yan Yuan 21)

Comment These three questions could be said to constitute the major content of self-cultivation. To undertake self-cultivation is to aspire to *Ren* and to attain Loyalty and Thoughtfulness. Strengthening morality is Loyalty, eliminating evil is Thoughtfulness and clarifying confusion is the nurture of the "wisdom" that prevents a rash act.

2.33 Zizhang asked about strengthening morality and clarifying confusion. The Master said: "Emphasize Loyalty and Integrity and follow Righteousness, that is how to strengthen morality. When you like someone you wish them to live, when you grow to dislike them, you wish them dead. So that you wish them both dead and alive, that is what confusion is! As the poem says: 'It is not to seek riches and honor but because of a change of heart!' " (Yan Yuan 10)

Comment It is important to maintain one's direction during self-cultivation and to avoid the influence of temptations, misgivings and emotions, otherwise it is easy to fall into an ocean of perplexity from which it is difficult to extricate oneself.

(Perseverance)

2.34 The Master said: "I am unlikely to meet a person of virtue, but were I to meet a person of perseverance, that would be enough. Those who have not but pretend they have; those who are empty but pretend they are full, those who are poor but pretend they are rich; it is difficult for these people to persevere!" (Shu Er 26)

Comment It is difficult for the vain to persevere. One of the virtues that self-cultivation seeks to promote is that of perseverance. A sentence that discussed sages and gentlemen originally preceded this quotation. This has been inserted elsewhere.

2.35 The Master said: "For example, when a mountain of earth lacks but the last basketful and is stopped; it is I that have stopped it! For example, on level ground, when the first basketful has been spread but spreading continues; it is I that have continued!" (Zihan 19)

Comment Whether or not self-cultivation is finally successful, depends, as with everything else, upon whether you can keep going to the end.

2.36 The Master said: "The commander of an army may be removed but you may not alter the will of the ordinary man." (Zihan 26)

Comment A person's will may sometimes be in contention with an emperor or a regime.

2.37 The Master said: "When cold winter comes it is then that you know that the pine and cypress are the last to wither." (Zihan 28)

Comment Only at the last do you know who it is that will truly hold out. Even if you do hold out to the last success is not guaranteed and the conclusion may still be that it withers.

(3) Fulfillment

2.38 The Master said: "Who can leave except through the door? Why not follow this path?" (Yong Ye 17)
Comment This is an example of fulfillment. Fulfillment is to experience and appreciate *Ren* in the practice of life. Nobody can leave a room other than through the door. This is the only route, over the threshold and outside lies the "Grand Principle."

2.39 Zizhang asked about the behavior of people of virtue. The Master said: "They no longer follow in the footsteps of others but have not entered the chamber!" (Xian Jin 20)
Comment This is one of the passages in the *Analects* that is comparatively difficult to explain. A person of virtue should really be "the complete person"—a perfect person, almost a "sage." The virtuous person's comprehension of *Ren* is self-conscious, he has no need to study with others but does not resemble the higher level of the sage. Kongzi explains here with the aid of an example from life.

2.40 The Master said: "Aspire to the Grand Principle, stand on Virtue, abide by *Ren*, take pleasure in the arts." (Shu Er 6)
Note The six Confucian arts are ceremony (rites), music, archery, chariot driving, calligraphy and mathematics.
Comment Life as a whole, whether it be in day to day living or in study, is all part of the process of the attainment of *Ren*.

2.41 The Master said: "The wise delight in water and those with *Ren* love mountains; the wise are active and those with *Ren* are calm. The wise are happy and those with *Ren* live long." (Yong Ye 23)

Comment *Ren* is all-embracing and ever-present even in mountains and amongst water, you just have to see whether you can experience it for yourself.

2.42 Yan Yuan and Zilu were in attendance upon the Master. The Master said: "Why not tell me your aspirations?" Zilu said: "Not to regret the loss of the horse and carriage and fur robes that I have enjoyed with my friends." Yan Yuan said: "Not to boast of my good works or to declare my achievements." Zilu asked the Master: "May we hear your aspirations?" The Master said: "To bring peace of mind to the old, trust to friends and care to the young." (Gongye Chang 26)

Comment It is the understanding of *Ren* that is being discussed here. Zilu is thinking of the sharing of pleasure, Yan Yuan is thinking of modesty but Kongzi is thinking of universal calm and order.

2.43 Zilu, Zeng Xi, Ran You and Gongxi Hua were sitting in attendance. The Master said: "I am older than you but do not let that prevent you from speaking. You often say 'Nobody understands me!' If people understood you, what would you then do?"

Zilu was the first to answer and said: "A nation of 1,000 chariots caught between other large states is subjected to military pressure and there is famine. Were I to deal with it, within three years I would make its people effective in warfare and understand custom." The Master smiled.

The Master then asked: "Ran You, what would you do?" Ran You replied: "Were I to govern an area of a circumference of 60 or 70, or 50 or 60 *li*, within three years there would be food and warmth for the people and as to ceremony and music, that would need to wait upon a ruler."

The Master then asked: "Gongxi Hua, what would you do?" Gongxi Hua replied: "I dare not say what I would do but I would study a little more. When there were sacrifices in the temples or ceremonies of oaths of alliance taken by vassal princes, I would be willing to wear ceremonial robes and hat and be a minor master of ceremonies." The Master then asked: "Zeng Xi, what would you do?" Zeng Xi was playing the harp and was slowing to the end of a piece, he put down the harp with a "clang" and said: "My views are not the same as those of the other three!" The Master said: "What does that matter? Each must have his own say!" Zeng Xi said: "On a spring evening in the third month, I would dress in new spring clothes and then with five or six adults and six or seven children bathe in the Yi river, take the breeze on the platform of sacrifices for rain and then return home singing." Kongzi sighed and said: "I think the same as Zeng Xi!"

Zilu, Ran You and Gongxi Hua withdrew first and Zeng Xi asked Kongzi: "What did you think of the answers of those three?" The Master said: "Each described their own aspirations." Zeng Xi said: "In that case why did you laugh at Zilu?" The Master said: "A nation should be governed with Propriety, but when he spoke it was with a total lack of modesty, that is why I laughed." Zeng Xi again asked: "Then what Ran You said, was that the way to govern a state?" The Master said "How can an area of a circumference of 60 or 70, or 50 or 60 *li* not be considered a state?" Zeng Xi further asked: "Then what Gongxi Hua asked, is that the way to govern a state?" The Master said: "If sacrifices at the Temple of Ancestors and oaths of alliance taken by vassal princes are not the concerns of a ruler, then what are they? If people like Gongxi Hua can be a minor master of ceremonies, then who can take the post of principal master of ceremonies?" (Xian Jin 26)

Comment The description of individual aspirations was also a description of individual understandings of *Ren*. Zilu discussed strengthening military power, while Ran You spoke of making the state wealthy and Gongxi Hua discussed ceremony and music. In Kongzi's eyes all this was merely a means. The ultimate ideal of *Ren* was to achieve the return of mankind to a natural state of joy—like the spring evening outing described by Zeng Xi or, over two thousand years later like the German philosopher Martin Heidegger's use of the description of life in a verse from one of Freidrich Hölderlin's poems "Yet, poetically, man dwells on this earth"—the highest realm of the universal "Great Community."

2. The path of the Gentleman

A Gentleman may be defined as a person with *Ren;* the person without *Ren* is the Lesser man or rogue. The Gentleman has his own unique rules of conduct just as a rogue has his own brand of behavior.

(1) Gentlemanly standards

(*Ren* in the heart)

2.44 The master said: "Are there Gentlemen without *Ren*? Amongst rogues, I have never seen any who possessed *Ren*." (Xian Wen 6)

Comment The distinction between gentlemen and rogues lies in whether or not they have *Ren* in their hearts.

2.45 The Master said: "There are three aspects to the path of a

Gentleman but I have not mastered them: those with *Ren* are not anxious, the wise are not confused and the brave do not fear." Zigong said: "The Master speaks of his own path!" (Xian Wen 28)

Comment Kongzi made similar statements many times. The Gentleman possesses *Ren*, but he must also possess wisdom and courage.

2.46 Sima Niu asked what a Gentleman was. The Master said: "The Gentleman is neither anxious nor fearful." Sima Niu said: "To be without anxiety and without fear, is that to be called a Gentleman?" The Master said: "When self-reflection finds no guilt what is there to be fearful or anxious about?" (Yan Yuan 4)

Comment Someone who has no guilty conscience and is therefore neither anxious nor fearful approaches *Ren* and becomes a Gentleman.

2.47 The Master said: "The Gentleman strives to achieve the Grand Principle and not for food. In plowing there is hunger; in study there is salary. The Gentleman's concerns are for the Grand Principle and not for poverty." (Duke Ling of Wei 32)

Comment The Gentleman's single-minded concentration upon the achievement of *Ren* to the exclusion of all else, is naturally fine, but the official career as the sole means of making a living is the weak point of traditional Confucians. The origin of the lack of a sense of political independence in Chinese intellectuals lies here.

2.48 Zilu asked how to be a Gentleman. The Master said: "Cultivate oneself and act with a sense of respect." Zilu said: "Is that enough?" The Master said: "If one cultivates

THE NEW ANALECTS: CONFUCIUS RECONSTRUCTED

oneself it can bring peace and happiness to others." Zilu said: "Is that enough?" The Master said: "Cultivating oneself can also make the people peaceful and happy. Yao and Shun were defective in bringing peace and happiness to the people through self-cultivation." (Xian Wen 42)

Comment From "self-cultivation" to "bringing peace" and from thence to "bringing peace to the people" equates to the journey from *Ren* to *Sheng* (a state of sageness approaching divinity) and from Gentleman to Sage.

2.49 The Master said: "I shall never see a Sage, but it is enough to be able to see a Gentleman." (Shu Er 26)

Comment In Kongzi's eyes, a man could become a Gentleman through his own efforts, but moving from *Ren* to *Sheng* and instituting government through *Ren* everywhere, was a matter for a Sage and required the Mandate of Heaven.

(Wide study brings knowledge of Propriety)

2.50 The Master said: "The Gentleman reads and studies widely, acts within the constraints of Propriety and thus does not stray from the path of correct principle." (Yong Ye 27)

Comment Wide learning is an essential prerequisite for being a Gentleman, as is an understanding of Propriety. In essence, the purpose of both wide learning and an understanding of Propriety is to achieve *Ren*.

2.51 The Master said: "The Gentleman reads and studies widely, acts within the constraints of Propriety and thus does not stray from the path of correct principle." (Yan Yuan 15)

Comment This quotation appears in the *Analects* twice in almost the same wording.

2.52 The Master said: "The Gentleman does not gorge himself, does not seek comfort in his dwelling, works hard, guards his speech and corrects himself through the company of the virtuous. This may be called learning well." (Xue Er 14)

Comment So called "learning well" is a willingness to learn from the virtuous.

2.53 The Master said: "When simplicity exceeds grace it leads to roughness; when elegance exceeds simplicity it leads to empty bombast. When both simplicity and elegance are complementary, that is what makes a Gentleman." (Yong Ye 18)

Comment "Elegant simplicity" is in fact a kind of temperament, a temperament formed through "achieving Propriety through learning." "Learning" has its own inner meaning, and people become cultured through the achievement of Propriety.

2.54 The Master said: "The Gentleman takes Righteousness for his character, Propriety for his actions, modesty for his self-expression and Integrity for his achievement. That is a Gentleman!" (Duke Ling of Wei 18)

2.55 The Master said: "Not to understand the Mandate of Heaven is to be unable to become a Gentleman; not to understand Propriety is to be unable to stand by oneself; not to divine the speech of others is to be unable to understand people." (Yao Yue 3)

Comment Apart from understanding Propriety, the Gentleman should also know about people and the Mandate of Heaven.

(Cautious speech and swift action)

2.56 The Master said: "The Gentleman should be cautious in speech and quick in action." (Li Ren 24)

Comment Kongzi placed great importance on guarded speech. He emphasizes it throughout the *Analects* and makes it one of the criteria against which the Gentleman is measured.

2.57 Zigong asked how to be a Gentleman. The Master said: "First practice what you preach and then speak of it." (Wei Zheng 13)

Comment This is a development of "cautious in speech and quick in action." There are two possible interpretations: first, act first and speak later; second, do what you can do yourself and then demand it of others.

2.58 The Master said: "A Gentleman feels shame when his speech exceeds his actions." (Xian Wen 27)

Comment The opposite of praise for "cautious speech." Kongzi had an extreme dislike of boastful speech. Boasting and "honeyed words and fine appearance" are both empty of meaning and are a manifestation of a lack of sincerity.

2.59 The Master said: "Those who speak seriously are worthy of esteem, but are they Gentlemen? Or are they those who just appear to be serious?" (Xian Jin 21)

Comment The fact that somebody speaks sincerely or pleasantly is not enough to prove that they are a Gentleman. How do you distinguish the Gentleman? The method that Kongzi suggested was to "Observe their speech, examine their conduct." (Gongye Chang 10)

2.60 The Master said: "The Gentleman does not recommend

someone on their speech alone, nor does he discard all they have said on the basis of their character." (Duke Ling of Wei 23)

Comment This is the attitude with which the Gentleman treats others and conducts himself in society. It is also the standard by which others judge the Gentleman.

(The spirit of non-competition)

2.61 The Master said: "The Gentleman does not compete. If he must, then let it be at archery! First he greets and then takes position. Afterwards he joins the toasts. He has competed but is still a Gentleman." (Ba Yi 7)

Comment The Gentleman may not compete but how he could exist in the competitive commercial world of today is a fresh problem.

2.62 The Master said: "The Gentleman is reserved and does not compete, he mixes but does not form a clique." (Duke Ling of Wei 22)

Comment The Gentleman does not form a clique because he does not compete. It is advantage that the Gentleman does not compete for, and a clique or party is a group based upon advantage. In a society like the present, comprised as it is of political parties, anyone intending to be Gentleman is going to find it more and more difficult.

2.63 The Master said: "The Gentleman is not a tool." (Wei Zheng 12)

Comment Not being a tool is not to seek to be an instrument or to be regarded as an instrument. This is one of Kongzi's most important ideas. Unfortunately, historically the dreams of the Confucians have always been liable to become the "instruments" of the ruler, seemingly in contravention of the teachings of their master.

(Three reverences, three warnings, three faults)

2.64 The Master said: "The Gentleman reveres three things: the Mandate of Heaven, people of standing and the sayings of the sages. The rogue has no understanding of the Mandate of Heaven and thus has no reverence. Nor does he revere people of stature and he treats the sayings of the sages with contempt." (Jishi 8)

Comment The "three reverences" of the Gentleman show respect for nature's heavenly will, for the secular power of royalty and for the moral precepts for which the sages are the spokesmen.

2.65 The Master said: "The Gentleman should beware of three things: in lusty youth, lechery; in vigorous manhood, brawling; in feeble old age, greed." (Jishi 7)

Comment The vicissitudes of life are something that the inexperienced can neither understand nor describe. Normally Kongzi speaks of morality rather than physiology, this is an exception.

2.66 The Master said: "There are three things to avoid when in the company of a Gentleman: to speak out of turn, that is impetuosity; to fail to speak when it is your turn, that is concealment; to speak before gauging the countenance, that is lack of discernment." (Jishi 6)

(Other)

2.67 The Master said: "If a Gentleman is not serious he will lack dignity and his study will lack grounding. He should conduct himself with Loyalty and Integrity and he should have no friends less than himself. He should not fear to correct his mistakes." (Xue Er 8)

Comment The overall requirement for the conduct of a Gentleman.

2.68 The Master said: "A Gentleman has nine considerations: in looking whether or not he sees clearly; in listening whether or not he has understood; in countenance whether or not it is mild; in appearance whether or not it is modest; in speech whether or not it is sincere; in affairs whether or not he is diligent; when there are problems whether or not he should enquire; in anger whether or not there may be consequences and when there is advantage whether or not it has been secured righteously." (Jishi 10)

Comment A specific guide to the Gentleman's approach to society.

2.69 The Master said: "As the Gentleman exists in the world, there is no path that he must follow and no path that he may not follow, but he must adhere to Righteousness." (Li Ren 10)

Comment A Gentleman may be flexible in the actualities of life but inwardly he must not "contravene *Ren.*"

2.70 The Master said: "The Gentleman abides by the principle and is not caught up in the detail." (Duke Ling of Wei 37)

Comment The same meaning as the previous quotation.

2.71 The Master said: "A Gentleman fears only his own lack of ability, not that others may not understand him." (Duke Ling of Wei 19)

Comment The same meaning, which Kongzi expressed many times, e.g. "Fear not that others do not understand you, fear only that you do not understand them." (Xue Er 16); "Fear not that others know you not, fear only your lack of ability." (Xian Wen 30)

2.72 The Master said: "The Gentleman grieves that after death his name may no longer be spoken of." (Duke Ling of Wei 20)

Comment A Gentleman may cope with loneliness but the state of his posthumous reputation is a matter of great concern.

2.73 Zigong said: "Master, are there things that you hate?" The Master said: "Indeed there are: I hate those who speak evil of others, I hate those who mock their betters, I hate those who are courageous but are without Propriety, and I hate those who are resolute but obstinate and inflexible." The Master then asked: "Zigong, are there things that you hate?" Zigong said: "I hate those who appropriate the work of others as their own, I hate those who regard lack of modesty as courage and I hate those who attack others but regard themselves as upright." (Yang Huo 24)

Comment A Gentleman both loves and hates. He naturally hates those things that are forbidden to the Gentleman. It is interesting to note that as a teacher, Kongzi could not stomach lack of respect for status and that, being a student, Zigong detested plagiarism.

(2) Gentlemen and rogues

(Conduct)

2.74 The Master said to Zixia: "You must be a Gentleman Confucian, not a rogue Confucian!" (Yong Ye 13)

Comment People are divided into gentlemen and rogues

as also are Confucians. Consequently those who style themselves Confucians are not necessarily gentlemen. There are many rogues amongst them.

2.75 The Master said: "The Gentleman is expansive and magnanimous but the rogue is petty and prey to anxiety." (Shu Er 37)

Comment One of the distinctions between gentlemen and rogues lies in their differing attitudes of mind.

2.76 The Master said: "The Gentleman is grand but not arrogant and the rogue is both grand and arrogant." (Zilu 26)

Comment Because of differing attitudes of mind Gentlemen and rogues differ in outward expression.

(Treatment of people)

2.77 The Master said: "The Gentleman makes demands of himself but the rogue makes demands of others." (Duke Ling of Wei 21)

Comment This is a major difference between the Gentleman and the rogue. The Gentleman is always hard on himself but the rogue likes battening on others.

2.78 The Master said: "The Gentleman embodies the good in man and not the evil. The rogue is the opposite." (Yan Yuan 16)

Comment The different attitude adopted towards the treatment of others is another major distinction between Gentlemen and rogues.

2.79 The Master said: "The Gentleman is in harmony with all but maintains his discrimination; the rogue does not discriminate but lacks the harmony." (Zilu 23)

Comment "In harmony but with discrimination" is the characteristic model for the Gentleman's relationship with others. "Indiscriminate and unharmonious" is the true image of the rogue's relationship with others.

2.80 The Master said: "The Gentleman is sociable but does not collude but the rogue colludes and is not sociable." (Wei Zheng 14)

Comment This example is substantially close to the quotation above. Because the Gentleman is "in harmony but with discrimination" he is therefore "sociable but does not collude." Similarly, since the rogue is "indiscriminate and unharmonious," he can only "collude and not be sociable."

2.81 The Master said: "It is easy to serve a Gentleman but difficult to gain his praise. If service does not conform to the Grand Principle he will be displeased. In employing people the Gentleman measures them. It is difficult to serve a rogue but easy to gain his praise. If service does not conform with morality he is pleased, but in employing people the rogue demands perfection." (Zilu 25)

Comment It is difficult to gain the praise of a Gentleman or to work with a rogue.

(The management of affairs)

2.82 The Master said: "The Gentleman knows Righteousness, the rogue merely advantage." (Li Ren 16)

Comment In the management of affairs the fundamental distinction between Gentlemen and rogues is whether or not the attribute of *Ren* is present. In the practice of *Ren,* Righteousness is a kind of responsibility or duty. The pursuit of advantage is one of man's natural instincts; but from thereon to seek Righteousness is an enlightenment; put ideologically, it is then the use of the "search for Righteousness" to "pursue advantage"—the advantage of the collective, of social strata or of mankind.

2.83 The Master said: "The Gentleman reaches for the heights, the rogue plumbs the depths." (Xian Wen 23)

2.84 The Master said: "The Gentleman does not indulge in the petty but undertakes the heavy responsibility. The rogue cannot undertake heavy responsibility but indulges in the petty." (Duke Ling of Wei 34)
Comment A Gentleman must be entrusted with major matters and never minor, in much the same way that the qualities of a roof beam should not be employed in the making of tables and chairs. Rogues cannot be employed in major matters but may be in minor. Society is comprised of a combination of Gentlemen and Lesser men or rogues each in their place and able to live in harmony.

2.85 The Master said: "The Gentleman embraces Virtue and the rogue clings to his native hearth; the Gentleman has in mind the penalties of the law and the rogue thinks of favor." (Li Ren 11)

2.86 Zilu said: "Does a Gentleman esteem courage?" The Master said: "The Gentleman puts Righteousness first. For a Gentleman to possess courage but not Righteousness would be disorder. A rogue with courage but not Righteousness would be a robber." (Yang Huo 23)
Comment Courage without Righteousness—no matter whether Gentleman or rogue, both can make mistakes, and the mistakes of the Gentleman are not necessarily

any the less than those of the rogue. The Gentleman and the rogue are admonished together only in this particular quotation in the *Analects*.

(Steadfastness)

2.87 When provisions ran out in the state of Chen, his followers fell sick and none could stand. Zilu angrily asked the Master: "Do Gentlemen also become desperate in adversity?" The Master said: "Gentlemen are steadfast in the face of adversity; rogues cannot bear it." (Duke Ling of Wei 2)

Comment During all the journeys that Kongzi made, the exhaustion of his supplies in the states of Chen and Chu was the most serious test of his life. At this crucial point even the most loyal of his disciples began to waver. Kongzi encouraged and stabilised them with the concept of the "steadfastness of a Gentleman."

CHAPTER 3 PRACTICE

1. Ruling the nation through government

To practice *Ren* in society is to govern with Humanity. The humane rule of a nation has its own set of skills, with the rule of Virtue at its center, together with the establishment of trust, the encouragement of education, the correction of titles and the selection of worth.

(1) Governing with Humanity

3.1 The Master said: "The people are more to *Ren* than they are to fire and water. I have seen those who have died from fire and water, but never those who have died from *Ren*." (Duke Ling of Wei 35)
Comment This is a well-known analogy but with many interpretations. The traditional interpretation is adopted here, that like water and fire, *Ren* is something upon which people depend upon for their livelihood.

3.2 The Master said: "If a ruler emerges he will come to *Ren* after a generation." (Zilu 12)
Comment In Kongzi's view, the universal implementation of *Ren* is an inevitable trend. No matter how a ruler comes to power, sooner or later, he must adopt the path of humane government.

3.3 The Master said: "That which is gained through wisdom and ability, if it is not preserved by *Ren,* though gained, it will be lost. That which is gained through wisdom and ability though it be preserved by *Ren* and yet does not display the dignity of government, will not earn the respect of the people. That which is gained through wisdom and skill, is preserved by *Ren*, displays the dignity of government, and yet is implemented without Propriety is imperfect." (Duke Ling of Wei 33)

Comment Humane government is the key to the peace and stability of a nation. In the long-run power achieved through force cannot be maintained by force.

3.4 The Master said: "A liking for belligerence and a dislike of being poverty-stricken leads to disorder. When people are without *Ren,* hatred flourishes and that is disorder." (Taibo 10)

Comment Belligerence and a dislike of being poverty-stricken are a source of social disorder, whilst an absence of *Ren* can exacerbate social disorder. Is Kongzi admonishing the populace here, or is he warning the ruler? The latter it seems.

(2) The rule of Virtue

3.5 The Master said: "The rule of Virtue is like the North star, fixed in its position and surrounded by other stars." (Wei Zheng 1)

Comment The rule of virtue is a core concept of Kongzi's ideas about humane government. For the state to be ruled with *Ren,* it requires that those who govern should first reach a state of *Ren*, so that they are a model, an example to the populace. If those that govern are without *Ren* (inhumane), it is difficult to imagine a society that would be able to implement a "government of *Ren*." This is the crux of "the rule of Virtue."

3.6 The Master said: "Lead through decree, control through punishment and the people will avoid punishment and be without shame; lead with Virtue, control through Propriety and there will be honor and character." (Wei Zheng 3)

Comment The different consequences that arise from the "rule of Virtue" and the "rule of punishment."

3.7 Duke Jing of Qi asked Kongzi about governance. Kongzi replied: "Lords should be lords; ministers should be ministers; fathers should be fathers; sons should be sons." Duke Jing said: "Excellent! Were lords not to be lords, ministers not to be ministers, fathers not to be fathers and sons not to be sons, there would be grain still but would I be able to eat it?" (Yan Yuan 11)

Comment The concept of *Ren* has different concrete manifestations in different social relationships, including the relationship between lord and minister and father and son. The relationship between characters is fixed, but the role that each person plays can frequently change. You can be a lord, or a minister, a father, or a son. In the eyes of Kongzi ruling a nation meant ensuring that everybody shouldered the responsibility that was appropriate to their role in society.

3.8 Duke Ye asked about governance. The Master said: "Make those that are near joyful and those that are far submit." (Zilu 16)

Comment This is the ideal of government through *Ren*. The population within the borders should live in peace and prosperity without the need for punishment; distant tribes should submit on their own initiative without the need for punitive expeditions.

3.9 Ji Kangzi asked Kongzi about governance and said: "Were those without the Grand Principle to be slaughtered and those with it to be fostered, how would that be?" The Master replied: "Where is the use of slaughter in governance? If you, yourself, desire virtue then the people will be virtuous as well. The character of a ruler resembles the wind and that of the lower orders is like grass, when the wind blows the grass will bend." (Yan Yuan 19)

Comment Virtuous government opposes slaughter, and advocates securing obedience through Virtue. In Kongzi's eyes, government is a process that should educate and remold the people, with the premise that those who govern should be models of morality.

3.10 The Master said: "'Were the virtuous to rule for 100 years, violence would be overcome and slaughter abandoned.' There is truth in this saying!" (Zilu 11)

Comment Kongzi opposed violence and believed that in the space of 100 years a nation could rid itself of violence and killing. Looking back today over 2,000 years, his view of the politics of mankind is rather over-optimistic.

3.11 Yan Yuan asked about rule. The Master said: "Use the calendar of the Xia, ride the chariot of the Yin. Wear the cap of the Zhou, perform the music of the Shao dance. Forbid the tunes of Zheng and distance oneself from those who flatter. The tunes of Zheng are lascivious and flatterers are dangerous." (Duke Ling of Wei 11)

Comment This is a concrete requirement for the implementation of virtuous government placed by Kongzi upon those who govern. On the face of it, it is a return to the ancient past. In fact it is a call for a return to a tradition of hardship and simplicity.

3.12 Zizhang asked Kongzi: "How may government be administered?" The Master said: "Respect the five good principles and reject the four evils, thus can government be administered." Zizhang said: "What are the five good principles?" The Master said: "That the ruler should be benevolent but not wasteful, he should cause the people to labor without hatred, that they should not be avaricious in their desires, that splendor should not be accompanied by arrogance, and that majesty should not be cruel." Zizhang said: "What is benevolent but not wasteful?" The Master said: "To cause the people to profit from their own interests, is that not benevolence without waste? To choose labor that can be undertaken at the right season, who may hate that? To desire *Ren* and to achieve it, what more may be desired? That the ruler, no matter in the many or the few, in the large or the small, should not be neglectful, is this not splendor without arrogance? That a ruler should be careful in his dress and comport himself with gravity so that people hold his dignity in awe, is this not majesty without cruelty?" Zizhang said: "What are the four evils?" The Master said: "To slaughter without civilizing is called cruelty: to demand success without warning is called violence; to demand completion without supervision is called disaster, to be stingy in disbursements is called pettiness." (Yao Yue 2)

Comment This is the most concrete explanation of government through Virtue given by Kongzi. At its core lies "love the people." *Ren* is the basis of government through Virtue.

(3) The nation built on Integrity

3.13 Zigong asked about governance. The Master said: "Sufficient food, sufficient arms and the trust of the people." Zigong said: "If, of these three, one had to be excluded, which would be first?" The Master said: "Arms." Zigong said: "If another had to be excluded, which would be second?" The Master said: "Food. From ancient times there has always been death, but without the trust of the people the state cannot stand." (Yan Yuan 7)

Comment In any form of state and under any regime there exists a formal or informal "contract" between the ruler and the people. In ancient times it was "trust," today we call it "constitution."

3.14 The Master said: "To lead a state of a thousand chariots requires proper attention to affairs and maintenance of trust, economy and love of the people, and labor according to the agricultural calendar." (Xue Er 5)

Comment The nation built on trust is the foundation of "rule through Virtue."

(4) Strengthening the nation through teaching

3.15 The Master visited the state of Wei. Ran You drove his carriage. The Master said: "The people are many!" Ran You said: "Since the people are many what more should be done?" The Master said: "Prosper them." Ran You said: "Once prosperous, then what more?" The Master said: "Teach them." (Zilu 9)

Comment Kongzi believed that prosperity preceded education. In other words, that if the people were not prosperous education and civilization would be difficult. The corollary to this is that in the state ruled by *Ren*, economic development is the prime task but that science and education is also a necessary component. The problem is, who should educate the people? The ruler, the wise, or the people themselves?

3.16 The Master said: "Once the people have been taught by the wise for seven years they may be called to arms." (Zilu 29)
Comment Part of "teaching the people" was military training. From this it can be seen that the Confucianism had both its civil and military aspects.

3.17 The Master said: "To use untrained people in warfare may be called abandoning them." (Zilu 30)
Comment This complements the previous quotation. To use the people in warfare once they have been trained, is also a manifestation of "the love of *Ren* for the people."

3.18 The Master said: "The people may know how but need not know why." (Taibo 9)
Comment This is one of the most historically controversial of Kongzi's opinions, and is considered to hold the idea of the "ignorant masses." In fact, this must have been Kongzi's original intention. What is being discussed is how the state should be ruled and "educating the people" is one of the means through which the state is ruled.

3.19 The Master said: "Adhering to the mean of moderation is of the quality of Virtue, it is of the utmost! It has long been rare amongst the people." (Yong Ye 29)
Comment Another major task in the education of the people is to cause them to maintain an attitude of moderation between the extremes of life. The doctrine of the mean was later expounded and emphasized by the Confucian school of philosophy. Nevertheless it only appears this once in the *Analects*.

(5) Setting an example

3.20 Ji Kangzi asked Kongzi about governance. The Master said: "Governance is to be upright. If one is upright, who dares then not to be upright?" (Yan Yuan 17)

Comment If a ruler wishes to educate the people, he must first make himself a model and set an example. A populace which has been "educated" will, in the proper course of events, demand that the ruler should set an example. This became a basic rule of traditional Chinese politics.

3.21 The Master said: "If one can correct oneself, what difficulty lies in governance? If one cannot correct oneself how then can one correct others?" (Zilu 13)

Comment The theme of this quotation is entirely the same as the one above.

3.22 The Master said: "If one is upright, there is obedience without the necessity for an order; if one is not upright, though there may be an order, there is no obedience." (Zilu 6)

Comment If a ruler cannot set an example it will directly obstruct the laws of the state.

3.23 Ji Kangzi was troubled by robbers and sought advice from Kongzi. Kongzi replied: "If you were not yourself so covetous, though robbers were to be rewarded they would not steal." (Yan Yuan 18)

Comment This remark was rather pointed and said to the hearer's face. We do not know whether he was angered or not. In fact, Kongzi's basic meaning was that the ruler should set a good example to the people.

3.24 Ji Kangzi asked: "How can one make the people respectful, loyal and industrious?" The Master said: "Treat them with gravity and they will respect; treat them with the compassion due to old and young and they will be loyal; choose able men to teach the less able and they will be industrious." (Wei Zheng 20)

Comment Whether or not the people are "respectful" or "loyal" depends upon whether or not the ruler himself is grave and possesses feelings. Similarly, whether or not the people are industrious depends upon the guidance of the ruler.

3.25 Zilu asked about governance. The Master said: "First example, then diligently encourage all." Zilu sought elucidation. The Master said: "Avoid laziness." (Zilu 1)

3.26 The Master said: "When those in power lack magnanimity, lack respect for ceremony, and do not display grief when mourning, how can I bear to look upon it?" (Ba Yi 26)

Comment This is a direct criticism of those in power at the time. In fact, at the time, Kongzi would have been regarded as a dissident.

(6) Forthright advice to the ruler

3.27 Duke Ding asked: "Is there a single word which may invigorate the state?" Kongzi replied: "There is probably no such word! But people say: 'It is difficult to be a ruler and not easy to be a minister.' Were one to know the difficulties of being a ruler, would that not almost be the one word that could invigorate the state?" Duke Ding asked further: "Is there a single word that can destroy the state?" Kongzi replied: "There is probably no such word!

But people say: 'I find no joy in being a ruler except that none contradict me.' If he speaks with Virtue and none contradict, is that not a Virtue too? But if there is no Virtue and none contradict is that not almost the single word that can destroy the state?" (Zilu 15)

Comment The first problem encountered in the governance of the state ruled by *Ren* is that of the relationship between ruler and minister. What Kongzi emphasizes in this relationship is Loyalty. Loyalty and forthright speech are interrelated. As, for example, in Xian Wen 7: "Can one be Loyal and yet not admonish?" Whether or not a state flourishes depends upon the wisdom of the ruler but the fall of a state has always occurred because its ministers have dared not speak the truth.

3.28 Zilu asked about serving a ruler. The Master said: "Do not deceive but one may dare to offend with forthright advice." (Xian Wen 22)

Comment This is a developed clarification of the quotation above.

(7) Give priority to the correction of titles

3.29 Zilu asked: "If the ruler of Wei asked you to rule, what would you do first?" The Master said: "I would first have to correct the titles!" Zilu said: "Would you so? That would be pedantic! What titles would you correct?" The Master said: "Such insolence, Zilu! A ruler should be reticent about that which he does not know. If title and status are not correct then speech will not accord with reason, if speech does not accord with reason then matters will not be resolved and if matters are not resolved, then neither ceremonies nor music will thrive; if neither ceremonies nor music thrive then punishments will not be appropriate; if punishments are not appropriate then the people will be confused. So it is that a ruler must speak with authority. A ruler cannot be casual in what he says." (Zilu 3)

Comment The background to this is that Zilu was about to take up an official post in the state of Wei and especially sought Kongzi's views. At the time, Duke Chu of Wei (the crown prince) had clashed with his father, Kuai Kui, over the succession to the throne and Kongzi gave his own opinion of this. Kongzi believed that the major task in the state of Wei should be to "correct the titles," that is to say, to establish the individual role of members of society and to clarify their responsibilities, otherwise it would be difficult for society to operate normally.

3.30 The Master said: "When the Grand Principle existed under heaven, ceremony, music, and punitive expeditions all derived from the Son of Heaven; when it was absent, ceremonies, music and punitive expeditions derived from the vassal princes and after ten generations there was little that had not collapsed. When derived from ministers, there was little that had not collapsed after five generations; when derived from household retainers there was little that had not collapsed after three generations. When the Grand Principle exists under heaven, the governance of the state is not in the hands of ministers and the commonality do not criticize." (Jishi 2)

Comment In Kongzi's view political disorder derived from chaos amongst "titles," in modern parlance confusion over job descriptions, where the responsibilities incumbent upon each member of society were out of position or misplaced.

(8) Raise the upright and select the worthy

3.31 Duke Ai of Lu asked: "What is it that makes the people obedient?" Kongzi replied: "Raise the upright above the unjust and the people will obey; raise the unjust above the upright and the people will not." (Wei Zheng 19)

Comment Raising the upright and selecting the worthy is not just in order to choose talented people for government but also to establish an example to the people worthy of their imitation.

3.32 Asked about wisdom, the Master said: "It is to understand man." Fan Chi did not understand. The Master said: "To raise the upright above the unjust, may make the unjust upright." Fan Chi withdrew and said to Zixia: "I just saw the Master and asked about wisdom, the Master said: 'To raise the upright above the unjust, may make the unjust upright.' What does it mean?" Zixia replied: "A profound remark! During the rule of Shun, Gao Tao was raised from the people and those without *Ren* were put at a distance; during the rule of Tang, Yi Yin was raised from the people and those without *Ren* were also put at a distance." (Yan Yuan 22)

Comment This bears the same general sense as the previous quotation and emphasises the effect of raising the upright and selecting the worthy and validates it with historical examples. In the original, this quotation was preceded by a sentence covering Fan Chi's question about *Ren*, now inserted elsewhere.

3.33 Zhonggong was to be a retainer of Ji Kangzi and asked about governance. The Master said: "Be a model for junior officials, forgive minor transgressions and raise the talented." Zhonggong further asked: "How can one know the talented so that they may be raised?" The Master said: "Raise those whom you know. Those whom you do not know, are they likely to be overlooked by others?" (Zilu 2)

(9) More haste less speed

3.34 Zixia was to become an official at Jufu in the state of Lu and asked about governance. The Master said: "Do not act in haste, do not seek petty advantage. Haste does not achieve its aim and petty advantage hinders achievement." (Zilu 17)

Comment This concept occupies an important position in Kongzi's theories of statecraft. Since the aim of governance is the realization of government through *Ren*, it can be a long process. "More haste," therefore "less speed."

3.35 The Master said to Yan Yuan: "If one is employed in office then one acts as such, if one is not employed then one retires from public life. Only you and I understand this!" Zilu said: "If the Master were to command three armies, with whom would you choose to be?" The Master said: "Not with the heroically reckless and foolhardy, but with the cautious and those who succeed through skill in planning." (Shu Er 11)

Comment Like warfare, the avoidance of haste in government needs not only courage but strategy as well.

(10) Other

3.36 The Master said: "If you do not occupy the post, do not make the policy." (Taibo 14)

Comment Different characters in society can have

different responsibilities, being misaligned can cause political chaos.

3.37 Someone asked Kongzi: "Why do you not follow a career in government?" The Master said: "The *Book of Documents* says 'Filial Piety! It is respect for parents and love for brothers. It is to be found in governing.' It too is government, what more need there be before it is considered so?" (Wei Zheng 21)

Comment Kongzi believed that even if one did not pursue a career an official, it was possible to take part in politics. The height of politics was to exercise Filial Piety and Fraternal Piety and to extend *Ren* to all.

3.38 Zizhang asked about governance. The Master said: "Exercise it without negligence, implement it with Loyalty." (Yan Yuan 14)

3.39 The Master said: "The ceremony of archery is not on account of hitting the target, because strengths differ, this was the way of the ancients." (Ba Yi 16)

Comment The point of the "ceremony of archery" lay not in the archery but in the ceremony. For the same reason, a state flourished not through military power but through the rites of ceremony and music.

3.40 The Master said: "In the hearing of legal cases, I am like others. What must be done is the elimination of lawsuits." (Yan Yuan 13)

Comment A major task of governing a state is the hearing of cases, but the ideal of government through *Ren* is that there should be no cases to hear.

2. Personal conduct and conduct in society

The crux of personal and social conduct for those with *Ren* lay in how they coped with riches and fame, how they made friends and treated others, how they behaved as officials and in their leisure.

(1) Honor and Riches

3.41 The Master said: "All men desire honor and riches but if they are acquired improperly they cannot be enjoyed; all men fear poverty and abasement but if they are suffered unjustly they cannot be cast off. If the Gentleman departs from *Ren* how can he be known as one? A Gentleman may not offend against *Ren* for even the length of a meal, it should remain thus when hurried and thus even when desperate." (Li Ren 5)

Comment In Kongzi's view riches and poverty were matters of "fate" and of "heaven's will." It was also a case of "life and death are determined by fate and riches and honor by heaven" (Yan Yuan 5). Only by upholding Righteousness can the Gentleman take riches in his stride and poverty without complaint. *Ren* is what personifies the Gentleman, and what he would not abandon for a single moment, however difficult the circumstances.

3.42 The Master said: "If riches are to be had I would even act as the servant who clears the way with a whip. If they are not to be had, then I have other pursuits." (Shu Er 12)

Comment The topic under examination is still the question of riches and honor. Kongzi addresses the question of riches and honor calmly and realistically and he has an alternative.

3.43 The Master said: "To eat coarse grain, drink cold water and to sleep pillowed on one's arms, there is joy in that. But to gain riches and honor unjustly is like a passing cloud." (Shu Er 16)

Comment Another aspect of riches and honor is the ability to accept hardship. Sometimes it is not difficult to resist the attraction of wealth and honor but maintaining one's optimism in poverty is not easy either.

3.44 Zigong said: "To be poor but not to flatter and to be rich but not arrogant, how is that?" The Master said: "It is well, but not as good as being poor but happy or rich and appreciating ceremony." Zigong said: "The *Classic of Poetry* says: 'Like slicing and polishing bone, cutting and grinding ivory,' is that what is being spoken of?" The Master said: "Zigong, now I can begin to discuss the *Classic of Poetry* with you. You can deduce what is to come from what I have already told you." (Xue Er 15)

Comment The rich and honored must not only be "without arrogance" but must, even more, appreciate ceremony; if riches and honor are not possible then not only must one not flatter but one must also maintain a sense of joy. This kind of mental state is not inborn but comes through an endless process of grinding and polishing as hinted at in the *Classic of Poetry*.

3.45 The Master said: "It is difficult to be poor without complaint but easy to be rich without arrogance." (Xian Wen 10)

Comment The same meaning as above. It is over the question of rich and poor that human nature is most easily displayed.

3.46 The Master said: "Be resolute in conviction and diligent in study. Hold to the way of virtue until death. Do not enter states where there is danger nor dwell in those in chaos. Serve where the Grand Principle exists but retire where there is not. In states that have the principle, poverty and abasement are a matter of shame. Where there is no principle, riches and honor are a matter of shame." (Taibo 13)

Comment Riches and honor may be sought but on the basis of whether or not the state holds to the Grand Principle.

(2) Fame

3.47 Zizhang asked: "How may an official be called successful?" The Master said: "What is the success of which you speak?" Zizhang replied: "To be famed abroad and to be known at court." The Master said: "That is fame, not success. To be successful is to be upright in character and to love justice, to guard one's words and gestures and to be considerate of others. This would be to be successful abroad and successful at court. What you call fame has the appearance of *Ren* but offends in action, and yet considers itself undoubtedly possessed of *Ren*. This would be to be merely famous abroad and famous at court." (Yan Yuan 20)

Comment Another problem that must be faced in the area of riches and honor is that of fame and success. In the eyes of Kongzi, success was internally and externally consistent and the name took second place to the reality; with fame there was a contradiction between words and action, it was a vain boast. The Gentleman sought the former and the rogue or Lesser man the latter. Those who succeeded approached *Ren*, the merely famous were distant from it.

3.48 The Master said: "Fear not that others do not know you, fear only that you do not know others." (Xue Er 16)
Comment When success and fame are absent the Gentleman must be able to maintain a certain detachment. He should only fear that he is deficient in character and ability and never be concerned about whether or not others understand him. Kongzi emphasizes this theme and the sense of the following few quotations is much the same.

3.49 The Master said: "Fear not that others do not know you, fear only your own lack of ability." (Xian Wen 30)

3.50 The Master said: "Fear not that you have no position, fear only that you lack the ambition. Fear not that you are unknown but strive for the qualities that will make you known." (Li Ren 14)

3.51 The Master said: "The worthy avoid the tumultuous world and then the disordered state, they avoid the offensive countenance and then offensive speech. Of such worthies there are seven!" (Xian Wen 37)
Comment This is a strategy that the worthy use to cope with life; in troubled times to avoid riches and honor, to avoid fame and to seek only to live a life of cultivated seclusion.

3.52 The Master said: "There are those who encounter virtuous behavior and pursue it, who encounter ill behavior and avoid it as they would avoid boiling water; I have met such people and heard such talk. There are those who live in seclusion and cultivate their aspirations, who pursue their aims with Righteousness; I have heard such talk but never met such a person." (Jishi 11)

Comment The pursuit of virtue and the avoidance of evil is a fundamental human instinct and relatively easily accomplished. Living apart from a troubled world with aspirations unchanged, requires strength of will and is not easily done.

(3) On being a Scholar

3.53 Zigong asked: "How may one be a Scholar?" The Master said: "Act with humility, in your missions abroad do not bring disgrace upon the orders of the ruler, that is to be a Scholar." Zigong said: "May I dare to ask what next?" The Master said: "To be regarded as filial within the clan and as fraternal within the village." Zigong asked further: "May I dare to ask what next?" The Master said: "To be true to one's word and for one's acts to bear fruit. Like the rattle of stones, shallow obstinacy is the mark of the rogue who can yet be a lower class of Scholar." Zigong asked: "Those who govern today, how may they be regarded?" The Master said: "Oh! As small-minded and unworthy to be considered a Scholar!" (Zilu 20)

Comment The Scholar was the lowest rank of the Zhou dynasty nobility, just above a commoner. If someone could not be a Gentleman he could at least be a decent Scholar. Kongzi and Zigong are discussing the various levels in the standards of behavior of yeomen. However, it is worth noting that a Gentleman may be a Scholar and so may a rogue.

3.54 Zilu asked: "How may one be a Scholar?" The Master said: "Learn from and encourage each other, enjoy each other's company, that is how to be a Scholar. Encourage with friends, enjoy with brothers." (Zilu 28)

3.55 The Master said: "The Scholar who prefers the peaceful life is no Scholar!" (Xian Wen 2)

Comment Kongzi also said: "The Lesser man clings to his hearth." (Li Ren 11) It looks as if the Scholar should not be over-attached to home and family.

3.56 The Master said: "The Scholar who aspires to the Grand Principle but is ashamed of eating badly or being ill-clothed is not worthy of engaging in discussion." (Li Ren 9)

Comment The Scholar with real aspirations will probably not be over-particular about food and clothing.

(4) On being an official

3.57 Zigong said: "Were there a beautiful piece of jade would one put it in a cabinet or sell it for a good price?" The Master said: "Sell it! Sell it! I've been waiting for somebody who knew what's what!" (Zihan 13)

Comment Being an official was the only path open to those who possessed *Ren*. Though they may have had a strategy for government, the world was in the hands of sovereign rulers. Kongzi was very realistic on this point. Unless the strategies were implemented by rulers, there would be no opportunity for them to be put into practice.

3.58 Fan Chi sought instruction on the sowing of crops. The Master said: "I am no old peasant." Fan Chi asked further about the planting of vegetables, the Master said: "Nor am I an old gardener." Fan Chi withdrew and the Master said: "What a rogue Fan Chi is! If those in power attach importance to rite and ceremony then the people will not dare show disrespect; if those in power have a proper regard for Righteousness then the people will not dare disobey; if those in power attach importance to sincerity then the people will not dare to be dishonest. Were it like this, then people would flock from the four corners of the earth bearing their children on their backs to seek shelter. What need to sow oneself then?" (Zilu 4)

Comment In this quotation, Kongzi criticizes Fan Chi's choice of life's work. In Kongzi's view the role of the Gentleman was to administer a government of *Ren* throughout the land and not to sow seed or plant vegetables. A Gentleman who had received many years of education should undertake administrative work and not physical labor. In fact, Fan Chi was not wrong in his wish to learn about agriculture. Someone who knew nothing of sowing and planting would probably be unable to run a country. This was certainly the view of Mao Zedong 2,000 years later.

3.59 Zizhang wished to know how to obtain a position. The Master said: "Enquire widely and put aside that which is in doubt, expound with care what remains and faults will be few; observe widely and avoid danger and implement what remains with care and regrets will be few. When speech is without fault and action without regret, there is your official salary." (Wei Zheng 18)

Comment Care in speech and action are the route to office and the path to follow when in office.

3.60 The Master said: "In serving a ruler, first perform his tasks and then enjoy his bounty." (Duke Ling of Wei 38)

Comment The Gentleman who serves as an official also

has his own professional morality.

3.61 The Master said: "If, after three years of study one has not attained a position, it will be even less easy thereafter." (Taibo 12)

3.62 The Master said: "If a state possesses the Grand Principle, one can speak and act forthrightly, if it lacks it one may act forthrightly but speak with circumspection." (Xian Wen 3)
Comment After achieving office, the Gentleman must still maintain his own personal integrity and retain a balanced judgment.

3. 63 Yuan Xian asked Kongzi about shame. The Master said: "When a state possesses the Grand Principle there are official emoluments; when a state lacks it and there are still official emoluments, that is shame." (Xian Wen 1)
Comment A similar meaning, Kongzi also said: "When a state lacks principle and yet there are riches and honor, that is shame" (Taibo 13). Sentences which dealt with "overcoming," "punitive expeditions," "complaint" and "desire," that originally stood at the end of this quotation have been included elsewhere.

(5) Respect for teachers

3.64 The Master said: "In the exercise of *Ren,* even one's teacher takes second place." (Duke Ling of Wei 36)
Comment Kongzi advocated respect for teachers but he elevated *Ren* above them, with the meaning of "I love my teacher but I love Humanity and Righteousness more."

3.65 The musician, Master Mian, came to see Kongzi. When he

reached the steps, the Master said: "These are the steps." When he reached the mat, the Master said: "This is the mat." When all had sat down, the Master told him: "So-and-so is here and so-and-so is here." Master Mian left and Zizhang asked: "Is this the way of conversing with masters of music?" The Master said: "It is indeed the way in which one should receive a teacher." (Duke Ling of Wei 42)

Comment At the time, most musicians were blind. Kongzi's respect for a teacher was not only respect for his own teacher but respect for all those who taught as a profession.

3.66 The Master said: "I have never refused to instruct those who brought me ten strips of dried meat as a fee." (Shu Er 7)

Comment Kongzi taught all his life and earned his living thereby. It could be said that he was the first private teacher in Chinese history.

3.67 The Master said: "In teaching there are no distinctions." (Duke Ling of Wei 39)

Comment As the first professional teacher in Chinese history, one might say that Kongzi turned no one away, drew no distinction between high and low, or rich and poor, took no account of political tendencies and was filled with a sense of equality. For Kongzi, the ultimate goal of education was to arouse a feeling of compassion in his pupils, so how could he possibly refuse anyone who sought *Ren*?

(6) On friendship

3.68 The Master said: "Where aspirations differ there can be no common ground." (Duke Ling of Wei 40)

Comment The first principle of friendship is that of "common aspiration." If aspirations differ it becomes difficult to associate. Aspiration is a common yearning for *Ren*.

3.69 The Master said: "It is good to live with *Ren*, if one chooses not to, how can one attain wisdom?" (Li Ren 1)

3.70 The Master said: "There are three kinds of good friends and three kinds of bad. The good are the upright, the sincere and the well-informed. The bad are those who flatter, those who feign friendship and those who are full of empty words." (Jishi 4)

Comment In making friends there are choices, good friends lead one towards virtue and bad towards depravity. In reality, the good friend is a Gentleman and the bad a rogue.

3.71 The Master said: "If one cannot be with those who take the middle way must one then necessarily be with either the wild or the timid? The wild forge ahead and the timid hold back." (Zilu 21)

Comment There are, perhaps, three kinds of people in society: The neutral middle, the wild, and the timid. It is best to associate with the neutral middle but there are advantages in friendship with both the wild and the timid. The wild are positive and go-ahead, always on the up; the timid hold back cautiously and can, through disengagement, teach us about the avoidance of moral contamination.

3.72 The Master said: "Give pride of place to Loyalty and Integrity. Make no friends less than oneself. Where there are faults do not fear to correct them." (Zihan 25)

Comment It may sound rather Machiavellian to say that, as a principle, you should make no friends less than oneself, but the measure of what is good and what is bad here, is not riches and honor or power, but the degree of enlightenment about *Ren*.

3.73 The Master said: "One may study with others but not seek the Grand Principle with them; one may seek the Grand Principle with them but not achieve success; one may achieve success with them but yet not a balance in advantage." (Zihan 30)

Comment One should not be too ruthless in friendship, and there are stages to friendship.

3.74 The Master said: "One may discuss the profound with those of moderate learning but not with those of less learning." (Yong Ye 21)

Comment Kongzi believed that there were disparities in people's mental capacity and that there were profound concepts which not all could understand. There had to be choice and discrimination in friendship and that in association there had to be distinctions in treatment.

3.75 The Master said: "Not to converse with those with whom one should converse is to lose a person; to converse with those with whom one should not converse is to lose conversation." (Duke Ling of Wei 8)

Comment Losing a friend and losing conversation are two frequent mistakes in friendship.

3.76 Zigong asked about friendship. The Master said: "Advise each other out of Loyalty and lead through Virtue, draw back from that which is impermissible and do not incur shame." (Yan Yuan 23)

Comment However deep a friendship may be, there are limits. Friends should be urged not to overstep the mark.

3.77 On the death of a friend, if there were none who could arrange the funeral, the Master would say: "Put it in my hands." (Xiang Dang 22)

(7) Knowledge of people

3.78 The Master said: "If all hate them, examine the reason; if all love them, examine the reason also." (Duke Ling of Wei 28)

Comment No matter whether as a ruler or administrator or as one living in society knowledge of people is important. Kongzi stresses the need for personal observation rather than merely relying upon the opinion of a bystander even if it were the "voice of the masses." The following quotation explains the reasoning.

3.79 Zigong asked: "If all the village liked him, how would that be?" The Master said: "It is hard to be certain." "If all the village hated him, how would that be?" The Master said: "It is hard to be certain. It would be better if the virtuous liked him and the bad hated him." (Zilu 24)

Comment The best way of determining good and bad character is not to see whether or not there is a unanimous good opinion but to see whether or not the good speak well of him and the bad speak ill of him.

3.80 The Master said: "Consider their motives, observe their history, examine that which contents them. What then may be hidden? What then may be hidden?" (Wei Zheng 10)

Comment Three essentials for the examination of character. Motive for behavior, personal history and spiritual goals.

3.81 The Master said: "There are shoots that do not grow to produce grain and there is grain that does not ripen." (Zihan 22)

Comment It is easy to detect shoots that do not grow to produce grain, but grain that does not ripen often confuses the eye.

3.82 The Master said: "Though you had the talents of Duke Zhou himself but were arrogant and mean-minded, the remaining qualities would be of no avail." (Taibo 11)

Comment Only the "complete man" can achieve perfection but there are small defects which are permissible and some major characteristics, such as arrogance and stinginess, which are not.

3.83 The Master said: "Only the wisdom of the superior and the stupidity of the inferior are beyond improvement." (Yang Huo 3)

Comment This is another of Kongzi's widely disputed remarks. Basically, there is no dispute over the fact that there is both high and low intelligence, the problem lies with "beyond improvement." If "superior wisdom" and "inferior stupidity" refer to social class, then the remark sounds as if it was support for the maintenance of a permanent system of social class; if it refers just to individual levels of intelligence, then it suggests that there are limits to the extent to which education can improve mental capacity.

3.84 The Master said: "One may respect the next generation, why should one expect the next generation not to equal the present? If they are still unknown by the age of 40 or 50, that may be insufficient to earn respect." (Zihan 23)

Comment Kongzi clearly believed in social evolution. He was firmly of the opinion that society was the better for being "ancient," however, he also believed that man grew stronger with each passing generation. Given the comparative brevity of life in ancient times, to set the limit for a final assessment of a person's ability at 40 or 50 should be regarded as very generous.

3.85 The Master said: "To be loathed at 40, that really is the end!" (Yang Huo 26)

Comment Kongzi also said "There is clarity at 40." That is to say that by 40 the virtuous are naturally resolute in virtue and the wicked are incorrigible.

3.86 The master said: "Only women and rogues are difficult to train! Near and they show you no respect, far and they complain." (Yang Huo 25)

Comment This is another of Kongzi's much disputed sayings. To speak of women in the same breath as rogues is to display an attitude of contempt for women. Nevertheless, there is a certain truth in this. The intimacy between man and woman has something of the "honeyed sweetness" between rogues rather than the calm waters of the relationship between gentlemen. On the question of the correct treatment of women, Kongzi was clearly politically incorrect and insufficiently mature.

3.87 The Master said: "Tough on the outside and weak inside, when compared with a rogue, would that be like a thief who bores a hole through a wall?" (Yang Huo 12)

3.88 The Master said: "How should one serve a ruler with colleagues of base character? Having not yet gained it, fearful of not gaining; having gained it, then fearful of losing. Once they fear loss, they are capable of anything." (Yang Huo 15)

Comment A portrait of anxiety about personal gain and loss. The final sentence is the most important, much of the bad done today is done by people who are not too bad in themselves but who fear loss.

(8) Behaving with Integrity

3.89 The Master said: "Man's innate nature is common to all but becomes different through acquired experience." (Yang Huo 2)

Comment Though innate nature may be the same, what determines the kind of person you are in the end is the result of the experience acquired from one's own behavior in life. Consequently, to seek *Ren* one must first learn how to behave.

3.90 The Master said: "Man lives through being upright, those that are not upright survive by luck." (Yong Ye 19)

Comment To behave uprightly should be the first principle of existence.

3.91 Zilu asked about becoming the complete man. The Master said: "To have the wisdom of Zang Wuzhong, the moral continence of Meng Gongchuo, the courage of Bian Zhuangzi and the talent of Ran You, then to enrich it all with the qualities of ceremony and music, that would

THE NEW ANALECTS: CONFUCIUS RECONSTRUCTED

make a complete man." The Master also said: "Why should the complete man of today have to be like this? To see advantage but think of Righteousness, to see danger but be prepared to sacrifice one's life and to live in poverty but not forget the promises of a lifetime, all this too, can make the complete man." (Xian Wen 12)

Comment The complete man must not only have wisdom, moral character and talent, more importantly, he must have the spirit of "seeing advantage but thinking of Righteousness."

3.92 Zizhang asked about conduct. The Master said: "Speak with Loyalty and Integrity, act steadfastly and with respect for one's calling and though you may be amongst barbarians, it will suffice. If your speech lacks Loyalty and Integrity and your actions are ungrounded and unprofessional, though you may be on your own territory, can it then suffice? See this before you as you stand; see it written on the shafts of your carriage as you travel and it will suffice you hereafter." Zizhang inscribed all this on his girdle. (Duke Ling of Wei 6)

3.93 The Master said: "Man may glorify the Grand Principle but the Grand Principle may not glorify man." (Duke Ling of Wei 29)

Comment The relationship between man and the Grand Principle. The principle is the end, not the means. One may "glorify the Grand Principle" for a lifetime but never exploit it to seek fame or advantage.

3.94 The Master said: "Be heavy in demands upon oneself but light in criticism of others and there will be distance from hatred." (Duke Ling of Wei 15)

Comment See also Duke Ling of Wei 21, where the theme is the same and Kongzi said: "The Gentleman makes demands of himself, and the rogue of others."

3.95 The Master said: "To conduct oneself merely to secure advantage incurs much hatred." (Li Ren 12)
Comment One cannot just take the pursuit of advantage as a principle. Its pursuit will inevitably lead to interpersonal conflict. The mediation and avoidance of this conflict of advantage is based upon the practice of *Ren*.

3.96 The Master said: "Not always to expect to encounter deception, nor to baselessly suspect lack of sincerity, but to perceive the duplicity of others beforehand would that not be becoming of a worthy?" (Xian Wen 31)
Comment The worthy are honest but not stupid. Those with *Ren* also possess wisdom.

3.97 The Master said: "The man without consideration of the long term, will suffer in the short term." (Duke Ling of Wei 12)
Comment A statement about experience of life. Lack of a long term view causes anxiety in the short term. Problems in the short term more than ever require a long term view.

(9) Love of Virtue

3.98 The Master said: "I have never yet met a man who loved Virtue as much as he loved beauty in women." (Zihan 18)
Comment If you say that "love of Virtue" is part of human nature, then it should be as natural as "love of beauty,"

but what perplexes Kongzi is that love of Virtue requires considerable effort and has never been as easy as love of beauty. Love of Virtue and love of beauty, as requirements of human nature, are not on the same level.

3.99 The Master said: "What a business! I have never yet met a man who loved Virtue as much as he loved beauty in women!" (Duke Ling of Wei 13)

Comment This sentence is to be found twice in the *Analects*. It is not known whether the single statement was recorded by two different disciples or whether Kongzi repeated his complaint a number of times. The attraction of beauty has many times the strength of virtue and is perhaps the greatest challenge that Kongzi faced in putting *Ren* into practice.

3.100 The Master said: "Zilu, there are few who understand Virtue!" (Duke Ling of Wei 4)

3.101 The Master said: "The virtuous do not exist on their own, they attract the company of others of the same mind." (Li Ren 25)

3.102 The Master said: "One does not praise the strength of a thoroughbred horse, one praises its moral character." (Xian Wen 33)

Comment Using horse as a metaphor for man, moral character is more important than ability.

3.103 The Master said: "The outwardly amiable who lack a sense of right and wrong are the ruin of Virtue!" (Yang Huo 13)

Comment The Gentleman is not a kind old man, he

fights the rogues to the bitter end.

3.104 Someone asked: "How would it be to repay hate with Virtue?" The Master said: "Then how would you repay Virtue? Repay hate with uprightness and repay Virtue with Virtue." (Xian Wen 34)

Comment *Ren's* love of people is not indiscriminate. It repays the hatred of a rogue or enemy with uprightness and not with Virtue, this quotation is an example.

3.105 The Master said: "In the South they have a saying: 'If you will not persevere you cannot become a shaman.' That's well said! 'If you have not the perseverance to maintain Virtue it is difficult to avoid shame.'" The Master further said: "You don't need divination to work this out." (Zilu 22)

Comment This quotation includes Kongzi' comments on two classical sayings. The first is a proverb from the South which describes the need for perseverance in work; and the second is a quotation from the *Book of Changes* which emphasizes the need to persevere in the maintenance of Virtue. Kongzi produced the second quotation on the back of the first—with a sigh.

(10) Prudence in speech

3.106 The Master said: "The reticence of the ancients derived from shame that they might not keep their word." (Li Ren 22)

Comment Kongzi always regarded prudence in speech as one of the great Virtues of the Gentleman. Its very basis is "trustworthiness," the belief that you will keep your word.

3.107 The Master said: "Shameless speech makes implementation difficult!" (Xian Wen 20)

Comment This seems to be a continuation of the previous quotation. Those who routinely exaggerate will, when the time comes, be unable to deliver on their promises.

3.108 The Master said: "It is enough that one's words should express their sense." (Duke Ling of Wei 41)

Comment Another level of meaning to prudence in speech, for the Gentleman it is "caution in words." Kongzi loathed "fine words" and believed that it was enough that words should express their meaning.

3.109 The Master said: "Fine words bring confusion to morality and failure to endure the trivial damages the major plan." (Duke Ling of Wei 27)

Comment The ill of "fine words" lies in its confusion of morality in the same way that failure to endure the minor annoyance can damage the overall strategy. In life, the reason for prudence in speech is more for maintaining one's own moral character than it is for avoiding disaster.

3.110 The Master said: "I loathe the fact that purple has replaced red, that the decadent sounds of the Zheng state have disturbed the elegance of music and I loathe those that use facile eloquence to subvert the state." (Yang Huo 18)

Comment Fine words not only damage morality, they damage ceremony too and most of all, they can bring disaster to the state.

3.111 The Master said: "To listen to street gossip and spread it is an abandonment of morality!" (Yang Huo 14)

Comment Prudence in speech not only refers to caution of utterance but to care over what you listen to. The Gentleman of morality neither believes nor spreads rumors.

3.112 Zizhang asked about clarity of perception. The Master said: "If neither surreptitious calumny that soaks in like water or slander that cuts like a knife can flourish, that may be called clarity of perception. If neither surreptitious calumny that soaks in like water or slander that cuts the skin like a knife can flourish that may be called far-sighted too." (Yan Yuan 6)

Comment Prudence in speech is the avoidance of fine words, not believing rumor enables you to distinguish slander.

(11) Leisure

3.113 The Master said: "To live a crowded life, never to speak of Righteousness, and to indulge in petty wit, that is difficult!" (Duke Ling of Wei 17)

Comment Most of life is spent in leisure. How to live a life of leisure is a very real problem for the Gentleman. Kongzi saw many people who wasted their lives in idleness and he lamented it bitterly.

3.114 The Master said: "To eat well each day, to have nothing to occupy the mind, that is difficult! A game of chess would be worthy!" (Yang Huo 22)

Comment Kongzi believed that learning to play chess was better than wasting time in idleness. Man should always aspire to something, if not to learning then at least to a skill.

3.115 The Master said: "I do not know what is to be done with those who do not say 'what is to be done.'" (Duke Ling of Wei 16)

Comment This seems to apply to those unwilling to think for themselves, those with "nothing to occupy the mind" of the previous quotation. Even Kongzi, "the greatest teacher of them all," felt that there was nothing that could be done and that they were ineducable.

3.116 The Master said: "There are three pleasures that are beneficial and three that are harmful. Those that benefit are cultivating the body and mind through ceremony and music, praising the virtue of others and engaging in friendship with the virtuous; the harmful are love of wild arrogance, love of amusement and love of banqueting." (Jishi 5)

Comment Kongzi clearly defines the beneficial and the harmful aspects of the pleasures of the leisured life.

CHAPTER 4 CASES

1. Evaluation of disciples

Through his evaluation of his many disciples and particularly through his praise and criticism of Yan Yuan, Zilu and Zigong, Kongzi indicates how it is possible to attain the realm of *Ren*.

(1) Yan Yuan

4.1 The Master said: "How worthy is Yan Yuan! A helping of coarse rice, a scoop of fresh water and he lives in humble surroundings. Others would find his situation unbearable but he continues in his delight. How worthy he is!" (Yong Ye 11)
Comment Yan Yuan was Kongzi's favorite disciple and the pupil most able to comprehend his ideas. Kongzi believed Yan Yuan had almost attained the state of *Ren*, that he embodied all the merits of somebody who possessed *Ren* and that he directly reflected all its characteristics. Kongzi's praise of Yan Yuan is also a glorification of *Ren*.

4.2 The Master said: "Yan Yuan can go for three months without contravening *Ren* for a moment, the others can only manage a day or a month." (Yong Ye 7)
Comment Yan Yuan's other praiseworthy quality, his ability to sustain *Ren*. "Three months without contravening *Ren*" is, whether in thought or action, a state that the average person has no way of achieving.

4.3 The Master said: "I teach Yan Yuan all day. He raises no questions and appears stupid. He withdraws and reflects and then presents inspiring views. He is by no means stupid." (Wei Zheng 9)

Comment Yan Yuan possessed the Gentleman's characteristic of "prudent speech." Kongzi praised him but he also preferred his disciples not to be stupid or utterly without original ideas.

4.4 The Master said: "Is not Yan Yuan somebody who is there to help me? When he speaks with me there is nothing that is not a delight." (Xian Jin 4)

Comment The thrust of this quotation is similar to the one above, but there is a hint of criticism in the tone in which Kongzi expresses his admiration for Yan Yuan's total acceptance of his own ideas.

4.5 The Master said: "Of those who listen to my teaching but are not idle, perhaps there is only Yan Yuan?" (Zihan 20)

Comment Kongzi had a reputation for love of learning. Yan Yuan's love of learning was no whit inferior to that of his teacher. Kongzi loved Yan Yuan because he recognized himself in him.

4.6 The Master said of Yan Yuan: "A pity! I saw his progress but I never saw him cease." (Zihan 21)

Comment This may be Kongzi in his old age sighing regretfully when recalling Yan Yuan who had died early. The deepest impression that Yan Yuan had left upon Kongzi was that of his love of learning.

4.7 Ji Kangzi asked: "Who amongst the disciples loves learning the most?" The Master replied: "Yan Yuan loved learning. But alas his life was short. There are none now who resemble him." (Xian Jin 7)

Comment In Kongzi's view Yan Yuan, of all his disciples, loved learning the most and was also his best pupil.

4.8 Duke Ai of Lu asked Kongzi: "Who amongst the disciples loves learning the most?" The Master replied: "Yan Yuan loved learning. He never took out his anger on others and never made the same mistake twice. But alas, his life was short. There are none now who resemble him and I know of none who have his learning." (Yong Ye 3)

Comment Kongzi almost always gave the same answer when different people asked him about Yan Yuan. We can see that his admiration and liking for Yan Yuan never changed. It is interesting that in this quotation, apart from love of learning, Kongzi mentions two other qualities that Yan Yuan possessed: not taking his anger out on others and not making the same mistake twice—the first is a matter of self examination and the second of the correction of faults, both characteristic of the virtuous conduct of a Gentleman.

4.9 The Master was besieged in the town of Kuang in the state of Wei and Yan Yuan was left behind. The Master said: "I thought you were dead!" Yan Yuan replied: "While the Master lives, how could I dare to die?" (Xian Jin 23)

Comment Passing through Kuang on his way from the state of Wei to the state of Chen, Kongzi was surrounded by its inhabitants in an unexpected incident. Yan Yuan was with him throughout and was the last to escape. When they met again, their conversation turned to life and death. Yan Yuan responded very well to Kongzi's anxiety and concerns. But at the time Yan Yuan could not have realized that he would be the first to die.

4.10 Yan Yuan died and the Master said: "Oh! Heaven has bereaved me, heaven has bereaved me!" (Xian Jin 9)

Comment Yan Yuan died in his prime, some say at the age of 31 and others say at the age of 41. Kongzi was desolated with grief, both for the feeling between teacher and pupil and for the loss of a proponent of the Grand Principle, hence his cry "Heaven has bereaved me."

4.11 The Master wept bitterly at the death of Yan Yuan. His followers said: "The Master grieves too much!" The Master said: "If I do not grieve for him, for whom shall I grieve?" (Xian Jin 10)

4.12 On the death of Yan Yuan, his father Yan Lu asked the Master to sell his carriage so that he might buy an outer coffin for his son. The Master said: "Whether they have talent or not, I regard them all as my sons. When my son, Kong Li, died, there was an inner coffin and no outer. I cannot go on foot for the sake of an outer coffin, for I cannot follow the procession of the ministers on foot." (Xian Jin 8)

Comment This is a tragic tale of the conflict between Propriety and emotion. Kongzi opposed an outer coffin for Yan Yuan and would not give up his carriage, very likely because Yan Yuan was a commoner by birth and had never held an official post; to have buried him with an inner and outer coffin would have been a breach of the rules of Propriety. In order to comfort Yan Lu, Kongzi cited the example of his own son as well as mentioning that he himself could not go on foot lest he could not keep up with ministerial processions. He was tactful in intent and grief-struck in feeling.

4.13 Yan Yuan died and his fellow disciples wanted a grand funeral for him. The Master said: "No." The disciples continued in their wishes. The Master said: "Yan Yuan looked on me as a father, but I cannot treat him as a son. That is not my fault but of those other disciples." (Xian Jin 11)

Comment Confucians advocated grand funerals but Kongzi's refusal to agree to a grand funeral for Yan Yuan was still rooted in his misgivings at "breaching Propriety." Nevertheless, on this occasion, Kongzi demonstrated some flexibility; he let the disciples manage the funeral and took no part himself. Kong Li had not had a grand funeral, so for Kongzi to say that he could not treat Yan Yuan as his own son was a form of self-justification.

(2) Zilu

4.14 The Master said: "If I cannot go by road then I must go by water. Of my followers, perhaps only Zilu would come with me." Zilu heard this and was pleased. The Master said: "Zilu has more courage than I do but his other talents are difficult to discern." (Gongye Chang 7)

Comment It might be said that Zilu was Kongzi's most loyal disciple but he was not the most perfect. His greatest quality was courage. In this respect even Kongzi knew he could not equal him. However, Zilu was still some distance away from *Ren* and wisdom.

4.15 The Master said: "Of those who wear tattered silk gowns, only Zilu can take his place without shame amongst those clad in fine furs. 'Being neither jealous nor greedy, what ill is there in that?'" Zilu heard this and recited it over and over again. The Master said: "Merely to follow this path, what good is there in that?" (Zihan 27)

Comment Zilu's courage again draws the heartfelt praise of Kongzi but he cannot progress to the attainment of *Ren* and wisdom and causes Kongzi some regret.

4.16 Meng Wubo asked: "Does Zilu possess *Ren*?" The Master said: "I do not know." Meng Wubo asked further. The Master said: "Zilu could command military supplies in a state of 1,000 chariots but I do not know whether he possesses *Ren*." Meng Wubo asked about Ran You. The Master said: "In a place of 1,000 households or a state of 100 chariots Ran You could be a governor, but I do not know whether he possesses *Ren*." Meng Wubo asked about Gongye Chang. The Master said: "Gongye Chang could attend court in ceremonial robes and greet important guests, but I do not know whether he possesses *Ren*." (Gongye Chang 8)

Comment Kongzi once again makes it clear that Zilu had not attained *Ren*. Of course, he is very tactful and does not say "he won't do," merely "I don't know." In Kongzi's view, Ran You and Gongxi Hua, the other two disciples had also not attained *Ren*.

4.17 Ji Kangzi asked: "Could Zilu administer a government?" The Master said: "Zilu is very decisive. What difficulty could he have in administering a government?" Ji Kangzi asked: "Could Zigong administer a government?" The Master said: "Zigong is clear minded. What difficulty could he have in administering a government?" Ji Kangzi again asked: "Could Ran You administer a government?" The Master said: "Ran You is talented above others, what difficulty could he have in administering a government?" (Yong Ye 8)

Comment Although he has not attained *Ren*, Kongzi still praises Zilu for his decisiveness and confirms his political skills. He also has high praise for Zigong and Ran You.

4.18 Ji Ziran asked: "May Zilu and Ran You be called chief ministers?" The Master said: "I thought that you were asking about others but you ask about Zilu and Ran You. A chief minister serves his ruler on the basis of the Grand Principle and if he cannot, he resigns. Zilu and Ran You may be presently regarded only as minor ministers." Ji Ziran then asked: "Are they then utterly loyal?" The Master said: "They would not commit parricide or regicide." (Xian Jin 24)

Comment Although Kongzi considers that Zilu and Ran You have not attained the level of *Ren*, as disciples they have achieved a baseline in conduct and efficiency.

4.19 The Master said: "Why does Zilu have to play his harp here?" On this account the disciples had no respect for Zilu. The Master said: "Zilu may have reached the hall but he is not yet in the chamber." (Xian Jin 15)

Comment "In the hall but not yet the chamber" is Kongzi's overall evaluation of Zilu. Entry through the sacred door is no guarantee of sagehood.

4.20 The Master said: "There is only one man who will make a judgement after just hearing one side of a case and that is Zilu!" Zilu made no promises that could not be delivered. (Yan Yuan 12)

Comment Is this praise for Zilu's courage and decisiveness or concern at his simplistic attitude of mind and impetuosity of character? Seemingly something between the two.

4.21 Zilu asked: "When one hears something, should one act immediately?" The Master said: "While father and elder brothers exist, how can one act immediately?" Ran You asked: "When one hears something, should one act immediately?" The Master said: "Act immediately!" Gongxi Hua said: "Zilu asked: 'When one hears something, should one act immediately?' and the Master replied: 'While father and elder brothers exist'; Ran You asked: 'When one hears something, should one act immediately?' and the Master replied: 'Act immediately!' I am puzzled, may I ask for clarification?" The Master said: "Ran You is hesitant, so I encouraged him, Zilu is impetuous, so I discouraged him." (Xian Jin 22)

Comment Kongzi was well aware of the character defect of Zilu's impetuosity and deliberately, over time, tried to cure it. To the same question put by different disciples he returned different answers, the significance lay in the focused nature of his teaching.

4.22 The Master lay ill. Zilu ordered the disciples to act as official mourners. The Master recovered a little and he said: "For a long time Zilu has practised trickery! I am not entitled to official mourners, nor should any pretend to act as official mourners, who am I deceiving? Am I deceiving heaven? I would rather die at the hands of the official mourners than at the hands of the disciples. Even if I cannot be buried with the ceremony due to a minister, am I likely to die in a ditch?" (Zihan 12)

Comment At the time Kongzi was not a minister and was not entitled to official mourners. However, by ordering the disciples to act as if they were official mourners, Zilu sought to upgrade the classification of Kongzi's funeral. Zilu heartfelt intention had been to make the funeral obsequies as impressive as possible but in so doing he had nearly forfeited all trust and had caused Kongzi great dissatisfaction. Zilu was loyal and uncomplicated in character but here and there there were one or two self-satisfying little tricks.

4.23 Zilu wished Zigao to become governor of the district of Fei. The Master said: "That would be to do ill to somebody's son!" Zilu said: "There are people there, there are the gods of earth and grain, why should it be that only book-learning is regarded as true learning?" The Master said: "This is the reason that I dislike those who play with words." (Xian Jin 25)

Comment Kongzi believed that it would do harm to Zigao, who had not studied very hard, to send him to an official post. Zilu believed that governing the people, land and agriculture was study in itself and that book-learning alone did not have to be regarded as true learning. Kongzi thought that Zilu was quibbling. In fact, Zilu's point of view was not utterly unreasonable.

4.24 Min Ziqian was in attendance on Kongzi, and was well spoken and respectful; Zilu was busy and active; Ran You and Zigong spoke with relaxed confidence. The Master was pleased but said: "As for Zilu, he may come to no good end." (Xian Jin 13)

Comment Kongzi had a particularly deep feeling for Zilu but was concerned by his reckless impetuosity. This might have been a joke, but unfortunately, in the end, Zilu perished in a mutiny in the state of Wei.

(3) Zigong

4.25 Zigong asked: "What do you think of me?" The Master said: "You, you are like a vessel." Zigong asked: "What kind of vessel?" The Master said: "A *hulian*, a precious sacrificial vessel." (Gongye Chang 4)

Comment If you can say that Kongzi saw *Ren* in Yan Yuan and courage in Zilu then he must have seen wisdom in Zigong. A *hulian* is both beautiful and valuable. In comparing Zigong to a *hulian*, Kongzi is obviously showing his esteem for his abilities, but Kongzi also said elsewhere that "A Gentleman is not a vessel," demonstrating that in some respects Zigong had not yet fulfilled Kongzi's hopes.

4.26 The Master said: "Yan Yuan excels in conduct and learning but is impoverished. Zigong is unhappy with his lot but flourishes as a merchant and always guesses the market price." (Xian Jin 19)

Comment Kongzi respected Zigong's intelligence, particularly his commercial acumen. What he regretted was the fact for all that Yan Yuan had attained *Ren*, he spent his life in poverty. Can it really be that "Those with *Ren* do not prosper" and "Riches mean not *Ren*" is heaven's will?

4.27 The Master said to Zigong: "As between you and Yan Yuan, who is the most outstanding?" Zigong replied: "Yan Yuan is, how could I dare hope to compare with him? I can infer two from one, but he can infer ten from one." The Master said: "You cannot match him, neither you nor I can match him." (Gongye Chang 9)

Comment The wisdom of Zigong is expressed in the clarity of his hard-won self-knowledge. He was aware of the gap in learning that existed between him and Yan

Yuan and he was even more aware that Yan Yuan stood much higher in the eyes of his teacher than he did. Kongzi was also intelligent, and because he was unwilling to hurt Zigong's feelings, said that both he himself and Zigong were no match for Yan Yuan.

4.28 Zigong enjoyed talking of others. The Master said: "Zigong, are you so perfect? I lack that sort of leisure." (Xian Wen 29)

Comment The intelligent person very easily detects the defects in others and always enjoys talking about other people. It rather looks as if Zigong was prone to this bad habit. Kongzi is reminding Zigong that in one's conduct one must not only guard one's speech, it is even more important not to be cruel about other people.

4.29 Zigong said: "I do not wish others to impose upon me, nor do I wish to impose upon others." The Master said: "Zigong, this is something that you have not yet mastered." (Gongye Chang 12)

Comment Zigong's statement comes close to the "Thoughtfulness" of "Loyalty and Thoughtfulness"—"Do not do to others that which you would not wish done to you," however, Kongzi clearly believed that Zigong had not yet reached that state.

(4) Other disciples

4.30 The Master said: "Truly filial is Min Ziqian! None disagree with the praise heaped upon him by his family." (Xian Jin 5)

Comment Kongzi saw Filial Piety in the person of Min Ziqian. Filial Piety is a concrete manifestation of *Ren*.

4.31 The ruler of Lu was rebuilding the treasury. Min Ziqian said: "How would it be according to the old plan? Why alter it?" The Master said: "This man does not speak much, but when he does he gets to the point." (Xian Jin 14)

Comment The crux is not whether or not it accords with "the old plan," but whether or not to indulge in an extravagant waste of bricks and timber.

4.32 The Master said of Gongye Chang: "One could marry one's daughter to him. He has been in prison but that was not his fault." The Master's daughter later married him. (Gongye Chang 1)

Comment It is said that Gongye Chang was Kongzi's son-in-law. Kongzi knew that he had been in prison but still married his daughter to him. From this we can see the great confidence that Kongzi had in his moral character.

4.33 The Master said of Nan Rong: "In a state with principle he could hold a position without fear of dismissal; in a state without principle he could withdraw without fear of execution." Later the Master married his elder brother's daughter to him. (Gongye Chang 2)

Comment In this quotation and the previous one, Kongzi sets the unchanging standard by which the Chinese chose their sons-in-law: first, honest and reliable; second, with the ability to earn a living; third, prudent and risk averse.

4.34 The Master dispatched Qidiao Kai to take up a post. Qidiao Kai replied: "I have not the confidence for this." The Master was pleased. (Gongye Chang 6)

Comment Why was Kongzi pleased at Qidiao Kai's answer? Because of his modesty and prudence? Because of the clarity of his self knowledge? Or because he had other great ambitions? There is no explanation and no way of being certain. What is certain, however, is that Qidiao Kai was in no hurry to become an official and was willing to stay with Kongzi and continue to study, perhaps this was one of the reasons why Kongzi was so pleased.

4.35 The Master said: "Zhonggong may be an official." (Yong Ye 1)

Comment Why did Kongzi consider that Zhonggong was suitable to be an official? It can be seen from the quotation below that he believed that Zhonggong possessed a mind of moral quality.

4.36 Somebody said: "Zhonggong has *Ren* but no eloquence." The Master said: "What is the use of eloquence? Eloquent argument merely arouses detestation. What is the use of eloquence without understanding *Ren*?" (Gongye Chang 5)

Comment It appears that Zhonggong conformed very closely to the Gentleman's standard of "cautious in speech but swift in action."

4.37 The Master said of Zhonggong: "If the hide of a sacrificial bullock is red and its horns are straight, though one may not wish to sacrifice it, will the gods of hill and river be willing to give it up?" (Yong Ye 6)

Comment The ancient ceremonies of sacrifice required the selection of fine bullocks with straight horns and a red hide, plough oxen could not be used as a substitute. Zhonggong came from a poor background but was of outstanding character. Consequently Kongzi used the analogy of the "sacrificial bullock" indicating that he was so outstanding that the gods would love him, implying that rulers would always employ him.

4.38 The Master said of Zijian: "This is the man to be a Gentleman! If there are no Gentlemen in the state of Lu, how did he attain the character of a Gentleman?" (Gongye Chang 3)

4.39 The Master said: "I have never met a man of resolve." Somebody said: "There is Shen Cheng." The Master said: "Shen Cheng is a man of desires, how can he be resolute?" (Gongye Chang 11)

Comment Kongzi's evaluation of Shen Cheng includes an element of the principle of "Resolve derives from absence of desire."

4.40 Yuan Xian was steward to the Master who gave him 900 measures of rice in payment; he declined it. The Master said: "Do not refuse it, share it with your village!" (Yong Ye 5)

Comment Yuan Xian worked for Kongzi and Kongzi wished to pay him. Even when Yuan Xian declined, Kongzi still wished to pay him. Kongzi was accustomed to receiving fees for teaching and he always paid the disciples for their services. It looks as if Kongzi had a modern consciousness of payment for services rendered.

4.41 Gongxi Hua was serving in an official post in the state of Qi. Ran You asked the Master for rice on Gongxi's mother's behalf. The Master said: "Give her six *dou* and more." Ran You asked for an increase. The Master said: "Give her two more *dou*." In the end Ran You gave her 800 *dou*. The Master said: "Gongxi Hua went to the state of Qi in a fine carriage drawn by fat horses and clad in a warm fur robe. I have heard it said that the Gentleman only aids those in desperate need and not the wealthy." (Yong Ye 4)

Comment "Help those in need and not the rich" is the charitable principle proposed by Kongzi and still applied today. In this quotation, Kongzi's dissatisfaction is directed at Ran You rather than at Gongxi Hua.

4.42 Ji Kangzi was richer than the Duke of Zhou but his steward Ran You continued to amass riches for him and add to his wealth. The Master said: "He is no pupil of mine, the disciples may sound the drum and attack him." (Xian Jin 17)

Comment The relationship between Kongzi and Ran You was a love-hate one. One of the most administratively gifted pupils, Ran You circulated amongst the ruler and ministers of the state of Lu and carried out many tasks for Kongzi, including persuading the then ruler of Lu, Ji Kangzi, to ask Kongzi to return to Lu once more. Whilst acting as Ji Kangzi's comptroller, Ran You exercised his talents remarkably, sparing no pains in the collection of taxes and debts. This incensed Kongzi and his fierce denunciation of Ran You was because his conduct utterly violated the basic morality of *Ren*.

4.43 Ran You said: "It is not that I take no joy in your teaching, it is that I lack the capacity." The Master said: "Those who lack the capacity give up half-way. You have drawn a line and will make no further progress." (Yong Ye 12)

Comment This is about Ran You's self-justification. Kongzi clearly does not agree with his explanation that the reason he cannot attain *Ren* is because of his lack of capacity, but thinks that it is a question of "unwilling" rather than "unable."

4.44 Zai Wo slept during the day. The Master said: "You cannot carve rotten wood or paint a wall built from dung! What is the use of scolding him?" The Master said: "When first I knew people I listened and believed they would act as they said, now I listen and see what they do. In the case of Zai Wo I have changed my mind." (Gongye Chang 10)

Comment Zai Wo was another problematical disciple. He liked to challenge Kongzi's views and was able in reasoning, he often caused Kongzi difficulty in responding, and some of his conduct infuriated Kongzi. But it is clearly excessive to describe somebody as "rotten wood" and a "wall of dung" because he takes a mid-day nap. It looks as if the pent-up anger that Kongzi accumulated during the ordinary day erupted when there was an opportunity.

4.45 Boniu was ill. The Master visited him and grasped his hand through the window saying: "Is death our fate? That such a one should be so ill! That such a one should be so ill!" (Yong Ye 10)

Comment To fall sick and die is something that everybody has to face and to experience. It is outside *Ren* and something that even the Gentleman of cultivation who loves virtue and is prudent of speech cannot avoid. This is the source of Kongzi's sigh.

4.46 Zigong asked: "Of Zizhang and Zixia, who is the more worthy?" The Master said: "Zizhang is rather excessive and Zixia falls a little short." Zigong said: "Then Zizhang is better?" The Master said: "To exceed is the same as falling short." (Xian Jin 16)

Comment In evaluating the merits and defects of these two disciples, Kongzi demonstrates that what he really approves of is the quality of "balance" in personal conduct.

4.47 Ziyou became governor of Wucheng. The Master said: "Have you any people of ability there?" Ziyou said: "There is one called Tantai Mieming, he keeps to the straight and narrow and apart from official business never calls to pay his respects." (Yong Ye 14)

Comment It seems that calling unofficially to pay one's respects was one of the rules to be observed by the true Gentleman.

4.48 The Master visited Wucheng and listened to the sound of strings and song. The Master laughed and said: "Would you use a bullock knife to carve a chicken?" Ziyou replied: "I once heard you say: 'In studying ceremony and music the Gentleman comes to understand the love of man and the rogue becomes obedient.'" The Master said: "Disciples! Ziyou is right, I spoke in jest!" (Yang Huo 4)

Comment Irrespective of the size of the place, ceremony and music are the same. Kongzi spoke in jest but quickly realized that Ziyou was right to be so serious.

4.49 The Master said: "Those that studied ceremony and music with me early were common country people. Those that came later were Gentlemen. Were I to employ them I would prefer the former." (Xian Jin 1)

Comment This is Kongzi's evaluation of his disciples. However the historical interpretations of this passage often contain infelicities and there has been no resolution to the dispute this has caused. The following interpretation may be slightly more reasonable: Kongzi is regretting the unfairness and lack of opportunity for advancement suffered by his early pupils. Kongzi believed that these earlier pupils had studied for longer and had accomplished more and he had more affection for them, hence the remark about employment, —that he would definitely choose from this early group of pupils.

4.50 While in the state of Chen, the Master said: "Return! Return! The young disciples from my home-town are vigorous and spirited, moreover they have talent too, but they have yet to learn moderation." (Gongye Chang 22)

Comment Whilst Kongzi was in the state of Chen, opportunities for preferment in government occurred in the state of Lu. Kongzi encouraged his young disciples to return home to realize their own ambitions. He saw that they had grown up and were capable of accepting responsibility but pointed out that they still did not understand moderation.

4.51 The Master said: "The disciples that were with me in the states of Chen and Cai no longer cross my threshold." (Xian Jin 2)

Comment The return home of some of his disciples saddened Kongzi. Their constant companionship and support, especially during the food shortages in Chen and Cai had forged a lifelong bond of friendship between Kongzi and the disciples.

2. On music and poetry

The use of poetry and music as an instrument through which to experience the grand path to *Ren* and to explore the inner meaning of music and poetry so as to inspire and educate the disciples.

(1) On poetry

4.52 The Master said: "Young men! Why do you not study poetry? Poetry can express your inner feelings, can show you all in nature's world, can join you with others and can express your grief. It can serve your parents at home and your ruler abroad and teach you the names of birds, beasts, plants and trees." (Yang Huo 9)

Comment In Kongzi's eyes, poetry was not merely a matter of literary appreciation, it was more a path towards *Ren*. As an instrument for the propagation of *Ren* poetry had a number of social functions, of which the expression of feeling, the observation of nature, the community of man, and grief formed the basic characteristics of classical Chinese poetry.

4.53 The Master said: "Start with poetry, establish with ceremony and complete with music." (Taibo 8)

Comment This describes the process through which a Gentleman achieved maturity, however, it would also be possible to see it in terms of the rise of a state.

4.54 The Master said: "The three hundred poems of the *Classic of Poetry* are expressed in but one word, purity." (Wei Zheng 2)

Comment There are many love songs in the 300 poems of the *Classic of Poetry*, for Kongzi to summarize them as "purity" suggests a rather particular way of looking at things. The normal emotions and desires of mankind, were, in the view of Kongzi, a part of human nature that was not in itself in breach of *Ren*, and could be naturally and sincerely expressed as "purity."

4.55 The Master said: "The poem, the "Call of the Osprey," is joyful but not wanton, sad but not grief-stricken." (Ba Yi 20)

Comment This quotation takes as an example the first poem of the *Classic of Poetry*, the "Call of the Osprey," which describes the longing for each other of a man and a woman, and further elucidates the "purity" of the previous quotation. Kongzi regards the emotional longing which the poem describes as neither too much nor too little, but as "just right" and to be taken as a model.

4.56 Zixia asked: "What is the meaning of the poem 'The smiling countenance enchants, how pretty the glancing eyes, the simple face beneath magnificently adorned'?" The Master said: "If you wish to paint a picture, you must first have a white ground." Zixia said: "Then Propriety comes later?" The Master said: "Zixia, you are the one who can inspire! Now I can discuss the *Classic of Poetry* with you." (Ba Yi 8)

Comment Kongzi and Zixia are discussing the *Classic of Poetry* and from the descriptions of beautiful women in some of the poems realize the principle of first *Ren*, then Propriety. *Ren* is the simple original beauty of the woman and Propriety is the make-up that is applied later.

4.57 "The shadberry flowers quiver in the wind, how can I not long for you? But you are too far away." The Master said: "This is no real longing, if it were, what distance could there be?" (Zihan 31)

Comment It is likely that what is being discussed here is a poem no longer included in the *Classic of Poetry*. Kongzi shows unusual humor in his comment and there is no profound "enlightenment" to be had.

4.58 The Master said: "To have the ability to recite the 300 poems of the *Classic of Poetry*, yet to hold a post in government which one cannot manage; or to be an envoy and not to be able to conduct negotiation and conversation on one's own; what then is the use of being able to recite so many poems by heart?" (Zilu 5)

Comment Kongzi is emphasizing the social functions of the *Classic of Poetry* at the time. At the time of the Spring and Autumn annals, government, judiciary and diplomacy all required an ability to quote from the *Classic of Poetry* as appropriate. To have studied the poems but to be unable to use them was tantamount to not having studied at all.

4.59 The Master said to his son Kong Li: "Do you know the "Zhou Nan" and the "Shao Nan," if people do not know these two, isn't it like standing facing a wall?" (Yang Huo 10)

Comment "Zhou Nan" and "Shao Nan" are the names of poems of the *Classic of Poetry* and are local songs collected under the name of their locality. The point here is that if you do not study poetry, you can go nowhere.

4.60 Chen Kang asked the Master's son Kong Li: "Have you learned anything unusual?" Kong Li replied: "No. He was once standing in the hall as I was passing through and he asked me: 'Have you studied the *Classic of Poetry*?' I replied: 'No.' He said: 'If you do not study the *Classic of Poetry* you will not know how to converse.' So I withdrew and studied the *Classic of Poetry*. On another day he was standing there as I passed through and he asked: 'Have you studied Propriety?' I replied: 'Not yet.' He said: 'If you do not study Propriety you will not know how to stand by yourself.' I withdrew and studied Propriety. These are the two things that I have learned." Chen Kang was delighted and said: "I have received three answers for the price of one question: I have learned of the principles of the *Classic of Poetry* and of Propriety and I have also learned that a Gentleman does not favor his son." (Jishi 13)

Comment There are no "secret texts" in Confucianism, whether son or disciples, all study the *Classic of Poetry* and Propriety. Nevertheless, of the 3,000 disciples, it is estimated that there were very few who comprehended the Grand Principle through the study of poetry, calligraphy, ceremony and music; the vast majority merely acquired a little cultural knowledge and a "Diploma of the School of Confucius."

(2) On music

4.61 While in the state of Qi the Master heard the music of *Shao*, and for three months could not taste meat, saying: "I had not thought that music was ravishing to this extent." (Shu Er 14)

Comment *Shao*, a type of music, reputed to be the ancient music of the time of the legendary emperor Shun. Kongzi loved music primarily for the emotional pleasure that it brought. The joy that *Shao* music brought him clearly exceeded that of the taste of meat.

4.62 The Master said of *Shao* music: "It has both utter beauty and utter virtue." He said of *Wu* music: "It has utter beauty but it is not utterly virtuous." (Ba Yi 25)

Comment *Wu*, a type of music reputed to be that of the time of the Zhou dynasty emperor, King Wu of Zhou (?-1043 BC). Kongzi is comparing *Shao* music and *Wu* music. He considered that *Shao* music achieved perfection in form and content and that although *Wu* music was perfect in form it was deficient in content. Where lay the deficiency of *Wu* music? In its lack of *Ren*.

4.63 The Master said: "From the opening piece played by the Master of Music Zhi to the final piece, the "Call of the Osprey," my ears were filled with rich and beautiful melodies." (Taibo 15)

4.64 The Master discussed music with the Tutor of Lu and said: "I know the melodies: the opening piece is played together and the sound fills one's ears with joy; then it expands with a melodious tune and clear rhythm, continuously repeating until the end." (Ba Yi 23)
Comment Kongzi's music standard was absolutely that of a professional. His description is one that pieces of music follow today: statement of theme, development, recapitulation and conclusion.

4.65 The Master said: "Propriety! Propriety! Is it just jade and silk? Music! Music! Is it just bells and drums?" (Yang Huo 11)
Comment Kongzi is pointing out that the essence of music lies in Propriety and that the essence of Propriety lies in *Ren*.

4.66 The Master said: "It was only when I returned to Lu from the state of Wei that music was collected and arranged and that Ya and Song each had their place." (Zihan 15)
Comment Ya (elegant, formal) and Song (a song of praise) are two different types of music from the *Classic of Poetry*. Following his peregrination through the states, Kongzi returned to Lu from the state of Wei and devoted his efforts to the editing of ancient texts and to the classification of ancient music. He believed that music was not confined

to giving pleasure but that it also had a social function in stabilizing popular feeling and that government through *Ren* started from ceremony and music.

3. Analysis of cases

Demonstrating, through an analysis of difficult cases, how those possessed of *Ren* can handle similar problems when they meet them and how the criteria of *Ren* should be observed and implemented.

4.67 Zai Wo asked: "If somebody told one that possessed *Ren* that somebody had fallen down a well, would he then jump in and save him?" The Master said: "Why should he act so? The Gentleman can save him from the mouth of the well and need not jump in; a Gentleman may be deceived but he cannot act stupidly." (Yong Ye 26)

Comment Zai Wo often asked challenging questions and this is an example. The question is a logical trap: somebody has fallen down a well, jump in to rescue them and you will die with them, that is *Ren*, watching them die without attempting rescue is not *Ren*. Kongzi did not fall into the trap but circumvented it by asking in return: "Why should he act so?" His meaning was clear, there was no necessity for pointless sacrifice, even in the name of *Ren*.

4.68 Duke Ye told the Master: "In my home-town there was an honest man whose father stole a sheep and the son reported him." The Master replied: "The honest in my home-town are different: the father protects the son and the son protects the father, that is where the honesty lies." (Zilu 18)

Comment Duke Ye and Kongzi were discussing a legal case. Duke Ye believed the law took precedence over human relationships; for his part, Kongzi considered that ethics took precedence over the law of kings. On the face of it, Duke Ye's view is comparatively modern, the law takes no account of human relationships; in fact Kongzi's view that the law should be built upon human relationships and ethics is rather more profound.

4. A discussion of the politics of the time

Commentary and views on many of the political events of the time, demonstrating the points of view and attitudes that those possessed of *Ren* should adopt towards different problems.

(1) The rule of Ji Kangzi

4.69 The Master said of Ji Kangzi: "Eight ranks of eight dancers performing in the courtyard, if this can be tolerated, what may not be tolerated?!" (Ba Yi 1)

Comment Ji Kangzi was in power in the state of Lu and any criticism of him was a criticism of the ruler of Lu. Kongzi's anger was directed at Ji Kangzi's open overstepping of the mark in the "Rules of Ceremony." Ji Kangzi's family was that of a chief minister and according to the *Rites of Zhou* were only entitled to 16 dancers, whereas he had used 64 dancers, the prerogative of the Zhou emperor. Looked at another way, this also reflected the social situation that accompanied the "collapse of ceremony and destruction of music" at the time.

4.70 The three families of Ji, Meng and Shusun performed the

Yong music at the conclusion of ancestral sacrifices. The Master said: "How can the meaning of the poem 'Assisting at the sacrifice from the side are the princes, in the center solemnly celebrating is the Zhou king' be taken as referring to your family temples?" (Ba Yi 2)

Comment The three families of Ji, Meng and Shusun were the three noble families then in power in the state of Lu. The use of imperial music at family sacrifices is another example of their contempt for the ceremonial system of the Zhou court and of its destruction as well.

4.71 Ji Kangzi intended to sacrifice at Mount Tai. The Master said to Ran You: "Can you not advise against this?" Ran You replied: "No." The Master said: "Alas! In speaking of Mount Tai are there none who know Propriety so well as Lin Fang?" (Ba Yi 6)

Comment Sacrificing at Mount Tai was the prerogative of the Son of Heaven and the vassal princes. Ji Kangzi was merely the chief minister of the state of Lu, but nevertheless also intended to sacrifice at Mount Tai. This usurpation of Propriety infuriated Kongzi.

4.72 Ji Kangzi was about to mount a punitive expedition against Zhuan Yu. Ran You and Zilu sought out Kongzi and said: "Ji Kangzi is taking up arms against Zhuan Yu." The Master said: "Ran You, is there no mistake of yours in this? Zhuan Yu once sacrificed at Mount Dongmeng for the Zhou king and it lies within the realm of Lu, it is a minister at the court of Lu, why mount an expedition against it?" Ran You said: "Ji Kangzi desires it but we two ministers do not approve." Kongzi said: "Ran You! Zhou Ren once said: 'Do your duty to the utmost, if you cannot, then resign.' If you cannot help in calamity or support in collapse then what is the use of you two ministers? Moreover you are mistaken. If the tiger and the rhinoceros escape their pen or the tortoise shell and jade are broken in the box, whose fault is that?" Ran You said: "Zhuan Yu's city walls are impregnable and he lies close to Fei. If it is not taken now there will be sorrow for our children and grandchildren." Kongzi said: "Ran You, a Gentleman hates those who do not say outright what they want but seek some other means of obtaining it. I have heard it said that in respect of a nation or a family, poverty is not to be feared but inequality of riches is; deficiency is not to be feared but lack of stability is. If there is equality then there are neither rich nor poor; if there is harmony then there is neither much nor little; if the state is stable then there is no danger of it being overthrown. This being so, if those afar do not submit then *Ren*, Righteousness, Propriety and music must be used to secure their submission. Those that have submitted should be allowed to live in peace. At present, Ran You and Zilu, you two ministers assist Ji Kangzi but the distant will not submit and cannot be made to, the state is divided internally and cannot be defended and yet there are plans to use force within its borders. I fear that for Ji Kangzi disaster lies not with Zhuan Yu but within his own gate." (Jishi 1)

Comment There was argument between Kongzi on the one hand and Ran You and Zilu on the other about Ji Kangzi's intention to go to war. Kongzi believed that this war was absurd, not only did it lack any proper purpose but it also failed to deal with the external threat. More importantly, as Kongzi pointed out, the suffering of a nation lay in "inequality" which led to disharmony which in turn led to unrest. Consequently, the fate of a nation lay, not outside, but within itself.

4.73 Ji Kangzi made a gift of medicinal herbs to Kongzi. The Master said: "I lack the skill, I dare not taste them." (Xiang Dang 16)

4.74 The Master said: "The rulers of Lu have been out of power for five generations and the government has been in the hands of the ministers for four. In consequence, Ji, Meng, and Shusun, the descendants of Duke Huan of Lu will be weakened." (Jishi 3)

Comment This is Kongzi's summary of the "collapse of the monarchy" in the state of Lu at the time, it is also his forecast of the inevitable decline of the rulers of Lu.

(2) The politics of the state of Lu

4.75 Yang Huo wished to see Kongzi but when Kongzi declined to receive him, he sent a roast suckling pig. Choosing a time when he would be absent, Kongzi paid a return visit but met him on the road. Yang Huo said: "Come! I must speak with you." Saying: "Would it be in accord with *Ren* to possess precious political ability but to allow the state to go to pot?" Kongzi said: "It would not." "Would it be called wise to possess the skill but to have allowed opportunities to escape?" Kongzi replied: "It would not." Yang Huo then said: "Time flies and waits for no one!" Kongzi said: "Then I will take office!" (Yang Huo 1)

Comment As comptroller for the Ji family Yang Huo was, for a time, a figure to be reckoned with in the state of Lu. He had political ambitions and wished to entice Kongzi into his own service, however, he was clearly somebody whom Kongzi neither liked nor wished to have any dealings with. It seems clear that Yang Huo understood Kongzi very well, and used words like *Ren* and wisdom to persuade him but Kongzi remained unmoved. Nevertheless, their conversation stimulated Kongzi's political ambitions and at the age of over 50 he became minister for criminal justice and chief minister in the state of Lu, thus realizing his ideas of government through *Ren* and displaying the Confucian spirit of engagement with the world.

4.76 Gongshan Furao occupied Fei in rebellion and called for Kongzi who wished to go. Zilu was unwilling and said: "Why should you wish to go to Gongshan?" Kongzi said: "Can it be that calling for me is merely an empty gesture? If there are those who will employ me I will re-establish the Zhou dynasty in the East!" (Yang Huo 5)

Comment Like Yang Huo, Gongshan Furao, was a counsellor in the service of the Ji family and belonged to the group of "traitorous officials." He had been in charge of the Ji clan's fiefdom of Fei but had rebelled and occupied it. His motive in calling for Kongzi was the same as that of Yang Huo. Surprisingly, Kongzi was tempted, from which can be seen his anxiety to propagate his theories of government through *Ren*, even to the point of a certain lack of discrimination.

4.77 The Master said: "Zang Wuzhong sought to exchange the town of Fang for a title of nobility in the state of Lu for the clan of Zang. Although it is said that he did not coerce the ruler, I do not believe it." (Xian Wen 14)

Comment Wuzhong had offended Meng and had fled the state of Lu but had later returned to his fiefdom of Fang and on the condition that his descendants should join the ranks of the ministerial class he had offered up the fiefdom. Kongzi clearly did not approve of the way in which he attempted to use the fiefdom as a bargaining counter with the ruler of Lu.

4.78 Chen Chengzi assassinated Duke Jian of Qi. Kongzi bathed and went to court and reported to Duke Ai of Lu: "Chen Chengzi has assassinated his ruler, please send an expedition to punish him." The Duke replied: "Report this to the ministers of the three clans." Kongzi said later: "Having myself been a minister, I dared not report! The ruler then said: 'Report this to the ministers of the three clans!'" Kongzi then reported to the ministers of the three clans who did not agree that an expedition should be sent. Kongzi said: "Having myself been a minister, I dared not report!" (Xian Wen 21)

Comment Kongzi believed the regicide in the state of Qi to be a grave matter and although retired felt that he had to lay the matter before the ruler of Lu personally. The ruler thereupon instructed him to report it to the ministers of the three clans of Ji, Meng and Shusun. One can see from this a part of the reason why the power of the Lu monarchy fell into the hands of others.

4.79 Ran You returned from court. The Master said: "Why so late?" Ran You replied: "There were matters of state." The Master said: "They were merely affairs, had they been matters of state I would have known, even though I am no longer employed." (Zilu 14)

Comment Ran You was in the service of the Ji clan and Kongzi was dissatisfied with him, hence this conversation. Matters of state were "matters" and family affairs were "affairs." Kongzi is mocking Ran You for regarding the family affairs of the Ji clan as matters of the Lu state.

4.80 The stables burned down. The Master returned from court and asked: "Was any one injured?" He did not ask about the horses. (Xiang Dang 17)

Comment To ask after people but not horses, is "making man the basis."

(3) The decline of ceremony and music

4.81 The Master said: "The sacrificial beakers are beakers no longer, what has become of them? What has become of them?" (Yong Ye 25)

Comment The beaker is a ritual vessel used in sacrificial ceremonies. We do not know under what circumstances Kongzi emitted this cry, perhaps at the Temple of Ancestors or perhaps at a sacrificial ceremony. In short, the beakers made at that time no longer resembled the genuine beakers. It was this that had drawn a sigh from Kongzi, the Zhou dynasty system of ceremony and music was dying away.

4.82 The Master said: "After the first libation at the sacrifice to the imperial ancestors I could bear to watch no longer." (Ba Yi 10)

Comment Why was Kongzi unable to continue watching? The ceremony was the sacrifice to the ancestors carried out in ancient times by the Zhou dynasty Son of Heaven, it was an imperial Zhou dynasty sacrifice now being performed on their own by vassal princes, how could Kongzi possibly have continued to watch?

4.83 Someone asked Kongzi about the meaning of the imperial sacrifice to the ancestors. The Master said: "I do not know. But for those who do understand, knowing how to govern would be as easy as putting something here," pointing to the palm of his hand. (Ba Yi 11)

Comment Kongzi believed that Propriety was the guiding principle of government. Once a ruler understood Propriety he would then know how to govern.

4.84 Duke Ai of Lu asked Zai Wo what wood should be used to make the memorial tablets for the Earth god. Zai Wo said: "The Xia used pine, the Yin used cedar, the Zhou used chestnut, so that the people should tremble." The Master commented: "Do not discuss what is already complete, do not try to prevent what is already in the past, do not rake over what has already happened." (Ba Yi 21)

Comment The context here is not clear and historical interpretations differ. Kongzi's remarks seem to be directed at Zai Wo. Zai Wo said that the aim of the Zhou use of chestnut (*li*) wood to make tablets to the Earth god was to "make the people tremble" (*zhan li*). It is the homophonic relationship between the two words that lends significance to the Zhou use of chestnut. True though it may be it makes the "elegant and cultivated" Zhou dynasty appear as an ethnic dictatorship. Hence Kongzi's views.

(4) The vassal states

(The state of Qi)

4.85 The Master said: "Once there is reform in Qi, it reaches Lu; once there is reform in Lu, it will lead to the Grand Principle." (Yong Ye 24)

Comment The implementation of the Grand Principle throughout the land was, for Kongzi, the ideal of a lifetime. He believed that the hope and conditions for realizing this ideal were more favorable in Lu than in Qi. His confidence in the state of Lu was not entirely a matter of patriotism, one of the factors was that Lu was developing more slowly than Qi and retained more of the traditions of ceremony and music.

(The state of Wei)

4.86 The Master said: "The politics of Lu and Wei are as close as elder and younger brothers." (Zilu 7)

Comment The state of Wei was Kongzi's first stop on his peregrination through the states, and the first territory in which he planned to propagate "government through *Ren*." Later, when returning to Lu, he stayed in Wei for a while.

4.87 Duke Ling of Wei asked Kongzi about deployment on the field of battle. Kongzi replied: "I have heard a little about the arrangement of sacrificial vessels but I have never studied military matters." He left the next day. (Duke Ling of Wei 1)

Comment Kongzi had once attempted to induce Duke Ling of Wei to introduce government through *Ren* but he had only been interested in matters military, there was clearly no common frame of reference for any conversation between the two.

4.88 The Master met Nanzi and Zilu was displeased. The Master swore: "If I do something that I should not, may Heaven reject me! May Heaven reject me!" (Yong Ye 28)

Comment There was a suspicion that when Kongzi had visited the famous beauty Nanzi it had been by way of the concubine's bedchamber. This, combined with her unsavory reputation had caused Zilu some disquiet. Zilu cared a great deal for Kongzi's image in his own eyes and the eyes of others.

4.89 Wangsun Jia asked: "What is the meaning of 'It is better to propitiate the kitchen god than gods more honorably positioned'?" The Master said: "Not so. Offend Heaven and there will be nowhere to pray." (Ba Yi 13)

Comment Duke Ling's minister was clearly after actual political information rather than enquiring about learning. The better positioned gods were more honored than the kitchen god but sometimes the kitchen god was more useful. We do not know whether or not this was actually the point of the conversation. Kongzi's reply was that all calculations were wrong. It was only Heaven that man should really not offend.

4.90 While in Wei the Master played the chimes. A man with a basket on his shoulder passed by the door and said: "There is a load on your mind, it is in your playing!" He further said: "There is sadness there, in the tinkling of the chimes. Since nobody understands you, all you can do is to guard yourself. 'When the water is deep, you just have to cross with your clothes on, when it is shallow you can roll your robe up and wade across.'" The Master said: "Well said! There is nothing that you have said that may be argued with!" (Xian Wen 39)

Comment Nothing went well for Kongzi in Wei and his plans had been obstructed and when his spirits were low he played the chimes to amuse himself, but his playing inevitably revealed his mood. The basket carrier who passed the door does not seem to have been a typical peasant since he could detect Kongzi's mood, quote from the *Classic of Poetry* and gently mock his passion for politics.

4.91 The Master spoke of Duke Ling of Wei's lack of principle and Ji Kangzi said: "Since it is so, how is it that he has not fallen?" Kongzi said: "Zhongshu Yu receives guests from abroad, Zhu Tuo is in charge of temple sacrifices and Wangsun Jia commands the army, with such talent how can he fall?" (Xian Wen 19)

Comment Neither the combination of stupid ruler with wise minister nor wise ruler with stupid minister is a national disaster. But with stupid ruler and stupid minister, disaster is not far off.

4.92 Qu Boyu sent an emissary to Kongzi. Kongzi sat with him and asked: "What has your Master done recently?" The emissary replied: "My Master desires to diminish his faults but has not yet succeeded." The emissary left and the Master said: "Such an emissary! Such an emissary!" (Xian Wen 25)

Comment Kongzi considered Qu Boyu to be a rare worthy. His praise for the emissary was also praise for the man himself.

4.93 Ran You said: "Would the Master assist the ruler of Wei?" Zigong said: "I will ask him." He entered and asked: "What manner of people were Boyi and Shuqi?" The Master replied: "They were ancient worthies." He further asked: "Did they bear hatred?" The Master said: "What hatred lies in seeking *Ren* and gaining it?" Zigong withdrew and said: "The Master will not do it." (Shu Er 15)

Comment This is an incident which occurred when Kongzi was staying in Wei once more on his way back to Lu. The ruler of Wei, namely Duke Chu of Wei, was Duke Ling of Wei's grandson, Zhe, whose father had been banished for plotting the assassination of Nanzi, Duke Ling's wife. Zhe had become ruler on the death of Duke Ling. His father had now returned from exile and was in contention with him for the throne. In the struggle for the throne between the two, Kongzi took the side of the father. This was not because the father was particularly virtuous but because succession to the position of ruler was governed by laws of succession which could not be broken. Kongzi believed that the Duke of Wei should imitate Boyi and Shuqi who had both abdicated in favor of their father and had achieved moral satisfaction thereby.

(Jin)

4.94 Bi Xi summoned Kongzi, and the Master intended to go. Zilu said: "In the past, I have heard you say 'The Gentleman does not visit those who themselves have done evil.' Bi Xi has rebelled and occupied the city of Zhongmou but you are going, why is this?" The Master said: "That is so, the words are mine. But is there not 'strength' that cannot be ground down or 'whiteness' that cannot be dyed black? Am I a gourd that hangs there and cannot be eaten?" (Yang Huo 7)

Comment This resembles Gongshan Furao of Lu's post-rebellion summons to Kongzi, Jin's Bi Xi also summons Kongzi after his rebellion. It is interesting that Kong's reaction is the same in each case: to go. Kongzi's passion for the implementation of government through *Ren* is so strong that it leads to lack of discrimination, though, fortunately, in each case he is dissuaded by Zilu.

(Outer barbarians)

4.95 The Master said: "The barbarians beyond the central plain who have rulers are less than the states of the central plain who have no ruler." (Ba Yi 5)

Comment Historical interpretations of this passage differ but it is certain that Kongzi's ideas tended towards the sinocentric and that he despised "barbarian" ethnic groups. He also believed levels of civilization differed amongst ethnic groups in the same way that he believed that man was divided into grades.

4.96 The Master wished to dwell amongst the barbarians. Someone said: "They are backward and unenlightened, what then?" The Master said: "How can there be backwardness and lack of enlightenment where a Gentleman chooses to dwell?" (Zihan 14)

Comment Although Kongzi despised the ethnic minorities on the borders he in no way considered that their backwardness was unchangeable. The mark of civilization was the existence of Gentlemen and it was Gentlemen who spread civilization.

(5) Mocked by the hermits

4.97 Weisheng Mu said to Kongzi: "Why are you always so busy? Is not perhaps to show off your eloquence?" The Master said: "I dare not become a person of flowery words and fine speeches, I just hate the stubbornness of people." (Xian Wen 32)

Comment This exchange probably took place when Kongzi was young. Kongzi, then in the state of Lu and busy with study and teaching, was determined to change the world.

4.98 Chang Ju and Jie Ni were plowing a field together, when Kongzi passed by and told Zilu to ask the way to the ford. Chang Ju said: "Who is it that is holding the reins?" Zilu said: "It is Kong Qiu." "Kong Qiu of Lu?"asked Chang Ju. Zilu said: "It is." "Then he should know the way to the ford!" said Chang Ju. Zilu then asked Jie Ni. Jie Ni said: "And who might you be?" Zilu replied: "I am Zilu." "The pupil of Kong Qiu?" asked Jie Ni. "I am." replied Zilu. Jie Ni then said: "The world rains disaster and who will change it? Rather than follow one who wishes to escape evil people, would it not be better to be as carefree as those who flee society?" So saying, he carried on plowing. Zilu returned and told Kongzi who said in disappointment: "Man cannot live with birds and beasts, if one cannot live with people with whom may one be? Heaven has its principle and I cannot change it." (Weizi 6)

Comment This incident occurred during Kongzi's peregrination through the states with his pupils. On the journey, Kongzi came across the two hermits who clearly disapproved of his political views and ridiculed his positive enthusiasm for engagement with the world. Kongzi was also aware of the deep divisions that existed between himself and these two lofty hermits. Both sides were similar in wisdom but held dissimilar attitudes to life.

4.99 Zilu fell behind and met an old man carrying a bamboo weeding tool suspended from a pole over his shoulder. Zilu asked: "Have you seen the Master?" The old man replied: "My limbs are heavy and I cannot tell one crop from another, tell me, who is the Master?" So saying, he stuck his pole in the ground and began weeding. Zilu stood there and saluted him. The old man took Zilu home, killed a chicken to eat with millet and introduced his two sons. The next day Zilu took to the road and told Kongzi. The Master said: "He was a hermit." He told Zilu to go back and see him. Zilu returned but the old man had left. Zilu said: "It is not right not to be an official. The manners between young and old should not be abandoned, how can the relationship between ruler and minister be of no concern? To be concerned just with the purity of self throws human relationships into chaos. The Gentleman becomes an official so as to practice Righteousness. As to the difficulty of implementing the Grand Principle, that has been known all along." (Weizi 7)

Comment Like the two hermits of the previous quotation, the old man with a pole over his shoulder was no ordinary person. It is interesting that the ancient hermits labored in the fields themselves, thus freeing themselves from dependence upon an official salary from the court and maintaining their spiritual independence. The final passage "Zilu said," may, from its style, be an error for "the Master said." In the eyes of the Confucians the relationship between ruler and minister was one of the complete set of human relationships and thus could not be discarded. In truth, the fact that human relationships could not be abandoned in no way meant that the relationship between ruler and minister could exist in perpetuity. In fact, the "republicanism" of today is a new set of human relationships that replaces the relationship between ruler and minister.

4.100 In the state of Chu, a madman Jieyu met his carriage and passed Kongzi singing: "Phoenix! Oh. Phoenix! Why so downcast on this day of virtuous fate? The past is beyond repair but the future gives time to repent. Enough! Enough! Those in power are in peril!" Kongzi dismounted seeking to talk to him but he escaped and Kongzi was unable to speak with him. (Weizi 5)

Comment There is no "The Master said" in this passage. It was not that Kongzi did not wish to speak but that the other side did not give him the opportunity. In fact, what was there that Kongzi could have said in the face of this madman's mockery? It was not that he could not see the dangers of the immediate situation but that different people make different choices. In this instance Kongzi spoke without speaking.

5. Praise and Criticism

In his discussions of learning and politics with his disciples, Kongzi gave his judgments, good or bad, on many historical and contemporary figures. In his judgments and discussions Kongzi always used *Ren* as the criterion.

(1) Contemporaries

(Personalities of the state of Lu)

4.101 An official of the state of Chen asked whether Duke Zhao of Lu understood Propriety, the Master said: "He does." After Kongzi had withdrawn, the official invited Wuma Qi to enter and said: "I have heard say that the Gentleman does not take sides, could it be that Kongzi is not impartial? The ruler of Lu took as his wife a woman of Wu of the same surname, the rulers of both states having the same surname, and called her Wu Mengzi. If the ruler of Lu understands Propriety, who does not?" Wuma Qi recounted this to Kongzi who said: "I am truly fortunate, if I make a mistake, somebody will always know." (Shu Er 31)

Comment When the Chen official asked Kongzi whether Duke Zhao of Lu "understood Propriety" it may, perhaps, have been out of patriotism or out of a desire not to embarrass and Kongzi gave a definite answer almost without thinking. However, in marrying a wife of the same name, Duke Zhao of Lu contravened the rule against marriage with a person of the same surname enshrined in the *Rites of Zhou* and was clearly no model for the "understanding of Propriety." When somebody else pointed out this contradiction to Kongzi he had to admit, in self mockery, that he was biased in favor of Duke Zhao. Propriety was an embodiment of *Ren* and, in Kongzi's eyes, had a universal value which surpassed states and rulers in importance.

4.102 The Master said: "Meng Zhifan never praises himself. When the army is in retreat he protects the rear, when it enters a town, he lashes his horse saying: 'I was not brave at the rear, it was just that my horse was slow.'" (Yong Ye 15)

Comment This Lu minister Meng Zhifan had the character of a Gentleman and could be the model for "Always at the very front in difficulty; hidden at the rear when things go well" (Yong Ye 22).

4.103 The Master said: "Meng Gongchuo has the qualities to be a household official in the Zhao clan or Wei clan of the state of Jin, but he could not be a minister in a small state like Teng or Xue." (Xian Wen 11)

Comment Elsewhere, Kongzi praises Meng Gongchuo for his "lack of desire" (Xian Wen 12), why say that he could be a household official in a large state but not a minister in a small one? Kongzi gives no detailed explanation but it must be to do with his "lack of desire."

4.104 Ji Wenzi never acted before thinking three times. Kongzi heard this and said: "Twice is quite enough." (Gongye Chang 20)

Comment Kongzi thought Ji Wenzi overcautious to the point of indecision.

4.105 Yuan Rang sat with legs outstretched waiting for Kongzi. Kongzi saw him and said: "Lacking Fraternal Piety when young, no achievement worthy of praise in adulthood; now old and refusing to die, what a disaster!" And, so saying, hit him on the legs with a stick. (Xian Wen 43)

Comment Kongzi very rarely swore. Yuan Rang is an exception, savagely abused and struck on the legs with a stick. Yuan Rang may very well have been obnoxious and provoked the highly cultivated Kongzi into an outburst of anger. *Ren* is the love of people, but how to love the obnoxious is a real problem.

4.106 A young man in Kongzi's hometown announced guests at a banquet. Somebody asked Kongzi: "Is this a young man who will do well?" The Master said: "Seeing him sitting in the place of an adult and seeing him alongside his elders, he appears bent on success, not on doing well." (Xian Wen 44)

Comment Kongzi's observation of people was acute and he was able to concentrate on the main elements. What he saw in this active young man was not a natural disposition towards *Ren* but an impatient ambition.

4.107 The people of Huxiang were difficult to engage in conversation. Kongzi received a boy and the disciples were puzzled. The Master said: "I praise his progress rather than confirm his backwardness. Why be excessive? If people clean themselves up to make progress, one should applaud their effort and not be constantly thinking of their past." (Shu Er 29)

Comment Another story of a boy. Kongzi took a different attitude to this boy of whom nobody thought well, and encouraged the progress demonstrated in his appearance, however slight it may have been.

(Personalities of the states)

4.108 Zizhang asked: "Minister Ziwen of the state of Chu became chief minister three times but displayed no joy; he was dismissed three times but displayed no indignation. Each time he left office he handed over everything to his successor. How is he to be considered?" The Master said: "As Loyal." Zizhang asked: "Is it *Ren*?" The Master said: "I do not know. How can this be described as *Ren*?" Zizhang asked again: "Cui Zhu assassinated the ruler of Qi and Chen Wenzi abandoned 40 horses and left the state of Qi. When he reached another state he said: 'Those in power here are just like Cui Zhu' and left. When he reached yet another state he said: 'Those in power here are just like Cui Zhu' and left again. How should he be regarded?" The Master said: "As pure." Zizhang said: "Could it be described as *Ren*?" The Master said: "I do not know. How could this be described as *Ren*?" (Gongye Chang 19)

Comment Ziwen, the chief minister of Chu and Chen Wenzi of the state of Qi were both held in high regard by Kongzi. One was loyal to his ruler and the other would not co-operate with a rebellious minister, they had attained "Loyalty" and "purity," but Kongzi did not consider that they had attained *Ren*.

4.109 The Master said: "Yan Pingzhong is skilled in making

friends. All revere him after knowing him a long time." (Gongye Chang 17)

Comment A model of worthiness.

4.110 The Master said: "Ning Wuzi is clever when the state is principled but appears stupid when it is not. His cleverness may be emulated but his stupidity may not." (Gongye Chang 21)

Comment The depths of wisdom.

4.111 Master said: "Shi Yu is truly upright, when a state is principled he is as straight as an arrow; when a state is unprincipled he is still as straight as an arrow. Qu Boyu is also a real Gentleman! When a state is principled he serves as an official, when it is not, you may roll him up like a scroll and hide him in your bosom." (Duke Ling of Wei 7)

Comment Upright or rolled up, advancing or withdrawing, the way a Gentleman deals with the world.

4.112 The Master said that Jing, the minister of Duke Wei was skilled at running an estate: "When it was just established and beginning to acquire wealth, he would say: 'More or less enough.' As it became richer, he would say: 'more or less complete.' When it was really wealthy, he would say: 'More or less perfect.'" (Zilu 8)

Comment Hardworking and content with one's lot, the way a Gentleman runs an estate.

4.113 Zhonggong asked the Master about Zisang Bozi. The Master said: "He is acceptable, his characteristic is simplicity." Zhonggong said: "Is it also acceptable to

govern the people with respectful conduct and simplicity in handling affairs? Would it be excessive to both conduct oneself in simplicity and handle affairs with simplicity?" The Master said: "Zhonggong, you are right." (Yong Ye 2)
Comment Simple and not elaborate, the Gentleman's way of going about things.

4.114 Zigong asked: "Why was Kong Wenzi awarded the posthumous title of 'Wen' (literary)?" The Master said: "Because he was intelligent and studious and saw no shame in seeking advice from those beneath him, that is why he was awarded the title." (Gongye Chang 15)
Comment Not afraid to seek advice, the Gentleman's method of study.

4.115 The Master asked Gongshu Wenzi about Gongming Jia: "Is it true? That he does not speak or smile and does not acquire wealth?" Gongming Jia said: "Whoever told you was mistaken. He speaks when the time is ripe, and people are not bored with what he says; he laughs when pleased, and people are not bored with his laughter; he acquires wealth when it is right to do so and people do not object." The Master said: "So that was the way it was. How could it have been otherwise?" (Xian Wen 13)
Comment Moral acquisition, how a Gentleman makes money.

4.116 Xun, the household official of Gongshu Wenzi, was, together with Gongshu Wenzi made a minister at court. When the Master heard, he said: "It is possible to receive the title of 'Wen' posthumously." (Xian Wen 18)
Comment Gongshu Wenzi's posthumous title was "Wen," hence Kongzi's remark.

4.117 The Master said: "Lacking the eloquence of Zhu Tuo and with only the good looks of Song Zhao it would be difficult to avoid disaster in today's society." (Yong Ye 16)

Comment Some Scholars believe that the eloquence of Zhu Tuo and the good looks of Song Zhao represented "honeyed words" and "fine appearance" respectively. Clearly neither of which met with Kongzi's approval. It may be that Kongzi's meaning here is: "fine words" are more important than "smart appearance" for anybody intending to get on in society.

(2) Historical personages

(The sacred kings)

4.118 The Master said: "Oh, great is King Yao! Such majesty! Heaven, great as it is, only he can follow. So vast that the people have not the words to praise him. Such magnificence is his achievement, such brilliance is his enlightened rule." (Taibo 19)

Comment Historically, Yao is China's mythological king and, naturally, the creator of "government through *Ren*." All Kongzi's ideals of government through *Ren* are concentrated in the person of the mythological kings.

4.119 The Master said: "Great it is that Shun and Yu possessed the land and did not scheme to acquire it." (Taibo 18)

Comment Shun followed Yao as king and Yu was the first ruler of the Xia dynasty. It is said that Yao abdicated in favor of Shun who, in his turn, abdicated in favor of Yu. In Kongzi's view kings should acquire the land through virtuous conduct and not through force of arms. Consequently the ancient system of abdication became part of the Confucian mythology. There are numerous historical interpretations of this passage.

4.120 The Master said: "Of those who brought order to the world through non-action there is probably only Shun! What was it that he did? He just sat on the south facing throne." (Duke Ling of Wei 5)

Comment The "order through non-action" that Kongzi praises here seems to be rather different from the "order through inaction" of the Daoists, as the passage below makes clear, Shun's "non-action" was made possible by his ability to select talent.

4.121 Shun had five ministers and ruled the land. King Wu of Zhou said: "I have ten able ministers to govern." Kongzi said: "Talent is difficult to find, is it not so? Talent flourished from the time of Yao and Shun and in the time of King Wu of Zhou. Of the ten ministers one was a woman and so there were only nine. King Wen of Zhou ruled two thirds of the land and still served the Shang court. The Virtue of the Zhou was true virtue." (Taibo 20)

Comment The reason that the sacred kings were able to govern by "order through non-action" lay in their ability to select talent. This passage seems to be a development in the explanation and expression of the previous passage.

4.122 The Master said: "I have no criticism of Yu, he lived simply and served the gods and spirits, he was clothed simply but was splendidly attired at sacrifices; his palace was humble but he devoted effort to irrigation. I have no criticism of Yu." (Taibo 21)

Comment Kongzi's praise of Yao and Shun knows no

bounds and he assesses Yu highly. Yet there is an element of distinction in the language used.

4.123 Nan Rong enquired of Kongzi: "Hou Yi was an archer and Ao was skilled in fighting by boat, they both came to a bad end. Yu and Ji ploughed and planted themselves and possessed the world." The Master did not answer. Nan Rong withdrew and the Master said: "Such a Gentleman! A man of such Virtue!" (Xian Wen 5)

Comment Hou Yi was the hero who shot at the sun. Ao was also famed for his strength and was killed by a ruler of the Xia dynasty. Yu was the ruler who founded the Xia dynasty and tradition has it that Ji was a forerunner of the Zhou dynasty and was expert in agriculture. Kongzi is full of praise for Nan Rong because he enunciated the basic concept of Confucian authority—that *Ren* should rule the land.

(Famous Ministers)

4.124 The Master said: "Taibo may be said to have achieved Virtue. Three times he yielded up the land and the people could not find the words with which to praise him." (Taibo 1)

4.125 Weizi was forced to flee and Jizi became a slave, Bigan remonstrated and was killed. Kongzi said: "There were three possessed of *Ren* in the Yin dynasty!" (Weizi 1)

4.126 The Master said of Zichan: "He has the four virtues of a Gentleman: he conducts himself seriously, he serves his ruler with respect, he treats the people with benevolence and uses them justly." (Gongye Chang 16)

Comment Zichan of the state of Zheng was a politician

of the previous generation whom Kongzi very much admired. Kongzi obviously detected traces of government through *Ren* in Zichan's methods of governance.

4.127 The Master said: "When the state of Zheng issued decrees, they were first drafted by Bi Chen, then discussed with Shi Shu, then polished by Ziyu and finally revised by Zichan." (Xian Wen 8)

4.128 Someone asked about Zichan. The Master said: "A man of great benevolence." They asked about Zixi and he said: "Oh, him! Oh, him!" They further asked about Guan Zhong and he said: "He was quite somebody, he confiscated the land of three hundred households belonging to Bo Shi at Pian Yi leaving him to eat coarse millet, and to the end of his life, Bo Shi bore no grudge." (Xian Wen 9)

Comment Kongzi's praise for Zichan of the state of Zheng seems unrestrained. However his assessment of Guan Zhong, the minister of the state of Qi is rather contradictory: on the one hand, he has profound respect for Guan Zhong's ability in government; on the other, he is extremely dissatisfied with some of his methods, as can be seen from some of the following passages.

4.129 Zilu said: "Duke Huan of Qi killed Prince Jiu, Shao Hu thereupon committed suicide but Guan Zhong did not. Is that *Ren*?" The Master said: "Duke Huan achieved nine alliances with the vassal princes without force of arms. That was the doing of Guan Zhong. That was his *Ren*! That was his *Ren*!" (Xian Wen 16)

Comment The fact that Guan Zhong did not die for his master and instead transferred his allegiance to Duke

Huan of Qi, seems to demonstrate that he failed to display complete Loyalty. However, in his assessments of people, Kongzi sees things as a whole and considers that Guan Zhong's *Ren* is the "great *Ren*" and that his political contribution cannot be dismissed.

4.130 Zigong asked: "Can Guan Zhong be considered as possessing *Ren*? Duke Huan killed Prince Jiu, Guan Zhong did not commit suicide but instead became a minister for Duke Huan." The Master said: "Guan Zhong served as a minister to Duke Huan and achieved hegemony over the vassal states and brought order to the land, even today the people still benefit from his actions. Had it not been for Guan Zhong I would be wild-haired and with my gown opening on the left. How could he kill himself in a ditch for nothing and nobody know of it, like some ordinary person?" (Xian Wen 17)

Comment Like Zilu, Zigong had criticisms of Guan Zhong's personal morality, but Kongzi stuck to his viewpoint that as a governor Guan Zhong had benefited the people of the land and that this was a kind of "great *Ren*." In this sense, the perfection or not of personal morality came second.

4.131 The Master said: "Guan Zhong was small minded!" Someone asked: "Was he frugal?" The Master said: "Guan Zhong maintained three establishments whose officials had no more than a single employment, can that be called frugality?" They further asked: "Being so, then did he understand Propriety?" The Master said: "If the ruler erected a screen in front of his entrance, then so did Guan Zhong. If the ruler had receptacles for empty wine cups at banquets for other rulers, then so did Guan

Zhong. If Guan Zhong understood Propriety, then who is there who does not?" (Ba Yi 22)

Comment Kongzi was in a tangle over Guan Zhong, despite arguing that he was unable to be utterly economical in his early years he found it impossible not to criticize his extravagance and overstepping of the bounds of Propriety.

(Worthies)

4.132 The Master said: "Boyi and Shuqi did not nurture old hatreds, hence grudges diminished." (Gongye Chang 23)

Comment Boyi and Shuqi were widely acknowledged ancient worthies and models of morality. Kongzi is praising their leniency and generosity to others.

4.133 Those worthies have become scattered amongst the people are: Boyi, Shuqi, Yuzhong, Yiyi, Zhuzhang. Liu Xiahui and Shaolian. The Master said: "Those who did not compromise their ideals nor bring shame upon themselves were, perhaps, Boyi and Shuqi?" As to Liu Xiahui and Shaolian, he said: "They compromised their ideals and brought shame upon themselves but they spoke in accordance with the law and acted after consideration, that was the way it was!" Of Yuzhong and Yiyi, he said: "Living as a hermit and speaking at will and yet to retain purity and self respect is to abandon the petty shifts of life. I am not the same, there is nothing that I may venture, and nothing that I may not venture." (Weizi 8)

Comment There are various ways of living, dispersed amongst the people or as a hermit. Kongzi knew that he differed from these hermetic eminences and that he could not live the life they did. He could not abandon his ideal of government through *Ren*.

4.134 The Master said: "Honeyed words and a fine appearance together with obsequiousness were regarded by Zuoqiu Ming as a disgrace. So do I regard it. To harbor hatred behind pleasant behavior was regarded by Zuoqiu Ming as a disgrace. And so do I, Kongzi, so regard it." (Gongye Chang 25)

Comment "Honeyed word and a fine appearance" had always been anathema to Kongzi, together with obsequiousness they constituted empty and insincere behavior.

(Other)

4.135 The Master said: "Duke Wen of Jin was duplicitous but not upright; Duke Huan of Qi was upright but not duplicitous." (Xian Wen 15)

4.136 The Master said: "Zang Wenzhong kept a pet turtle in an elaborately ornamented building, how clever can that be?" (Gongye Chang18)

Comment Kongzi regarded this elderly Lu official as a negative example. Elaborately ornamented buildings were confined to imperial palaces and temples. This passage describes a "breach of Propriety" and the next describes how Zang failed to advance merit.

4.137 The Master said: "Is not Zang Wenzhong one who obtained an official position by stealth? He knew of Liu Xiahui's worthiness but did not recommend him as well." (Duke Ling of Wei 14)

4.138 The Master said: "Who says that Weisheng Gao is straightforward? Someone once asked him for some vinegar and he begged it off a neighbor and passed it on."

(Gongye Chang 24)

Comment It seems that Kongzi regarded Weisheng Gao's method of "doing good works" as not quite right.

4.139 Zizhang said: "What does the *Book of Documents* mean when it says 'King Gao Zong of Shang dynasty mourned for three years and did not speak of government'?" The Master said: "Not only King Gao Zong, all the ancients were so. When a ruler died, for three years all the officials took their instructions from the chief minister." (Xian Wen 40)

Comment The custom of children mourning their parents for three years had existed for a long time. There was no exception for a ruler. Before a new ruler ascended the throne he had to spend three years in mourning.

4.140 The Master said: "In my dealings with people, whom have I vilified and whom have I praised? Where there is praise, it has been given after due consideration. It is these people who enabled the Xia, Shang and Zhou dynasties to follow the right path. " (Duke Ling of Wei 25)

CHAPTER 5   CONSIDERATION

1. The Mandate of Heaven

Ren is rooted in human nature and is in harmony with the natural law. The implementation of *Ren* on earth was the Mandate of Heaven and Kongzi firmly believed that it was his mission to realize the mandate.

5.1 The Master was besieged in Kuang and said: "King Wen of Zhou is dead, does the task of transmitting the ceremonies and music of Zhou then fall to me? If heaven wishes to let ceremonies and music die out, then later generations will have no grasp of it; if Heaven does not intend it to die out, then what is there that the people of Kuang can do to me?" (Zihan 5)

Comment Kongzi's overpowering sense of mission sprang from the simple concept: that heaven required him to pass on the culture of the ceremonies and music of Zhou. If this was heaven's intention, then he would never encounter the unexpected since he was the only one on earth who both understood and had the ability to pass on this culture of ceremonies and music.

5.2 The Master said: "Since heaven has granted me Virtue, what is there that Huan Tui can do to me?" (Shu Er 23)

Comment Huan Tui had dispatched soldiers to kill Kongzi as he passed through the state of Song. History does not tell us why, but Kongzi once again displayed no fear, convinced as before that since heaven had bestowed a mission on him, what was there that could either obstruct or harm him?

5.3 Gongbo Liao brought a case against Zilu before Ji Kangzi. Zifu Jingbo told Kongzi, saying: "Although Ji Kangzi has been spellbound by Gongbo Liao, yet I still have the power to slay Gongbo Liao and display his corpse in the market place." The Master said: "If the Grand Principle is to be implemented in the land, that is a matter for the Mandate of Heaven; if the Grand Principle is to be cast aside, that, too, is a matter for the Mandate of Heaven. What is there that Gongbo Liao can do about the Mandate of Heaven?" (Xian Wen 36)

Comment Kongzi saw the implementation of the Grand Principle as historically inevitable, this being so, no person or event could alter the course of history.

5.4 The Master said: "Nobody understands me!" Zigong said: "Why do you say that?" The Master said: "I have neither complaint against heaven, nor rebuke for man, I study the ways of the world and attain the will of heaven. Is it only heaven that understands me!" (Xian Wen 35)

Comment Those with a mission sometimes feel isolated, Kongzi is no exception.

5.5 The Master said: "I desire not to speak." Zigong said: "If you do not speak, then what may your disciples pass on?" The Master said: "Must heaven needs speak? Yet the four seasons proceed and all things grow. Must heaven needs speak?" (Yang Huo 19)

Comment *Ren* is rooted in human nature and is in harmony with the natural law. Human nature may speak but natural law cannot. Absolutely nothing seems to remain within Kongzi's doctrines of any theories about "nature and the will of heaven."

THE NEW ANALECTS: CONFUCIUS RECONSTRUCTED

5.6 The Master said: "The phoenix comes no more, the river drawing no longer emerges from the Yellow River. Is that all of my life complete?" (Zihan 9)

Comment The Phoenix, a mythical bird whose appearance symbolizes the arrival of a "sacred king" on earth. It is said that during the time of the mythical emperor Fuxi, a dragon-horse emerged from the Yellow River, bearing the design of the Eight Trigrams in the markings on its back, and thus known as the "river drawing" (*he tu*). This was an omen which also foretold the arrival of a "sacred king" on earth. In his later years, Kongzi's conviction and overpowering sense of mission contained a thread of doubt. He knew that, in his life-time, he would not see the implementation of the Grand Principle through the victory of government through *Ren*. He says nothing of the next generation.

2. Demons and spirits

Kongzi's attitude to extra-empirical entities such as demons and spirits was always a sensible one of "they may exist but do not discuss."

5.7 When performing a sacrifice one should behave as if the object of the sacrifice were present, when sacrificing to spirits one should behave as if the spirits were present. The Master said: "If I cannot attend a sacrifice, it is as if the sacrifice had not been performed." (Ba Yi 12)

Comment "One should behave as if the spirits were present"—not necessarily out of reverence but out of an attitude of sensibility. When one has not attended a sacrifice one should not behave as if one had.

5.8 Zilu asked about serving demons and spirits. The Master said: "When you have not yet served man, why ask about serving demons and spirits?" Zilu asked: "May I dare ask about death?" The Master said: "If you do not understand life, how can you understand death?" (Xian Jin 12)

Comment Kongzi deliberately circumvented Zilu's question about demons and spirits, perhaps because he did not wish to reply, or, more possibly, because it was difficult to answer. Kongzi's doctrines deal with the principles of the secular world, so his reply to Zilu is a secular truth.

5.9 Fan Chi asked about wisdom. The Master said: "Observe Righteousness in dealing with people, respect demons and spirits but be distant from them, that is wisdom." (Yong Ye 22)

Comment One can see Kongzi's basic attitude towards demons and spirits from the fact that he regarded distancing oneself from them as wisdom. Fan Chi's question about *Ren*, which followed this passage is included elsewhere.

5.10 The Master lay ill. Zilu prayed to demons and spirits for him. The Master said: "Do they exist?" Zilu said: "They do. The *Eulogies* say 'Pray to the spirits of heaven and earth for you.'" The Master said: "I have prayed for a long time." (Shu Er 35)

Comment Kongzi, though not superstitious, does not deny the existence of demons and spirits and leaves a little space for them in his mind.

5.11 The Master said: "It is flattery to sacrifice to those demons and spirits who should not receive sacrifice; it is weakness not to act righteously when you should." (Wei Zheng 24)

Comment In ancient times all demons and spirits had

clan affiliations, and different clans sacrificed to different gods, rather like a symbol of national consciousness or ideology.

3. The Master speaks of himself

Kongzi's criticism of himself.

5.12 On the streets of Daxiang they said: "Great is Kongzi! Vast in learning but known for nothing." The Master heard this and said to his disciples: "What am I known for? For driving a chariot? Or archery? Probably for driving a chariot." (Zihan 2)

Comment Kongzi had a sense of self-ridicule and mockery as well as a sense of fun. The time that he was lost in the state of Zheng he said that he was a "dog without a home"; describing himself as skilled in chariot driving is another example.

5.13 The court chamberlain asked Zigong: "Is the Master a sage? How can he be so talented?" Zigong said: "It is heaven that made him a sage and so talented." The Master heard and said: "Does the chamberlain understand me? When I was young my status was low and thus I learned many lowly skills. Do Gentlemen command so many skills? They do not!" (Zihan 6)

Comment Zigong believed that Kongzi's many talents were a gift from heaven, Kongzi himself considered that they derived from the acquired experiences of life.

5.14 Lao said: "The Master once said: 'I have never held office, hence my skills.'" (Zihan 7)

Comment A developed explanation of the previous passage about the many talents.

5.15 The Master said: "Zigong! Do you consider me a learned man of wide knowledge?" Zigong replied: "I do, can it not be so?" The Master replied: "It is not. I merely stick to a single thing." (Duke Ling of Wei 3)

Comment In reply to Zeng Can, Kongzi once also said: "My thinking has one essential which is consistent throughout." Kongzi may have been renowned for breadth of learning but he believed that his ideas were concentrated upon the upholding of the single word "*Ren.*"

5.16 The Master said: "Outside, one should serve dukes and ministers, at home one should serve father and elder brothers, in arranging funerals one should do one's utmost, one should never be incapacitated through drink. As far as I am concerned, is there more?" (Zihan 16)

Comment Kongzi considered himself ordinary and believed that proper behavior was this simple. This may have been a youthful assessment of himself.

5.17 The Master said: "Were I to hold an office of state, there would be results within a year and achievement within three." (Zilu 10)

Comment Kongzi was filled with confidence at his own political skills, a confidence which was in large measure derived from his belief in "the implementation of the Grand Principle throughout the land."

5.18 The Master said: "Disciples, do you think that there are matters that I conceal from you? There is nothing that I conceal from you. There is no action that I take that I do not share with you. That is the person I am." (Shu Er 24)

Comment Kongzi spoke the truth. He was frank and open throughout his life, his actions were straightforward and even discreditable events were recorded in the *Analects*.

5.19 The Master said: "How dare I speak of sageness and *Ren*? I can merely strive for them and teach them to others, that much I can do." Gongxi Hua said: "That is truly something that the disciples cannot learn." (Shu Er 34)

Comment It could be said that this passage represents Kongzi's own summation of his life. If *Ren* is "self-control and the bringing of speech and action into conformity with the demands of Propriety," rather like individual religious practice, then sageness more resembles "helping mankind by broadly bestowing benevolence upon the people" as a social practice. It is also true that during his life Kongzi lacked political accomplishment and himself said that he had not attained "sageness."

5.20 The Master said: "As to culture and learning, I am much like other people. I have not yet attained the accomplishments of a Gentleman." (Shu Er 33)

Comment Kongzi is being modest when he says that he has not become a Gentleman.

5.21 The Master said: "Describe but not inscribe, love and believe what is ancient. Secretly, I regard myself as rather like Lao Peng." (Shu Er 1)

Comment "Describe but not inscribe" has to be true. Had there not been the disciples' records at the time, there would have been no *Analects*. Why did Kongzi "describe but not inscribe"? Perhaps because that was the practice of the time. Laozi did not write things down either and without the records of others there would have been no transmission of the *Classic of Dao and De* (*Dao De Jing*).

5.22 The Master said: "To know through memorizing, to learn without loathing, to teach indefatigably, as far as I am concerned, is there more?" (Shu Er 2)

Comment Kongzi believed that he possessed no special qualities, merely that he had spent his life "learning without loathing and teaching indefatigably."

5.23 Duke Ye asked Zilu about Kongzi. Zilu did not answer. The Master said: "Why do you not say something like: when he is deeply engaged in something he forgets to eat, when he is happy he forgets anxiety and he is unaware of the approach of old age." (Shu Er 19)

Comment This is Kongzi's image of himself in old age: industrious as ever, happy and often forgetful of his age.

4. Time flows like water

Lamenting the perpetuity of time and the brevity of life.

5.24 On the bank of a river, the Master said: "Time flows like a river, days and nights stream ceaselessly away." (Zihan 17)

Comment The most difficult problem for all is the perpetuity of time and the brevity of life. Men as wise as Kongzi feel profoundly helpless and can but sigh.

5.25 A flock of birds rose, stretched their wings, flew and resettled again. The Master said: "These hen pheasants on the mountain bridge, how timely, how timely." Zilu threw them some food, the birds sniffed at it and flew away.

(Xiang Dang 27)

Comment This passage has always been incomprehensible. What does Kongzi sigh over when he sees these pheasants flying in the hills? Is he envious of their timeliness? Their independence? Or is he praising their beauty? Or a mixture of all three, a salute to life in the midst of nature.

5.26 The Master said: "I am old and weak! For a long time I have not dreamed of seeing Duke Zhou again." (Shu Er 5)

Comment Kongzi had always regarded Duke Zhou as a "sage," and had considered himself the transmitter of his ceremonies, music and culture. This passage not only demonstrates his reverence for Duke Zhou but also reflects an awareness of his approaching end.

OUTER SECTION:
THE REMARKS OF THE DISCIPLES

CHAPTER 6   EVALUATION

1. During life

Knowledge and evaluation of Kongzi by his contemporaries.

6.1 The guardian official of the fiefdom of Yi sought a meeting with Kongzi, saying: "I have never yet not met a Gentleman who has arrived here." The disciples took him to meet Kongzi. After he came out he said: "Why are you so disheartened? The world has lacked the Grand Principle for a long time but your master will be a bell that calls to the people of the world." (Ba Yi 24)

Comment It is impossible to deny that this nameless official of the fiefdom of Yi was prophetic. His explanation of the historical significance of Kongzi was both profound and accurate.

6.2 Zilu stayed overnight at Shimen outside the city gate. The next morning, the gatekeeper asked him: "Where from?" Zilu replied: "From Kongzi's." The gatekeeper said: "The one who knows it can't be done but does it?" (Xian Wen 38)

Comment "Knows it can't be done but does it," is probably the best description of the spirit of Kongzi. The reason that he was so persistent was not just because of his strength of will, it derived more from a kind of fierce sense of mission.

2. After death

The disciple's defence of the majesty of Kongzi's image.

6.3 Shusun Wushu said to the ministers at court: "Zigong is more worthy than Kongzi." Zifu Jingbo told Zigong of this. Zigong said: "It's rather like the wall round a house, my wall is shoulder height and you can look in and readily see the fine appearance of the house; the Master's wall is higher by several measures, unless you can find the door and enter, you cannot see the splendor of the temple or the beauty of the buildings. There are few that can find the door and enter. Is it not natural that Shusun Wushu speaks as he does?" (Zizhang 23)

Comment It is not known why Shusun Wushu was so dissatisfied with Kongzi that he had to attack him by praising Zigong. Zigong's answer demonstrates the depth of his feeling for Kongzi and the profundity of his understanding.

6.4 Shusun Wushu vilified Kongzi. Zigong said: "This cannot be done! Kongzi is not to be slandered. The virtues of others resemble a range of hills that can be crossed; those of Kongzi are like the sun and the moon and are insurmountable. What harm can befall the sun and the moon if people do not wish to see them? It merely shows how they overestimate their own abilities!" (Zizhang 24)

Comment The same one again, still intent on attacking Kongzi. On this occasion, Zigong is rather less polite.

6.5 Ziqin of the stae of Chen said to Zigong: "You are a man of respect and modesty, how can it be that Kongzi exceeds you in virtue?" Zigong said: "The Gentleman could show his wisdom in a single word and his ignorance in a single word. Speech must always be cautious! The unattainability of Kongzi resembles an ascent to heaven without stairs. If the Master secured appointments under the vassal princes and ministers it was like the saying: 'If there is establishment then the system that is established will succeed, if there is leadership then the people will follow, if there is pacification then the peoples at a distance will submit; if there is mobilization then people will respond. In life, glory. In death, grief.' This being so, how could I possibly attain his level?" (Zizhang 25)

Comment Zigong's reverence for Kongzi was heartfelt from beginning to end. Although he was full of regret and disappointment at the missed moments of opportunity for achievement in Kongzi's life, he believed that they in no way detracted from his greatness.

3. Doctrine

The disciples had their own individual understanding and perception of the profundity of Kongzi's thought.

6.6 Yan Yuan sighed: "The higher you aim the higher it is, the harder you drill the deeper it is. It seems in front and then is suddenly behind. With his patient guidance the Master expanded my knowledge with learning, constrained my speech and action with Propriety and made me keep going. When I had exhausted all effort a towering mountain still stood before me, and though I still wanted to continue climbing, there was no path." (Zihan 11)

Comment It is worth noting that Yan Yuan's understanding and feeling for Kongzi's doctrines differ from the normal run and have their own particular vision. As he sees it, Kongzi's doctrines are not only profound but mysterious as well. The pity is that Yan Yuan died young and was never able to pass on the more profound aspects of Kongzi's thought. As a result, the death of Yan Yuan rendered Kongzi particularly grief-struck, expressed in the phrase "Heaven has bereaved me!"

6.7 Zigong said: "The classical culture that the Master taught may be heard and understood; what the Master expounded about human nature and the heavenly law can be neither heard nor understood." (Gongye Chang 13)

Comment The study of *Ren* is also the study of the Mandate of Heaven. Heaven is the way of heaven; and the mandate is life itself. This is what Zigong here refers to as the study of "human nature and the heavenly law." After the death of Yan Yuan there was probably not one amongst the disciples capable of understanding "human nature and the heavenly law," even someone as intelligent as Zigong sighed in vain.

6.8 Gongsun Chao of Wei asked Zigong: "How did Kongzi acquire his learning?" Zigong said: "The teachings of King Wen and King Wu are with us still and have not been lost. The worthy know them in the main and the unworthy know them a little and these teachings of the kings are everywhere. How could the Master not have acquired learning? There is no set teacher who instructs." (Zizhang 22)

Comment Kongzi belonged to the category of wise man whose knowledge grows naturally. Not only are their insights penetrating but their knowledge is all-embracing. For them, study without a regular teacher is a necessity.

CHAPTER 7 REMINISCENCE

1. Geniality

Kongzi as he appears in the reminiscences of his disciples.

7.1 The Master was warm but severe, stern but not fierce, calm and courteous. (Shu Er 38)

7.2 The Master spoke with an elegant court accent which he used when reciting from the *Classic of Poetry* and the *Book of Documents* and when performing ceremonies. (Shu Er 18)
Comment Kongzi was an inhabitant of the state of Lu and would normally have spoken in the Lu dialect. On formal occasions however, he would have used the speech of court.

2. Behavior and bearing

Kongzi as he appeared on different occasions.

(1) At court

7.3 When ordered by the ruler to receive guests, Kongzi's countenance immediately became serious and his step quickened. He greeted those standing on one side and saluted those to right and left with both hands clasped, his robes swaying elegantly. When he hurried forward he seemed like a bird with wings outstretched. When the guests had left he never failed to report to the ruler: "The

guests no longer look back." (Xiang Dang 3)
Comment Greeting guests and envoys at the command of the ruler.

7.4 Kongzi entered the palace gate bowing humbly as if there were nowhere to hide. He did not stand in the center of the gate nor place his foot upon the raised threshold. His countenance became more serious as he approached the throne, his step quickened and his speech softened as if lacking breath. Entering the audience hall he raised the hem of his robe, bowed and ascended holding his breath. On withdrawing, his expression and bearing relaxed as he reached the bottom step. Away from the dais his step quickened like a bird spreading its wings. When he returned to his place it was with decorum and care. (Xiang Dang 4)
Comment How to enter and leave court.

7.5 The tablet of office is held humbly and as if heavy. Raised as if in greeting and put down as if bestowing a gift, all the while the expression serious as if in fear and trembling. When walking with shortened pace and quickened step, as if following a straight line. When receiving gifts from guests, the expression is amiable. In private meetings it is relaxed. (Xiang Dang 5)
Comment How to hold one's tablet of office when at court and how to receive guests.

7.6 When conversing with junior ministers at court, calm and composed; when conversing with senior minister, respectful and straight-forward. When the ruler is present, reverential and nervous. (Xiang Dang 2)
Comment The interaction between ministers and ruler at court.

(2) **In the country**

7.7 When in the country Kongzi behaved courteously and respectfully and as if not very eloquent. When at court or in a temple he spoke with dignity and composure but rather more carefully. (Xiang Dang 1)

Comment He seems not to have been the same man in the country as at court.

7.8 When the country people performed Nuo opera to welcome the gods and banishing demons Kongzi always took the principal place on the platform clad in his court robes. (Xiang Dang 14)

Comment Although Nuo opera was a folk rite, Kongzi took it seriously.

7.9 If, in singing with somebody else, it went well, Kongzi would ask him to sing again and would then join him. (Shu Er 32)

7.10 When asking an envoy to convey greetings to friends in other states, one salutes them twice in bidding farewell. (Xiang Dang 15)

7.11 Unless it were an offering of sacrificial meat, Kongzi did not bow to gifts from friends, even if they were horses or carriages. (Xiang Dang 23)

7.12 On days when he had wept at a funeral, the Master did not sing. (Shu Er 10)

7.13 The Master did not eat his fill when eating with those in mourning. (Shu Er 9)

7.14 When he met those dressed in mourning, or wearing an official cap or those who were blind, the Master would stand and when he passed them would do so quickly, even when there was no need because of their youth. (Zihan 10)

7.15 When Kongzi met those in mourning his countenance became grave even when he knew them well. When he met those who wore official caps or who were blind he treated them politely even though they were familiar. When riding in a carriage and he met somebody in mourning he would lean on the crossbar and incline his head. This he would also do when he met somebody bearing official written matter. When eating at a banquet he would always rise gravely and give thanks. He would greet thunder with reverence. (Xiang Dang 25)

3. Food, dress, housing and travel

(1) Dress

7.16 A Gentleman does not have a crimson or black border to his garments, nor does he wear garments of red or purple at home. In the summer unlined garments of coarse or fine hemp must be worn as outer clothes with an inner garment. Black clothes go with a sheepskin lined gown and white with a deerskin robe; yellow clothes go with a gown lined with fox fur; fur robes worn at home should be slightly longer but the right sleeve may be shorter. Quilts should be a length and a half of the body. Thick fox and raccoon skins may be made into cushions. Ornaments may be worn after mourning garments have been set aside. Ceremonial garments not made from cloth of the correct width must be tailored. It is not permitted to wear a sheepskin lined robe or a black official cap when paying visits of condolence. Formal court attire is obligatory when attending court on the first of each month. (Xiang Dang 6)

Comment There are two principles for the wearing of clothes; they may not offend against Propriety and they must be comfortable.

7.17 On days of abstinence, a cloth robe should be worn when bathing. On days of abstinence, diet should be changed, as should residence. (Xiang Dang 7)

(2) Food

7.18 When the ruler makes a gift of food, it should be tasted after being properly seated. When the ruler makes a gift of uncooked flesh it must be cooked and first offered to the ancestors. When the ruler makes a gift of livestock it must be raised. When eating with the ruler, the food must be tasted before the ruler offers prayer before the meal. (Xiang Dang 18)

7.19 Care must be taken with foodstuffs, fish and flesh should be sliced thinly. Food stored over-long turns sour and fish and meat rot, neither can be eaten. Food that becomes discolored or changes smell should not be eaten; food that is improperly cooked should not be eaten; food that is not appropriate to the hour should not be eaten; food that is not butchered correctly should not be eaten; food that is improperly seasoned should not be eaten. At a banquet, although food may be plentiful, the amount consumed should not be excessive. There is no such limit on wine though drunkenness should be avoided. Dried meat and wine obtained from a market should not be eaten. There will be ginger after the meal but not too much should be eaten. (Xiang Dang 8)

Comment There are two main aspects to the attention paid by Kongzi to eating, the quality of the ingredients and table manners. The first is a matter of health and the second a matter of Propriety.

7.20 At sacrificial ceremonies sacrificial meat presented by the ruler should not be left for a second day. Generally sacrificial meat should not exceed three days, if it does it should not be eaten. (Xiang Dang 9)

7.21 Do not converse while eating and do not talk while sleeping. (Xiang Dang 10)

7.22 Even with coarse food or vegetable soup a portion must be set aside for sacrifice to the ancestors as solemnly as on days of abstinence. (Xiang Dang 11)

7.23 At village drinking parties, the old leave first, then you may leave. (Xiang Dang 13)

(3) Housing

7.24 At home the Master was neat and his bearing relaxed. (Shu Er 4)

7.25 When the mat is not straight, do not sit. (Xiang Dang 12)

Comment There were no tables and chairs in the time of

Kongzi. Seating was on mats with cushions.

7.26 Do not sleep as straight as a corpse, or live as if always receiving guests. (Xiang Dang 24)

7.27 When ill and the ruler visits, lie with the head to the east, the body covered with the court robe and with sash extended. (Xiang Dang 19)

(4) Travel

7.28 At the summons of the ruler, do not wait for horse and carriage but proceed at once on foot. (Xiang Dang 20)

7.29 When mounting a carriage, stand erect and mount with the aid of the hand strap. Once in the carriage do not look around, do not talk loudly or gesticulate. (Xiang Dang 26)

4. Teaching by example in word and action

Teaching apart, Kongzi laid great stress upon setting an example in daily life.

7.30 The Master seldom spoke of profit and utility but spoke often in praise of destiny and *Ren*. (Zihan 1)

7.31 The Master took care over: fasting, warfare, and illness. (Shu Er 13)

7.32 The Master did not speak of strange happenings, of violence or chaos, or of demons and spirits. (Shu Er 21)

Comment Kongzi's attitude towards demons and spirits was one of distant respect, they existed but were not to be discussed, nor did he have much interest in other manifestations of the supernatural.

7.33 The Master taught only four subjects: literature and the art of discourse, conduct, Loyalty and Integrity. (Shu Er 25)

7.34 The Master abominated four things, wild guesswork, dogmatic insistence, obstinacy and belief in one's own infallibility. (Zihan 4)
Comment These are errors frequently encountered in the search for knowledge and truth.

7.35 The Master did not fish with a line of many hooks nor did he shoot at homing birds. (Shu Er 27)

5. The twists and turns of life

People and events of Kongzi's life recorded by the disciples.

7.36 Duke Jing of Qi sought to keep Kongzi in his employ and said: "I cannot treat you like Jishi in the state of Lu but I can treat you as if you were between a senior and a junior minister." Later he said: "I am old and can use you no longer." Kongzi departed. (Weizi 3)
Comment Kongzi spent a considerable time in the state of Qi as a young man and had the opportunity to promote his theories of "government through *Ren*" with Duke Jing. However, Duke Jing displayed no interest.

7.37 The state of Qi made a gift of dancing girls to the state of

Lu. Ji Huanzi accepted them and did not attend court for three days. Kongzi left. (Weizi 4)

Comment At the age of over 50 Kongzi had been minister of law and acting chief minister of the state of Lu and responsible for the administration of the court with the opportunity to try out his own ideas for "government through *Ren.*" However, it only lasted for 100 days and became difficult to implement thereafter. Finally, Kongzi was obliged to leave and set out on his "peregrination of the states." The affair of the dancing girls was, in fact, the fuse that set off the complete incident.

7.38 Ru Bei wished to call on Kongzi, but Kongzi declined to receive him on the grounds of illness. As the messenger came out of the gate, Kongzi took up his harp and sang to it so that Ru Bei could hear. (Yang Huo 20)

Comment It is not known why Kongzi disliked Ru Bei and refused to see him using illness as an excuse but deliberately leading him to understand that he did not wish to see him. There may have been political factors involved.

CHAPTER 8 EXPOSITION

1. Principal ideas

The exposition and elaboration by the disciples of some of Kongzi's principal ideas such as Filial Piety, Fraternal Piety and Propriety.

(1) Filial and Fraternal Piety

8.1 You Ruo said: "There are few who respect their father and mother and obey their elder brother and yet dare offend their superiors. There are also few who have never offended their superiors and yet dare stir up trouble and strife. The Gentleman devoted his effort to the root of things and once that was established then the correct path sprang from it. Filial and Fraternal Piety are the basis of *Ren*." (Xue Er 2)
Comment The manifestation of *Ren* within a person has to start from Filial and Fraternal Piety. Those who lack these two qualities can possess neither Loyalty nor Integrity and, in the end, become those "without *Ren*."

8.2 Sima Niu said sadly: "All have brothers, I alone lack them!" Zixia said: "I have heard it said that: 'Life and death are a matter of fate, riches and honor depend upon heaven.' If a Gentleman is prudent and without error in his conduct, and treats people with respect and Propriety, then all within the four seas become brothers and why should he be despondent at the lack of them?" (Yan Yuan 5)
Comment Filial Piety derives from *Ren* and Fraternal Piety

is the product of Filial Piety. With Fraternal Piety there is Integrity which once expanded naturally causes all within the four seas to be brothers.

8.3 Zeng Can said: "I heard the Master say: 'People rarely unburden their feelings, should they do so, it must be at the death of mother and father!'" (Zizhang 17)

8.4 Zeng Xi said: "I heard the Master say that the Filial Piety of Meng Zhuangzi could be emulated by others but it was difficult for them to attain the way in which he did not alter the rules and precepts of his father and older ministers." (Zizhang 18)
Comment It is not merely a question of obedience to parents during their lifetime, it is even more a question of persevering with "for three years make no alteration to the way of one's father" after they have died.

8.5 Ziyou said: "Mourn until grief is exhausted." (Zizhang 14)

(2) **Propriety**

8.6 You Ruo said: "The uses of Propriety place value upon the achievement of harmony. The principles of government of the former kings attached most value to this point and it was so in matters large and small. Where it did not work, it was because of exercising harmony only for harmony's sake and failing to impose the restraints of Propriety thus rendering it unworkable." (Xue Er 12)
Comment To value harmony is correct, but harmony just for the sake of harmony will never work.

8.7 You Ruo said: "To act with Integrity is to be close to

Righteousness and to keep one's word; to act with decorum is to be close to Propriety and thus to be distant from shame. To rely upon one's intimates is a support." (Xue Er 13)

2. Study and self-cultivation

The disciples' individual views on how best to study and undertake self-cultivation.

(1) **Study**

8.8 Zixia said: "There is *Ren* in broad study and a steadfast will, in careful questioning and deep thought." (Zizhang 6)
Comment The ultimate aim of study is to achieve a state of *Ren*.

8.9 Zixia said: "The craftsman works in a workshop in order to learn his trade, the Gentleman studies to realize the Grand Principle." (Zizhang 7)
Comment The Gentleman strives to learn in the same way that a craftsman learns his trade.

8.10 Zixia said: "To learn each day that which one did not know, every month to remember that which has been learnt, that may be called love of learning." (Zizhang 5)

8.11 Zeng Can said: "To be capable but willing to learn from the incapable, to be learned but willing to learn from the ignorant; to have but to appear to have not, to be full but to appear to be empty; to be insulted but not to take offence, this was the custom of a former friend." (Taibo 5)

(2) Self-cultivation

8.12 Zigong said: "The mistakes of a Gentleman are like an eclipse of the sun or moon. Everybody sees them but when they are corrected, all admire." (Zizhang 21)

Comment What is valued in a Gentleman is not that he does not make mistakes but that he could correct them.

8.13 Zeng Can said: "Each day I examine myself three times: have I exerted myself on behalf of others? Have I been honest in my dealings with friends? Have I revised and implemented the teachings of my master?" (Xue Er 4)

Comment How does one undertake "self-cultivation?" Zeng Can's method was daily "triple examination." A person was piously Filial and Fraternal at home and behaved with Loyalty and Integrity outside. As far as the disciples were concerned, the quality of study was of course important.

8.14 Zixia said: "Through respect for virtue one may transform one's basic nature; in serving one's parents one may exert all one's strength; in serving one's ruler one may offer one's life; in friendship one may keep one's word. Though it may be said that there is no learning in this, I call it learning." (Xue Er 7)

Comment Study and self-cultivation are both paths to the attainment of *Ren*. The virtuous man is naturally a man of study, the depth of his knowledge is irrelevant.

8.15 Zixia said: "In the large, the limits of morality may not be crossed, in the small one may to and fro." (Zizhang 11)

Comment Zixia opens up a loophole in the moral standards of a Gentleman and provides a little space for independent coming and going. Would Kongzi have agreed with this?

8.16 Zixia said: "The rogue will always conceal his mistakes." (Zizhang 8)

Comment Gentlemen correct their mistakes but rogues conceal them.

8.17 Zizhang said: "To possess Virtue yet not to promote it, to believe in the Grand Principle yet not to be steadfast in it, can this be morality? Can this be steadfastness?" (Zizhang 2)

8.18 Zeng Can was ill and Meng Jingzi visited him. Zeng Can said: "At the approach of death, the bird's cry becomes mournful; at the approach of death man's speech becomes virtuous. The Gentleman possesses three attributes worthy of regard: a polished appearance that distances him from coarseness; an upright expression that demonstrates sincerity; prudence in speech that puts vulgarity at a distance. As to sacrificial ceremonies, they are conducted by the official in charge." (Taibo 4)

8.19 Zeng Can was ill. He called his disciples together and said: "Lift my feet and hands! The *Classic of Poetry* writes: 'In fear and trepidation, as if standing at the edge of an abyss, or treading upon thin ice.' Henceforward I know that I shall come to no harm, oh, disciples!" (Taibo 3)

Comment This was probably Zeng Can's deathbed statement, celebrating the fact that he had managed to pass a peaceful life in the midst of chaos. That his limbs remained intact was a matter for congratulation and at the point of death to have remained morally complete was surely an even greater cause for congratulation.

Consequently, it can be no easy matter for the Gentleman to spend a life minutely careful and always "In fear and trepidation, as if standing at the edge of an abyss, or treading upon thin ice."

3. The Gentleman and the man of principle

The disciples discuss how best to become a Gentleman and a man of Principle.

(1) Gentleman

8.20 Zeng Can said: "Someone who can be entrusted with a young orphan or the fate of a nation, someone who does not waver in the face of a life or death crisis, is he a Gentleman? He is!" (Taibo 6)
Comment A Gentleman is trustworthy, he can shoulder a burden and he has Integrity.

8.21 Zeng Can said: "A Gentleman meets friends through literature and uses friendship to nurture his own *Ren*." (Yan Yuan 24)
Comment The aim of meeting friends through literature is still centered on *Ren*. Without "literature" (*wen*) there is no pleasure and without *Ren* there is no significance.

8.22 Ji Zicheng said: "A Gentleman merely needs to be of good character, why should he require any literary talent?" Zigong replied: "How regrettable are your remarks about Gentlemen, a team of horses could not catch them! Literary talent is character and character is literary talent. A tiger skin less its fur is the same as a dog or sheep skin less its wool." (Yan Yuan 8)

Comment Zigong's point of view on the relationship between character and literary ability is quite profound, it is that character and literary ability are hewn from the same material and are difficult to separate.

8.23 Zixia said: "There are three changes in aspect for a Gentleman: he appears dignified when viewed from a distance, he may appear warm and approachable when close up and serious in speech when giving instruction." (Zizhang 9)

Comment In the recollections of the disciples Kongzi appeared: "Warm but severe, stern but not fierce, calm and courteous." (Shu Er 38) See under 7.1.

8.24 Zixia said: "Though there may be something to be gained from minor skills they are of little account in the long run and for this reason the Gentleman does not employ them." (Zizhang 4)

(2) The man of principle

8.25 Zeng Can said: "The Scholar should have breadth of mind and strength of will, for his task is heavy and the road is long. To make the achievement of *Ren* his task, cannot the burden be but heavy? To cease only with death, cannot the road be but long?" (Taibo 7)

8.26 Zizhang said: "The Scholar will offer his life in the face of danger; will consider morality when he encounters advantage; will consider decorum at sacrificial ceremonies and grief in mourning. This is appropriate." (Zizhang 1)

4. Politics and government

The disciples discuss a number of problems concerning government: seeking office, governing a state, bringing prosperity to the people and the difficulties of being an official.

8.27 Ziqin asked Zigong: "When the Master visits a state he takes part in its government. Is this because he seeks to do so or because he is invited to do so?" Zigong said: "The Master is warm, virtuous, decorous, simple and modest, these qualities earn him the opportunity to take part. Perhaps the Master's way of seeking office differs from those of others?" (Xue Er 10)

Comment Kongzi sought office through virtue.

8.28 Zixia said: "In office if there is effort to spare, then study, in study if there is effort to spare, then seek office." (Zizhang 13)

Comment This passage makes clear the fact that the Confucian professional career cycled between learning and official office.

8.29 Zixia said: "The ruler must first gain the trust of the people, then he can demand their labor; otherwise they will feel oppressed. He must gain their trust before admonishing them; otherwise they will feel ill used." (Zizhang 10)

Comment Government through "Integrity."

8.30 Duke Ai of state Lu asked You Ruo: "There is famine this year and funds are insufficient, what is to be done?" You Ruo replied: "Why not cut taxes to one tenth?" Duke Ai said: "I have not enough with two tenths, how can I cut to a tenth?" You Ruo replied: "If the people have enough how then can the ruler not have enough? If the people have not enough how then can the ruler have enough?" (Yan Yuan 9)

Comment In Confucian economic theory the prime requisite for strengthening the nation is "enriching the people."

8.31 Zeng Can said: "Perform the funeral rites for one's parents with care, sacrifice with reverence to the ancestors and the morality of the people will grow stronger." (Xue Er 9)

Comment Guiding the people through Filial Piety.

8.32 Kongzi said: "The Master said: If you do not hold the office, do not make the policy." Zeng Can said: "The Gentleman should not think beyond his position." (Xian Wen 26)

Comment This passage should be regarded as Zeng Can's explanation and development of "If you do not hold the office, do not make the policy." What Kongzi said may be found under Taibo 14.

8.33 Meng Yizi appointed Yang Fu director of prisons and Yang Fu sought guidance from Zeng Can. Zeng Can said: "If those in power depart from the correct way, then the spirit of the people is lost. To know true reality is to feel pity rather than joy." (Zizhang 19)

8.34 Liu Xiahui was a prison official and was dismissed three times. Someone said: "Why do you not leave the state of Lu?" He replied: "If one serves a ruler properly, where might one go and not be dismissed thrice? If one is to serve a ruler unjustly, why must one needs leave the state of Lu?" (Weizi 2)

Comment This passage records the remarks of Liu Xiahui on the difficulties of being an official.

5. The path of friendship

The disciples' views and thoughts on friendship.

8.35 Ziyou said: "To serve a ruler over-assiduously may bring shame, to be over-assiduous in friendship leads to estrangement." (Li Ren 26)

8.36 A disciple of Zixia asked Zizhang about friendship. Zizhang said: "What does Zixia say?" The disciple replied: "He said: 'One can be friends with those with whom one may and reject those with whom one may not.'" Zizhang said: "This is not the same as I have heard. The Gentleman respects the worthy and tolerates all, praises the virtuous and pities the incapable. Were I to be worthy, what would there be that others could not tolerate and were I to be unworthy and people rejected me, how then could I reject others?" (Zizhang 3)

Comment The understanding of friendship expressed by Zizhang is much more profound than that of Zixia. Together with Ziyou, Zizhang and Zixia were the three most outstanding disciples of Kongzi's later years and there are already signs of the emergence of differing schools of thought here.

6. The disciples

Record of the sayings and deeds of disciples of the Kongzi school and of their opinions of each other.

8.37 Of disciples of virtue there were: Yan Yuan, Min Ziqian, Boniu, and Zhonggong. Of those of eloquence there were Zai Wo and Zigong. Of those with ability to govern there were Ran You and Zilu. Of those with literary ability there were Ziyou and Zixia. (Xian Jin 3)

Comment This passage provides an overall evaluation of Kongzi's disciples. It does not definitely seem to be Kongzi's own view but a summation made by later disciples.

8.38 When Zilu heard something new and was not immediately able to put it into practice his fear was that there would again be something else new. (Gongye Chang 14)

Comment Zilu was obviously impatient and liked to do things at once but the moment there was too much to understand he did not know what to do.

8.39 Ji Kangzi sent a messenger to ask Min Ziqian to be governor of Fei. Min Ziqian said to the messenger: "Please decline on my behalf. If you come again, I shall flee across the Wen river." (Yong Ye 9)

8.40 Nan Rong recited the poem *The White Tablet* several times and Kongzi betrothed his elder brother's daughter to him. (Xian Jin 6)

Comment The meaning of the lines "The flaws in a white tablet of jade may be ground away; the flaws in words cannot" in the *Classic of Poetry* is that while flaws in jade may be remedied errors in speech are difficult to retrieve. It is a warning to be circumspect in speech. Nan Rong seems to have been a very prudent man.

8.41 Zigao was rather simple minded; Zeng Can was rather slow-witted; Zizhang was rather outspoken and Zilu was rather impulsive. (Xian Jin 18)

Comment These evaluations seem to spring from the lips of Kongzi himself but there appears to be no lack of affection in his incisive comments.

8.42 Zeng Can said: "Zizhang is very grand in appearance but a difficult man with whom to seek *Ren*." (Zizhang 16)

Comment Zeng Can was somewhat critical of Zizhang but polite nevertheless. This evaluation of Zizhang may come from the records of Zeng Can's disciples.

8.43 Ziyou said: "My friend Zizhang has rare ability but he does not achieve *Ren*." (Zizhang 15)

Comment Ziyou's remark contains an implied criticism of Zizhang. Like Zeng Can he admires Zizhang's abilities but considers him to be some distance from *Ren*.

8.44 Ziyou said: "Zixia's disciples are very good at sweeping up and can manage replies to questions and greeting and seeing off visitors. But these are minor details, the basis is not there, what is to be done?" Zixia heard and said: "Ha! Ziyou speaks in error! The principles of the Master, how they should be transmitted and how strengthened, are like the distinction between grass and trees. How can the principles of the Master be distorted at will? Only a sage can teach them from beginning to end!" (Zizhang 12)

Comment Ziyou was also critical of Zixia. After Kongzi, Confucianism split into eight schools and an inkling of this can be seen here.

7. The mirror of history

The deeds and sayings of the former Kings, with a record of historical events, personalities and documentary knowledge.

8.45 Yao said: "Oh, Shun! The Mandate of Heaven has fallen upon you. Justly exercise impartiality! Should those within the four seas suffer, then heaven's bounty will be withdrawn from you forever." When Shun yielded his throne to Yu he passed this mandate to him. (Shang Tang) said: "I, King Lü of Shang, sacrifice a black bull and promise the Emperor of Heaven that I will not, of my own accord, dare pardon the guilty nor dare conceal the crimes of officials. All is known to the heart of the Emperor of Heaven. If I offend, do not visit it upon the people, if the people offend then the guilt is mine." (King Wu of Zhou) said: "The House of Zhou bestows great gifts upon its vassals and the virtuous are honored. Though there is a royal family, it is better to employ those with *Ren*. If the people offend, it is upon my head." Carefully institute a system of measures, set up laws and statutes, reform official posts and the writ of government will run throughout the land. Raise the nations that have fallen, continue the clans that have been destroyed, use the talents of the people that have been scattered and all the peoples under heaven will obey. Pay attention to the people, to supplies of food, to funeral ceremonies, and to sacrifices. Magnanimity will secure the support of the people. Integrity will secure their trust. Diligence will secure achievement and fairness will bring joy. (Yao Yue 1)

Comment The first part of this passage seems to be disciples' notes of a lecture about the sayings of the former kings, which describe the official proclamations made by Yao and Shun, Tang and Wu when they yielded or succeeded to the throne. The final passage appears to be a summation of Kongzi's lecture hall teaching outlining the basic principles of government. "Raise the nations that have fallen, continue the clans that have been destroyed, use the talents of the people that have been scattered," may be regarded as Kongzi's political clarion call, not necessarily as a program for a return to the old ways but more a call of the old clans of the Yin and Shang for the restoration of their power. As a descendant of the Yin and Shang, Kongzi retained a strong consciousness of Yin identity.

8.46 Zigong said: "The wickedness of Zhou was not as bad as recounted. Consequently a ruler does not place himself in a degrading position lest evil repute should engulf him." (Zizhang 20)

Comment Zigong mounts an unusual defense of the Shang tyrant King Zhou. There is no record of Kongzi's attitude here, he would probably agree, or at least not dissent. It should be noted that Kongzi was descended from the Yin and was one of the descendants of the Shang kings. There was still a family connection between Kongzi and King Zhou. Tradition has it that Wei Zhongyan, younger brother of Weizi, one of the concubinal brothers of King Zhou, and the first Song king, was a remote ancestor of Kongzi. The Shang kings all bore the surname "Zi." Kongzi's forbears had the name "Zi" up until six generations before Kongzi. The *Book of Rites* suggests that a title of nobility could be handed down for five generations at the most and that beyond five generations the original title is deemed exhausted and no longer regarded as an ancestral title. At this point a separate family was established and the name had to be changed to Kong.

8.47 Duke Zhou said to Duke Lu: "A ruler does not neglect his relatives nor cause ministers to complain at lack of trust. Provided that old friends are without blame they should not be discarded. One should not put one's faith in one man alone." (Weizi 10)

8.48 Duke Jing of Qi had 4,000 horses. When he died there were none who praised him for his virtue; Boyi and Shuqi died of hunger beneath the hill of Shouyang and people praise them still. Is that the meaning? (Jishi 12)

8.49 In the Zhou dynasty there were eight worthy of the title of Scholar: Boda, Boshi, Botu, Zhonghu, Shuye, Shuxia, Jisui and Jigua. (Weizi 11)

8.50 The wife of a ruler is called "Madam" (*furen*) by her spouse and a wife refers to herself as "Your child" (*xiao tong*); others address her as "Madam Ruler" (*jun furen*); in conversation with those from other states she is referred to as Madam Dowager (*gua xiaojun*) and those from other states refer to her as "Madam Ruler." (Jishi 14)
Comment The detail in these descriptions of differing styles of address for the wives of rulers perhaps suggest that they are in some way connected with Nanzi, the wife of Duke Ling of Wei.

8.51 The Master of Music Zhi fled to the state of Qi, Gan, the director of the second banquet ensemble fled to the state of Chu, Liao, the director of the third ensemble fled to the state of Cai, Que, the director of the fourth ensemble fled to the state of Qin. The master drummer Fang Shu reached the Yellow river and Wu, the drummer of the small drums reached the Han river. The deputy master of music Yang and Xiang, the master of the chimes reached the sea. (Weizi 9)

Comment This passage describes the scattering of a court orchestra and unconsciously brings to mind the phrase "The collapse of ceremony and the destruction of music."

COMPILER'S POSTSCRIPT

The following works have been consulted in the preparation of this book.

For textual analysis: Yang Bojun 杨伯峻, Lunyu Yishi 论语译注 (*The Analects Annotated*) (Beijing: Zhonghua Shuju, 1980)

For historical events and names: Zhang Dainian 张岱年, ed., *Kongzi Dacidian* 孔子大辞典 (*The Large Confucian Dictionary*) (Shanghai: Shanghai Cishu Chubanshe, 1993)

The comments are based upon the compiler's own research and understanding of the *Analects* together with decoding and interpretation of the original, based upon a view of the construction of the original text taken as a whole.

This book was first published in Simplified Chinese by SDX Joint Publishing Company in 2012.

TRANSLATOR'S POSTSCRIPT

The translation of Kongzi (Confucius), whether into modern Chinese (no text published in China or online today is without such a translation), or into English, is a process of expansion and extension. Over the last two millennia, many generations of Chinese scholars have labored in exegesis to produce such expansions.

To give an example of the scale of extension required to make the original fully intelligible to the modern reader of Chinese or English, a sparse original text of some 24 Chinese characters can extend to 50 characters of modern Chinese and 33 words of English. There are more extreme examples. If anything, classical Chinese is as remarkable for its brevity as it is for its obscurity.

The expansions can differ from commentator to commentator and depend to a considerable extent upon their interpretation of the original text which, in any case, was exiguous by its very nature. This may produce significant differences of meaning, as well as disagreement, between commentators, in some cases extending over centuries. However, since it is the function of the translator to translate what is before him, I have necessarily followed the expansions of the compiler, Qian Ning, though I have consulted other commentators for help.

The history of the translation of the *Analects* into English dates back to the end of the 17th century when extracts from the earlier Jesuit translations into latin were published in London. James Legge's 19th century translation into English is accessible online. These translations generally followed the traditional order and arrangement of the Chinese text and there was a tendency to treat the *Analects* as a collection of disparate individual aphorisms. In the *New Analects*, the compiler Qian Ning, approaches the text as a contextual and philosophical whole, as he explains in detail in his crucial preface. It is thus possible to see all that Kongzi said about, for example, music (and he was clearly of a musicological bent) and its function in society collected in one place.

There are countless modern translations of the *Analects* in their traditional form, but those who wish to consult a scholarly and yet eminently readable text can do no better than turn to the late Professor D.C.Lau's 1979 translation.

Tony Blishen

ANALECTS
ORIGINAL TEXT[1]

Xue Er I

1. The Master said: "To study and to put into practice is not that also a pleasure? When friends come from afar is that not also a joy? Not to feel resentment when misunderstood is not that the act of a Gentleman?"

2. You Ruo said: "There are few who respect their father and mother and obey their elder brother and yet dare offend their superiors. There are also few who have never offended their superiors and yet dare stir up trouble and strife. The Gentleman devoted his effort to the root of things and once that was established then the correct path sprang from it. Filial and Fraternal Piety are the basis of *Ren*."

3. The Master said: "Honeyed words and a fine appearance, where is the *Ren* in that!"

4. Zeng Can said: "Each day I examine myself three times: have I exerted myself on behalf of others? Have I been honest in my dealings with friends? Have I revised and implemented the teachings of my master?"

5. The Master said: "To lead a state of a thousand chariots requires proper attention to affairs and maintenance of trust, economy and love of the people, and labor according to the

---

[1] The *Analects* were originally arranged in 20 chapters. Each chapter took its title from its first two characters. For example, the first chapter "Xue Er" took its name from the first two characters of its opening phrase "To learn and to…," the second chapter from "Wei Zheng" and so on. In the reconstructed version the original chapter headings have been included in brackets after each quotation.

agricultural calendar."

6. The Master said: "The young observe Filial Piety at home and Fraternal Piety outside, possessed of Integrity and caution in speech, they become close to *Ren* through universal love. If there is effort to spare they use it to acquire wisdom."

7. Zixia said: "Through respect for virtue one may transform one's basic nature; in serving one's parents one may exert all one's strength; in serving one's ruler one may offer one's life; in friendship one may keep one's word. Though it may be said that there is no learning in this, I call it learning."

8. The Master said: "If a Gentleman is not serious he will lack dignity and his study will lack grounding. He should conduct himself with Loyalty and Integrity and he should have no friends less than himself. He should not fear to correct his mistakes."

9. Zeng Can said: "Perform the funeral rites for one's parents with care, sacrifice with reverence to the ancestors and the morality of the people will grow stronger."

10. Ziqin asked Zigong: "When the Master visits a state he takes part in its government. Is this because he seeks to do so or because he is invited to do so?" Zigong said: "The Master is warm, virtuous, decorous, simple and modest, these qualities earn him the opportunity to take part. Perhaps the Master's way of seeking office differs from those of others?"

11. The Master said: "While the father lives observe the son's aspirations; when the father is dead observe his conduct. If, after three years, he continues to follow in his father's footsteps, that is Filial Piety."

12. You Ruo said: "The uses of Propriety place value upon the achievement of harmony. The principles of government of the former kings attached most value to this point and it was so in matters large and small. Where it did not work, it was because of exercising harmony only for harmony's sake and failing to impose the restraints of Propriety thus rendering it unworkable."

13. You Ruo said: "To act with Integrity is to be close to Righteousness and to keep one's word; to act with decorum is to be close to Propriety and thus to be distant from shame. To rely upon one's intimates is a support."

14. The Master said: "The Gentleman does not gorge himself, does not seek comfort in his dwelling, works hard, guards his speech and corrects himself through the company of the virtuous. This may be called learning well."

15. Zigong said: "To be poor but not to flatter and to be rich but not arrogant, how is that?" The Master said: "It is well, but not as good as being poor but happy or rich and appreciating ceremony." Zigong said: "The *Classic of Poetry* says: 'Like slicing and polishing bone, cutting and grinding ivory,' is that what is being spoken of?" The Master said: "Zigong, now I can begin to discuss the *Classic of Poetry* with you. You can deduce what is to come from what I have already told you."

16. The Master said: "Fear not that others do not know you, fear only that you do not know others."

Wei Zheng II

1. The Master said: "The rule of Virtue is like the North star, fixed in its position and surrounded by other stars."

2. The Master said: "The three hundred poems of the *Classic of Poetry* are expressed in but one word, purity."

3. The Master said: "Lead through decree, control through punishment and the people will avoid punishment and be without shame; lead with Virtue, control through Propriety and there will be honor and character."

4. The Master said: "At fifteen I had the will to learn, at thirty I stood upon my own feet, at forty nothing disconcerted me, at fifty I knew the will of heaven, at sixty I was open to argument

and at seventy whatever I desired was within bounds."

5. Meng Yizi asked about Filial Piety. The Master said: "Do not violate Propriety." Fan Chi was once driving Kongzi and Kongzi told him: "Meng Yizi once asked me about Filial Piety and I told him: 'Do not violate Propriety.'" Fan Chi said: "What does that mean?" The Master said: "While they are alive serve one's parents with Propriety; after they are dead bury them with Propriety and sacrifice to them with Propriety."

6. Meng Wubo asked about Filial Piety. The Master said: "Feel anxiety for the sickness of parents."

7. Ziyou asked about Filial Piety. The Master said: "What is called Filial Piety today is just the keeping of parents. Dogs and horses are kept, and if there is no respect, where lies the difference?"

8. Zixia asked about Filial Piety. The Master said: "It is not easy to always maintain a smiling countenance towards one's mother and father. Can just helping with their affairs and letting them eat first be regarded as Filial Piety?"

9. The Master said: "I teach Yan Yuan all day. He raises no questions and appears stupid. He withdraws and reflects and then presents inspiring views. He is by no means stupid."

10. The Master said: "Consider their motives, observe their history, examine that which contents them. What then may be hidden? What then may be hidden?"

11. The Master said: "Revise the old to know the new and become a master."

12. The Master said: "The Gentleman is not a tool."

13. Zigong asked how to be a Gentleman. The Master said: "First practice what you preach and then speak of it."

14. The Master said: "The Gentleman is sociable but does not collude but the rogue colludes and is not sociable."

15. The Master said: "Study without thought is futile, thought without study is dubious."

16. The Master said: "Strike down heterodoxy, make it harmless."

17. The Master said: "Zilu! Let me teach you about knowledge. Knowing is knowing and not knowing is not knowing, that is knowledge."

18. Zizhang wished to know how to obtain a position. The Master said: "Enquire widely and put aside that which is in doubt, expound with care what remains and faults will be few; observe widely and avoid danger and implement what remains with care and regrets will be few. When speech is without fault and action without regret, there is your official salary."

19. Duke Ai of Lu asked: "What is it that makes the people obedient?" Kongzi replied: "Raise the upright above the unjust and the people will obey; raise the unjust above the upright and the people will not."

20. Ji Kangzi asked: "How can one make the people respectful, loyal and industrious?" The Master said: "Treat them with gravity and they will respect; treat them with the compassion due to old and young and they will be loyal; choose able men to teach the less able and they will be industrious."

21. Someone asked Kongzi: "Why do you not follow a career in government?" The Master said: "The *Book of Documents* says 'Filial Piety! It is respect for parents and love for brothers. It is to be found in governing.' It too is government, what more need there be before it is considered so?"

22. The Master said: "I do not know how it is possible to be a person and yet lack Integrity! If the shafts of carriages and carts lack joints how can they run?"

23. Zizhang asked: "Can one know ten dynasties hence?" The Master said: "The Yin dynasty succeeded to the ceremonial system of the Xia dynasty and its losses and gains may be known; the Zhou dynasty succeeded to the systems of the Yin and its losses and gains may be known. That which succeeds to the

Zhou, though it may be 100 generations hence, is also to be known."

24. The Master said: "It is flattery to sacrifice to those demons and spirits who should not receive sacrifice; it is weakness not to act righteously when you should."

Ba Yi III

1. The Master said of Ji Kangzi: "Eight ranks of eight dancers performing in the courtyard, if this can be tolerated, what may not be tolerated?!"

2. The three families of Ji, Meng and Shusun performed the Yong music at the conclusion of ancestral sacrifices. The Master said: "How can the meaning of the poem 'Assisting at the sacrifice from the side are the princes, in the center solemnly celebrating is the Zhou king' be taken as referring to your family temples?"

3. The Master said: "If man is without *Ren* what then of ceremony? If man is without *Ren* what then of music?"

4. Lin Fang asked about the basis of Propriety. The Master said: "That is a significant question! So far as ceremony is concerned frugality is better than extravagance; so far as funeral arrangements are concerned true grief is better than elaborate obsequies."

5. The Master said: "The barbarians beyond the central plain who have rulers are less than the states of the central plain who have no ruler."

6. Ji Kangzi intended to sacrifice at Mount Tai. The Master said to Ran You: "Can you not advise against this?" Ran You replied: "No." The Master said: "Alas! In speaking of Mount Tai are there none who know Propriety so well as Lin Fang?"

7. The Master said: "The Gentleman does not compete. If he

must, then let it be at archery! First he greets and then takes position. Afterwards he joins the toasts. He has competed but is still a Gentleman."

8. Zixia asked: "What is the meaning of the poem 'The smiling countenance enchants, how pretty the glancing eyes, the simple face beneath magnificently adorned'?" The Master said: "If you wish to paint a picture, you must first have a white ground." Zixia said: "Then Propriety comes later?" The Master said: "Zixia, you are the one who can inspire! Now I can discuss the *Classic of Poetry* with you."

9. The Master said: "I can speak of the ceremonies of the Xia dynasty but not of those of the state of Qi for lack of evidence; I can speak of the ceremonies of the Yin dynasty but not of those of the state of Song for lack of evidence. This is because of the lack of documents. Were they adequate, then I could provide the evidence."

10. The Master said: "After the first libation at the sacrifice to the imperial ancestors I could bear to watch no longer."

11. Someone asked Kongzi about the meaning of the imperial sacrifice to the ancestors. The Master said: "I do not know. But for those who do understand, knowing how to govern would be as easy as putting something here," pointing to the palm of his hand.

12. When performing a sacrifice one should behave as if the object of the sacrifice were present, when sacrificing to spirits one should behave as if the spirits were present. The Master said: "If I cannot attend a sacrifice, it is as if the sacrifice had not been performed."

13. Wangsun Jia asked: "What is the meaning of 'It is better to propitiate the kitchen god than gods more honorably positioned'?" The Master said: "Not so. Offend Heaven and there will be nowhere to pray."

14. The Master said: "The Zhou dynasty inherited the systems

of two previous dynasties, such a proliferation of documents! I follow the Zhou."

15. Kongzi visited the Temple of Ancestors and asked about everything. Somebody said: "Who says that this son of somebody from Zou knows Propriety? He visited the Temple of Ancestors and had to ask about everything." The Master heard and said: "That is Propriety."

16. The Master said: "The ceremony of archery is not on account of hitting the target, because strengths differ, this was the way of the ancients."

17. Zigong wished to abandon the practice of presenting a lamb for sacrifice on the 1st of each month. The Master said: "Give it! You may pity the lamb but I treasure the ceremony."

18. The Master said: "To serve a ruler to the utmost with Propriety, some may regard that as flattery."

19. Duke Ding of Lu asked: "How may rulers use their ministers and ministers serve their rulers?" The Master replied: "Rulers employ their ministers with Propriety and ministers serve their rulers with Loyalty."

20. The Master said: "The poem, the "Call of the Osprey," is joyful but not wanton, sad but not grief-stricken."

21. Duke Ai of Lu asked Zai Wo what wood should be used to make the memorial tablets for the Earth god. Zai Wo said: "The Xia used pine, the Yin used cedar, the Zhou used chestnut, so that the people should tremble." The Master commented: "Do not discuss what is already complete, do not try to prevent what is already in the past, do not rake over what has already happened."

22. The Master said: "Guan Zhong was small minded!" Someone asked: "Was he frugal?" The Master said: "Guan Zhong maintained three establishments whose officials had no more than a single employment, can that be called frugality?" They further asked: "Being so, then did he understand Propriety?" The Master said: "If the ruler erected a screen in front of his

entrance, then so did Guan Zhong. If the ruler had receptacles for empty wine cups at banquets for other rulers, then so did Guan Zhong. If Guan Zhong understood Propriety, then who is there who does not?"

23. The Master discussed music with the Tutor of Lu and said: "I know the melodies: the opening piece is played together and the sound fills one's ears with joy; then it expands with a melodious tune and clear rhythm, continuously repeating until the end."

24. The guardian official of the fiefdom of Yi sought a meeting with Kongzi, saying: "I have never yet not met a Gentleman who has arrived here." The disciples took him to meet Kongzi. After he came out he said: "Why are you so disheartened? The world has lacked the Grand Principle for a long time but your master will be a bell that calls to the people of the world."

25. The Master said of *Shao* music: "It has both utter beauty and utter virtue." He said of *Wu* music: "It has utter beauty but it is not utterly virtuous."

26. The Master said: "When those in power lack magnanimity, lack respect for ceremony, and do not display grief when mourning, how can I bear to look upon it?"

Li Ren IV

1. The Master said: "It is good to live with *Ren*, if one chooses not to, how can one attain wisdom?"

2. The Master said: "Those that do not possess *Ren* cannot exist long in poverty nor can they exist long in joy. Those that possess *Ren* are content in it and the wise benefit from it."

3. The Master said: "Only those that possess *Ren* can love others or hate others."

4. The Master said: "If one puts one's will into *Ren* there can be

no evil."

5. The Master said: "All men desire honor and riches but if they are acquired improperly they cannot be enjoyed; all men fear poverty and abasement but if they are suffered unjustly they cannot be cast off. If the Gentleman departs from *Ren* how can he be known as one? A Gentleman may not offend against *Ren* for even the length of a meal, it should remain thus when hurried and thus even when desperate."

6. The Master said: "I have not met those who love *Ren* nor those who hate those who are without *Ren*. Naturally, there are none better than those who love *Ren;* those who hate the absence of *Ren* have *Ren* of themselves and that prevents those without *Ren* imposing upon them. Will there come a day when effort may be devoted to *Ren*? I have not met those who lack this effort. Such people may exist, but I have not met them."

7. The Master said: "The faults of man differ from group to group. Through the examination of fault one may know whether there is *Ren* or not."

8. The Master said: "If I hear of the Grand Principal at dawn, I will willingly die at dusk."

9. The Master said: "The Scholar who aspires to the Grand Principle but is ashamed of eating badly or being ill-clothed is not worthy of engaging in discussion."

10. The Master said: "As the Gentleman exists in the world, there is no path that he must follow and no path that he may not follow, but he must adhere to Righteousness."

11. The Master said: "The Gentleman embraces Virtue and the rogue clings to his native hearth; the Gentleman has in mind the penalties of the law and the rogue thinks of favor."

12. The Master said: "To conduct oneself merely to secure advantage incurs much hatred."

13. The Master said: "Is it possible to use Propriety to govern the state with principle? Where is the difficulty in that? If Propriety

cannot be used to govern the state with principle, how can one speak of the application of Propriety?"

14. The Master said: "Fear not that you have no position, fear only that you lack the ambition. Fear not that you are unknown but strive for the qualities that will make you known."

15. The Master said: "Oh Zeng Can! My thinking has one essential, which is consistent throughout." Zeng Can replied: "True." The Master left and the disciples asked: "What did he say?" Zeng Can said: "The Master said his thinking has one essential which consists of Loyalty (*Zhong*, 忠) and Thoughtfulness (*Shu*, 恕). That is all."

16. The Master said: "The Gentleman knows Righteousness, the rogue merely advantage."

17. The Master said: "Meet the worthy and emulate them, meet the unworthy and examine oneself."

18. The Master said: "Serving one's parents resembles offering humble advice. When they are unwilling, maintain respect and do not disobey, feel anxiety but do not hate."

19. The Master said: "Do not travel far while parents live, should you travel let your whereabouts be known."

20. The Master said: "If, after three years, a son continues to follow in his father's footsteps, that is Filial Piety."

21. The Master said: "One must know the age of parents, both for joy and for dread."

22. The Master said: "The reticence of the ancients derived from shame that they might not keep their word."

23. The Master said: "There are very few who, having once been restrained by Propriety, continue in error!"

24. The Master said: "The Gentleman should be cautious in speech and quick in action."

25. The Master said: "The virtuous do not exist on their own, they attract the company of others of the same mind."

26. Ziyou said: "To serve a ruler over-assiduously may

bring shame, to be over-assiduous in friendship leads to estrangement."

Gongye Chang V

1. The Master said of Gongye Chang: "One could marry one's daughter to him. He has been in prison but that was not his fault." The Master's daughter later married him.
2. The Master said of Nan Rong: "In a state with principle he could hold a position without fear of dismissal; in a state without principle he could withdraw without fear of execution." Later the Master married his elder brother's daughter to him.
3. The Master said of Zijian: "This is the man to be a Gentleman! If there are no Gentlemen in the state of Lu, how did he attain the character of a Gentleman?"
4. Zigong asked: "What do you think of me?" The Master said: "You, you are like a vessel." Zigong asked: "What kind of vessel?" The Master said: "A *hulian*, a precious sacrificial vessel."
5. Somebody said: "Zhonggong has *Ren* but no eloquence." The Master said: "What is the use of eloquence? Eloquent argument merely arouses detestation. What is the use of eloquence without understanding *Ren*?"
6. The Master dispatched Qidiao Kai to take up a post. Qidiao Kai replied: "I have not the confidence for this." The Master was pleased.
7. The Master said: "If I cannot go by road then I must go by water. Of my followers, perhaps only Zilu would come with me." Zilu heard this and was pleased. The Master said: "Zilu has more courage than I do but his other talents are difficult to discern."
8. Meng Wubo asked: "Does Zilu possess *Ren*?" The Master said: "I do not know." Meng Wubo asked further. The Master

said: "Zilu could command military supplies in a state of 1,000 chariots but I do not know whether he possesses *Ren*." Meng Wubo asked about Ran You. The Master said: "In a place of 1,000 households or a state of 100 chariots Ran You could be a governor, but I do not know whether he possesses *Ren*." Meng Wubo asked about Gongye Chang. The Master said: "Gongye Chang could attend court in ceremonial robes and greet important guests, but I do not know whether he possesses *Ren*."

9. The Master said to Zigong: "As between you and Yan Yuan, who is the most outstanding?" Zigong replied: "Yan Yuan is, how could I dare hope to compare with him? I can infer two from one, but he can infer ten from one." The Master said: "You cannot match him, neither you nor I can match him."

10. Zai Wo slept during the day. The Master said: "You cannot carve rotten wood or paint a wall built from dung! What is the use of scolding him?" The Master said: "When first I knew people I listened and believed they would act as they said, now I listen and see what they do. In the case of Zai Wo I have changed my mind."

11. The Master said: "I have never met a man of resolve." Somebody said: "There is Shen Cheng." The Master said: "Shen Cheng is a man of desires, how can he be resolute?"

12. Zigong said: "I do not wish others to impose upon me, nor do I wish to impose upon others." The Master said: "Zigong, this is something that you have not yet mastered."

13. Zigong said: "The classical culture that the Master taught may be heard and understood; what the Master expounded about human nature and the heavenly law can be neither heard nor understood."

14. When Zilu heard something new and was not immediately able to put it into practice his fear was that there would again be something else new.

15. Zigong asked: "Why was Kong Wenzi awarded the

posthumous title of 'Wen' (literary)?" The Master said: "Because he was intelligent and studious and saw no shame in seeking advice from those beneath him, that is why he was awarded the title."

16. The Master said of Zichan: "He has the four virtues of a Gentleman: he conducts himself seriously, he serves his ruler with respect, he treats the people with benevolence and uses them justly."

17. The Master said: "Yan Pingzhong is skilled in making friends. All revere him after knowing him a long time."

18. The Master said: "Zang Wenzhong kept a pet turtle in an elaborately ornamented   building, how clever can that be?"

19. Zizhang asked: "Minister Ziwen of the state of Chu became chief minister three times but displayed no joy; he was dismissed three times but displayed no indignation. Each time he left office he handed over everything to his successor. How is he to be considered?" The Master said: "As Loyal." Zizhang asked: "Is it *Ren*?" The Master said: "I do not know. How can this be described as *Ren*?" Zizhang asked again: "Cui Zhu assassinated the ruler of Qi and Chen Wenzi abandoned 40 horses and left the state of Qi. When he reached another state he said: 'Those in power here are just like Cui Zhu' and left. When he reached yet another state he said: 'Those in power here are just like Cui Zhu' and left again. How should he be regarded?" The Master said: "As pure." Zizhang said: "Could it be described as *Ren*?" The Master said: "I do not know. How could this be described as *Ren*?"

20. Ji Wenzi never acted before thinking three times. Kongzi heard this and said: "Twice is quite enough."

21. The Master said: "Ning Wuzi is clever when the state is principled but appears stupid when it is not. His cleverness may be emulated but his stupidity may not."

22. While in the state of Chen, the Master said: "Return! Return! The young disciples from my home-town are vigorous

and spirited, moreover they have talent too, but they have yet to learn moderation."

23. The Master said: "Boyi and Shuqi did not nurture old hatreds, hence grudges diminished."

24. The Master said: "Who says that Weisheng Gao is straightforward? Someone once asked him for some vinegar and he begged it off a neighbor and passed it on."

25. The Master said: "Honeyed words and a fine appearance together with obsequiousness were regarded by Zuoqiu Ming as a disgrace. So do I regard it. To harbor hatred behind pleasant behavior was regarded by Zuoqiu Ming as a disgrace. And so do I, Kongzi, so regard it."

26. Yan Yuan and Zilu were in attendance upon the Master. The Master said: "Why not tell me your aspirations?" Zilu said: "Not to regret the loss of the horse and carriage and fur robes that I have enjoyed with my friends." Yan Yuan said: "Not to boast of my good works or to declare my achievements." Zilu asked the Master: "May we hear your aspirations?" The Master said: "To bring peace of mind to the old, trust to friends and care to the young."

27. The Master said: "Enough! I have never met anybody who, having seen his own faults, could then conduct self-examination."

28. The Master said: "In any village of ten families there is bound to be someone with my qualities of Loyalty and Integrity but not with my love of study."

Yong Ye VI

1. The Master said: "Zhonggong may be an official."

2. Zhonggong asked the Master about Zisang Bozi. The Master said: "He is acceptable, his characteristic is simplicity."

Zhonggong said: "Is it also acceptable to govern the people with respectful conduct and simplicity in handling affairs? Would it be excessive to both conduct oneself in simplicity and handle affairs with simplicity?" The Master said: "Zhonggong, you are right."

3. Duke Ai of Lu asked Kongzi: "Who amongst the disciples loves learning the most?" The Master replied: "Yan Yuan loved learning. He never took out his anger on others and never made the same mistake twice. But alas, his life was short. There are none now who resemble him and I know of none who have his learning."

4. Gongxi Hua was serving in an official post in the state of Qi. Ran You asked the Master for rice on Gongxi's mother's behalf. The Master said: "Give her six *dou* and more." Ran You asked for an increase. The Master said: "Give her two more *dou*." In the end Ran You gave her 800 *dou*. The Master said: "Gongxi Hua went to the state of Qi in a fine carriage drawn by fat horses and clad in a warm fur robe. I have heard it said that the Gentleman only aids those in desperate need and not the wealthy."

5. Yuan Xian was steward to the Master who gave him 900 measures of rice in payment; he declined it. The Master said: "Do not refuse it, share it with your village!"

6. The Master said of Zhonggong: "If the hide of a sacrificial bullock is red and its horns are straight, though one may not wish to sacrifice it, will the gods of hill and river be willing to give it up?"

7. The Master said: "Yan Yuan can go for three months without contravening *Ren* for a moment, the others can only manage a day or a month."

8. Ji Kangzi asked: "Could Zilu administer a government?" The Master said: "Zilu is very decisive. What difficulty could he have in administering a government?" Ji Kangzi asked:

"Could Zigong administer a government?" The Master said: "Zigong is clear minded. What difficulty could he have in administering a government?" Ji Kangzi again asked: "Could Ran You administer a government?" The Master said: "Ran You is talented above others, what difficulty could he have in administering a government?"

9. Ji Kangzi sent a messenger to ask Min Ziqian to be governor of Fei. Min Ziqian said to the messenger: "Please decline on my behalf. If you come again, I shall flee across the Wen river."

10. Boniu was ill. The Master visited him and grasped his hand through the window saying: "Is death our fate? That such a one should be so ill! That such a one should be so ill!"

11. The Master said: "How worthy is Yan Yuan! A helping of coarse rice, a scoop of fresh water and he lives in humble surroundings. Others would find his situation unbearable but he continues in his delight. How worthy he is!"

12. Ran You said: "It is not that I take no joy in your teaching, it is that I lack the capacity." The Master said: "Those who lack the capacity give up half-way. You have drawn a line and will make no further progress."

13. The Master said to Zixia: "You must be a Gentleman Confucian, not a rogue Confucian!"

14. Ziyou became governor of Wucheng. The Master said: "Have you any people of ability there?" Ziyou said: "There is one called Tantai Mieming, he keeps to the straight and narrow and apart from official business never calls to pay his respects."

15. The Master said: "Meng Zhifan never praises himself. When the army is in retreat he protects the rear, when it enters a town, he lashes his horse saying: 'I was not brave at the rear, it was just that my horse was slow.'"

16. The Master said: "Lacking the eloquence of Zhu Tuo and with only the good looks of Song Zhao it would be difficult to avoid disaster in today's society."

17. The Master said: "Who can leave except through the door? Why not follow this path?"

18. The Master said: "When simplicity exceeds grace it leads to roughness; when elegance exceeds simplicity it leads to empty bombast. When both simplicity and elegance are complementary, that is what makes a Gentleman."

19. The Master said: "Man lives through being upright, those that are not upright survive by luck."

20. The Master said: "To like it is better than to know it, to take pleasure in it is better than to like it."

21. The Master said: "One may discuss the profound with those of moderate learning but not with those of less learning."

22. Fan Chi asked about wisdom. The Master said: "Observe Righteousness in dealing with people, respect demons and spirits but be distant from them, that is wisdom." (Fan Chi) asked about *Ren*. Kongzi said: "*Ren* is to be at the forefront of difficulty but at the rear of advantage, that may be spoken of as *Ren*."

23. The Master said: "The wise delight in water and those with *Ren* love mountains; the wise are active and those with *Ren* are calm. The wise are happy and those with *Ren* live long."

24. The Master said: "Once there is reform in Qi, it reaches Lu; once there is reform in Lu, it will lead to the Grand Principle."

25. The Master said: "The sacrificial beakers are beakers no longer, what has become of them? What has become of them?"

26. Zai Wo asked: "If somebody told one that possessed *Ren* that somebody had fallen down a well, would he then jump in and save him?" The Master said: "Why should he act so? The Gentleman can save him from the mouth of the well and need not jump in; a Gentleman may be deceived but he cannot act stupidly."

27. The Master said: "The Gentleman reads and studies widely, acts within the constraints of Propriety and thus does not stray

from the path of correct principle."

28. The Master met Nanzi and Zilu was displeased. The Master swore: "If I do something that I should not, may Heaven reject me! May Heaven reject me!"

29. The Master said: "Adhering to the mean of moderation is of the quality of Virtue, it is of the utmost! It has long been rare amongst the people."

30. Zigong said: "Were one to bestow benefit upon the people so as to help all, how would that be? Might it be called *Ren*?" The Master said: "That would be more than *Ren*, it would be divine! Yao and Shun feared they were defective in this respect! *Ren* is to wish to stand oneself yet to help others to stand as well, to wish to attain oneself yet to help others attain as well. To come close to an understanding of others may be called the way of *Ren*."

Shu Er VII

1. The Master said: "Describe but not inscribe, love and believe what is ancient. Secretly, I regard myself as rather like Lao Peng."

2. The Master said: "To know through memorizing, to learn without loathing, to teach indefatigably, as far as I am concerned, is there more?"

3. The Master said: "What I fear is that Virtue may not be nurtured, that learning may not be pursued, that Righteousness may not be sought out and that evil may not be corrected."

4. At home the Master was neat and his bearing relaxed.

5. The Master said: "I am old and weak! For a long time I have not dreamed of seeing Duke Zhou again."

6. The Master said: "Aspire to the Grand Principle, stand on Virtue, abide by *Ren*, take pleasure in the arts."

7. The Master said: "I have never refused to instruct those who brought me ten strips of dried meat as a fee."

8. The Master said: "Do not explain before they struggle to understand, do not enlighten until they struggle for words. Do not persevere with those who cannot deduce four corners from the existence of one."

9. The Master did not eat his fill when eating with those in mourning.

10. On days when he had wept at a funeral, the Master did not sing.

11. The Master said to Yan Yuan: "If one is employed in office then one acts as such, if one is not employed then one retires from public life. Only you and I understand this!" Zilu said: "If the Master were to command three armies, with whom would you choose to be?" The Master said: "Not with the heroically reckless and foolhardy, but with the cautious and those who succeed through skill in planning."

12. The Master said: "If riches are to be had I would even act as the servant who clears the way with a whip. If they are not to be had, then I have other pursuits."

13. The Master took care over: fasting, warfare, and illness.

14. While in the state of Qi the Master heard the music of *Shao*, and for three months could not taste meat, saying: "I had not thought that music was ravishing to this extent."

15. Ran You said: "Would the Master assist the ruler of Wei?" Zigong said: "I will ask him." He entered and asked: "What manner of people were Boyi and Shuqi?" The Master replied: "They were ancient worthies." He further asked: "Did they bear hatred?" The Master said: "What hatred lies in seeking *Ren* and gaining it?" Zigong withdrew and said: "The Master will not do it."

16. The Master said: "To eat coarse grain, drink cold water and to sleep pillowed on one's arms, there is joy in that. But to gain

riches and honor unjustly is like a passing cloud."

17. The Master said: "Given a few more years, I would study the *Book of Changes* from the age of fifty and would be without great fault."

18. The Master spoke with an elegant court accent which he used when reciting from the *Classic of Poetry* and the *Book of Documents* and when performing ceremonies.

19. Duke Ye asked Zilu about Kongzi. Zilu did not answer. The Master said: "Why do you not say something like: when he is deeply engaged in something he forgets to eat, when he is happy he forgets anxiety and he is unaware of the approach of old age."

20. The Master said: "I am not one of those who understood all from birth. I like the past and seek out the knowledgeable."

21. The Master did not speak of strange happenings, of violence or chaos, or of demons and spirits.

22. The Master said: "Where there are three together, one must be my teacher. Choose that which has virtue and follow it and improve on that which lacks virtue."

23. The Master said: "Since heaven has granted me Virtue, what is there that Huan Tui can do to me?"

24. The Master said: "Disciples, do you think that there are matters that I conceal from you? There is nothing that I conceal from you. There is no action that I take that I do not share with you. That is the person I am."

25. The Master taught only four subjects: literature and the art of discourse, conduct, Loyalty and Integrity.

26. The Master said: "I shall never see a Sage, but it is enough to be able to see a Gentleman. I am unlikely to meet a person of virtue, but were I to meet a person of perseverance, that would be enough. Those who have not but pretend they have; those who are empty but pretend they are full, those who are poor but pretend they are rich; it is difficult for these people to

persevere!"

27. The Master did not fish with a line of many hooks nor did he shoot at homing birds.

28. The Master said: "There are those who knowing nothing yet can create, I am not one of them. Enquire widely, choose the best and follow it. Observe widely and note it. This is wisdom of the second order."

29. The people of Huxiang were difficult to engage in conversation. Kongzi received a boy and the disciples were puzzled. The Master said: "I praise his progress rather than confirm his backwardness. Why be excessive? If people clean themselves up to make progress, one should applaud their effort and not be constantly thinking of their past."

30. The Master said: "Is *Ren* distant? If I desire it, it is there."

31. An official of the state of Chen asked whether Duke Zhao of Lu understood Propriety, the Master said: "He does." After Kongzi had withdrawn, the official invited Wuma Qi to enter and said: "I have heard say that the Gentleman does not take sides, could it be that Kongzi is not impartial? The ruler of Lu took as his wife a woman of Wu of the same surname, the rulers of both states having the same surname, and called her Wu Mengzi. If the ruler of Lu understands Propriety, who does not?" Wuma Qi recounted this to Kongzi who said: "I am truly fortunate, if I make a mistake, somebody will always know."

32. If, in singing with somebody else, it went well, Kongzi would ask him to sing again and would then join him.

33. The Master said: "As to culture and learning, I am much like other people. I have not yet attained the accomplishments of a Gentleman."

34. The Master said: "How dare I speak of sageness and *Ren*? I can merely strive for them and teach them to others, that much I can do." Gongxi Hua said: "That is truly something that the disciples cannot learn."

35. The Master lay ill. Zilu prayed to demons and spirits for him. The Master said: "Do they exist?" Zilu said: "They do. The *Eulogies* say 'Pray to the spirits of heaven and earth for you.'" The Master said: "I have prayed for a long time."

36. The Master said: "Extravagance shows a lack respect, frugality is simplicity. I would rather simplicity than lack of respect."

37. The Master said: "The Gentleman is expansive and magnanimous but the rogue is petty and prey to anxiety."

38. The Master was warm but severe, stern but not fierce, calm and courteous.

Taibo VIII

1. The Master said: "Taibo may be said to have achieved Virtue. Three times he yielded up the land and the people could not find the words with which to praise him."

2. The Master said: "Respect without Propriety is to no avail, caution without Propriety is timidity, boldness without Propriety is sharpness of tongue. If the ruler is careful to bestow affection then the people will glory in *Ren*. If old friends are not abandoned then the people will not be heartless."

3. Zeng Can was ill. He called his disciples together and said: "Lift my feet and hands! The *Classic of Poetry* writes: 'In fear and trepidation, as if standing at the edge of an abyss, or treading upon thin ice.' Henceforward I know that I shall come to no harm, oh, disciples!"

4. Zeng Can was ill and Meng Jingzi visited him. Zeng Can said: "At the approach of death, the bird's cry becomes mournful; at the approach of death man's speech becomes virtuous. The Gentleman possesses three attributes worthy of regard: a polished appearance that distances him from coarseness; an upright expression that demonstrates sincerity; prudence in speech that

puts vulgarity at a distance. As to sacrificial ceremonies, they are conducted by the official in charge."

5. Zeng Can said: "To be capable but willing to learn from the incapable, to be learned but willing to learn from the ignorant; to have but to appear to have not, to be full but to appear to be empty; to be insulted but not to take offence, this was the custom of a former friend."

6. Zeng Can said: "Someone who can be entrusted with a young orphan or the fate of a nation, someone who does not waver in the face of a life or death crisis, is he a Gentleman? He is!"

7. Zeng Can said: "The Scholar should have breadth of mind and strength of will, for his task is heavy and the road is long. To make the achievement of *Ren* his task, cannot the burden be but heavy? To cease only with death, cannot the road be but long?"

8. The Master said: "Start with poetry, establish with ceremony and complete with music."

9. The Master said: "The people may know how but need not know why."

10. The Master said: "A liking for belligerence and a dislike of being poverty-stricken leads to disorder. When people are without *Ren,* hatred flourishes and that is disorder."

11. The Master said: "Though you had the talents of Duke Zhou himself but were arrogant and mean-minded, the remaining qualities would be of no avail."

12. The Master said: "If, after three years of study one has not attained a position, it will be even less easy thereafter."

13. The Master said: "Be resolute in conviction and diligent in study. Hold to the way of virtue until death. Do not enter states where there is danger nor dwell in those in chaos. Serve where the Grand Principle exists but retire where there is not. In states that have the principle, poverty and abasement are a matter of shame. Where there is no principle, riches and honor are a matter of shame."

14. The Master said: "If you do not occupy the post, do not make the policy."

15. The Master said: "From the opening piece played by the Master of Music Zhi to the final piece, the "Call of the Osprey," my ears were filled with rich and beautiful melodies."

16. The Master said: "I do not understand how there can be people who are arrogant and not upright, ignorant and dishonest, and loquacious and untrustworthy."

17. The Master said: "In study fear not to achieve and fear to lose."

18. The Master said: "Great it is that Shun and Yu possessed the land and did not scheme to acquire it."

19. The Master said: "Oh, great is King Yao! Such majesty! Heaven, great as it is, only he can follow. So vast that the people have not the words to praise him. Such magnificence is his achievement, such brilliance is his enlightened rule."

20. Shun had five ministers and ruled the land. King Wu of Zhou said: "I have ten able ministers to govern." Kongzi said: "Talent is difficult to find, is it not so? Talent flourished from the time of Yao and Shun and in the time of King Wu of Zhou. Of the ten ministers one was a woman and so there were only nine. King Wen of Zhou ruled two thirds of the land and still served the Shang court. The Virtue of the Zhou was true virtue."

21. The Master said: "I have no criticism of Yu, he lived simply and served the gods and spirits, he was clothed simply but was splendidly attired at sacrifices; his palace was humble but he devoted effort to irrigation. I have no criticism of Yu."

Zihan IX

1. The Master seldom spoke of profit and utility but spoke often in praise of destiny and *Ren*.

2. On the streets of Daxiang they said: "Great is Kongzi! Vast in learning but known for nothing." The Master heard this and said to his disciples: "What am I known for? For driving a chariot? Or archery? Probably for driving a chariot."

3. The Master said: "To wear a ceremonial hat made from hemp is in accordance with Propriety. Now, they are all made from silk and are simpler, I follow the many. Ministers once knelt in the lower hall to make obeisance, that is in accordance with Propriety. Now they make obeisance in the upper hall, that is overbearing. I do not follow the many and still kneel in the lower hall."

4. The Master abominated four things, wild guesswork, dogmatic insistence, obstinacy and belief in one's own infallibility.

5. The Master was besieged in Kuang and said: "King Wen of Zhou is dead, does the task of transmitting the ceremonies and music of Zhou then fall to me? If heaven wishes to let ceremonies and music die out, then later generations will have no grasp of it; if Heaven does not intend it to die out, then what is there that the people of Kuang can do to me?"

6. The court chamberlain asked Zigong: "Is the Master a sage? How can he be so talented?" Zigong said: "It is heaven that made him a sage and so talented." The Master heard and said: "Does the chamberlain understand me? When I was young my status was low and thus I learned many lowly skills. Do Gentlemen command so many skills? They do not!"

7. Lao said: "The Master once said: 'I have never held office, hence my skills.'"

8. The Master said: "Do I possess knowledge? I do not. If a rustic seeks my help, I am empty of knowledge, but I can infer the middle from the ends."

9. The Master said: "The phoenix comes no more, the river drawing no longer emerges from the Yellow River. Is that all of my life complete?"

10. When he met those dressed in mourning, or wearing an official cap or those who were blind, the Master would stand and when he passed them would do so quickly, even when there was no need because of their youth.

11. Yan Yuan sighed: "The higher you aim the higher it is, the harder you drill the deeper it is. It seems in front and then is suddenly behind. With his patient guidance the Master expanded my knowledge with learning, constrained my speech and action with Propriety and made me keep going. When I had exhausted all effort a towering mountain still stood before me, and though I still wanted to continue climbing, there was no path."

12. The Master lay ill. Zilu ordered the disciples to act as official mourners. The Master recovered a little and he said: "For a long time Zilu has practised trickery! I am not entitled to official mourners, nor should any pretend to act as official mourners, who am I deceiving? Am I deceiving heaven? I would rather die at the hands of the official mourners than at the hands of the disciples. Even if I cannot be buried with the ceremony due to a minister, am I likely to die in a ditch?"

13. Zigong said: "Were there a beautiful piece of jade would one put it in a cabinet or sell it for a good price?" The Master said: "Sell it! Sell it! I've been waiting for somebody who knew what's what!"

14. The Master wished to dwell amongst the barbarians. Someone said: "They are backward and unenlightened, what then?" The Master said: "How can there be backwardness and lack of enlightenment where a Gentleman chooses to dwell?"

15. The Master said: "It was only when I returned to Lu from the state of Wei that music was collected and arranged and that Ya and Song each had their place."

16. The Master said: "Outside, one should serve dukes and ministers, at home one should serve father and elder brothers,

in arranging funerals one should do one's utmost, one should never be incapacitated through drink. As far as I am concerned, is there more?"

17. On the bank of a river, the Master said: "Time flows like a river, days and nights stream ceaselessly away."

18. The Master said: "I have never yet met a man who loved Virtue as much as he loved beauty in women."

19. The Master said: "For example, when a mountain of earth lacks but the last basketful and is stopped; it is I that have stopped it! For example, on level ground, when the first basketful has been spread but spreading continues; it is I that have continued!"

20. The Master said: "Of those who listen to my teaching but are not idle, perhaps there is only Yan Yuan?"

21. The Master said of Yan Yuan: "A pity! I saw his progress but I never saw him cease."

22. The Master said: "There are shoots that do not grow to produce grain and there is grain that does not ripen."

23. The Master said: "One may respect the next generation, why should one expect the next generation not to equal the present? If they are still unknown by the age of 40 or 50, that may be insufficient to earn respect."

24. The Master said: "Can one fail to accept advice that conforms with principle? But it is the proper correction of fault that is to be valued. Can one not be happy at respectful praise? But it is examination that is to be valued. To be happy without examination, to accept advice but not to correct faults properly, there is nothing that I can do with this kind of person!"

25. The Master said: "Give pride of place to Loyalty and Integrity. Make no friends less than oneself. Where there are faults do not fear to correct them."

26. The Master said: "The commander of an army may be removed but you may not alter the will of the ordinary man."

27. The Master said: "Of those who wear tattered silk gowns, only Zilu can take his place without shame amongst those clad in fine furs. 'Being neither jealous nor greedy, what ill is there in that?'" Zilu heard this and recited it over and over again. The Master said: "Merely to follow this path, what good is there in that?"

28. The Master said: "When cold winter comes it is then that you know that the pine and cypress are the last to wither."

29. The Master said: "Those that know are not baffled, those that possess *Ren* are not anxious and those that have courage are not frightened."

30. The Master said: "One may study with others but not seek the Grand Principle with them; one may seek the Grand Principle with them but not achieve success; one may achieve success with them but yet not a balance in advantage."

31. "The shadberry flowers quiver in the wind, how can I not long for you? But you are too far away." The Master said: "This is no real longing, if it were, what distance could there be?"

Xiang Dang X

1. When in the country Kongzi behaved courteously and respectfully and as if not very eloquent. When at court or in a temple he spoke with dignity and composure but rather more carefully.

2. When conversing with junior ministers at court, calm and composed; when conversing with senior minister, respectful and straight-forward. When the ruler is present, reverential and nervous.

3. When ordered by the ruler to receive guests, Kongzi's countenance immediately became serious and his step quickened. He greeted those standing on one side and saluted those to right

and left with both hands clasped, his robes swaying elegantly. When he hurried forward he seemed like a bird with wings outstretched. When the guests had left he never failed to report to the ruler: "The guests no longer look back."

4. Kongzi entered the palace gate bowing humbly as if there were nowhere to hide. He did not stand in the center of the gate nor place his foot upon the raised threshold. His countenance became more serious as he approached the throne, his step quickened and his speech softened as if lacking breath. Entering the audience hall he raised the hem of his robe, bowed and ascended holding his breath. On withdrawing, his expression and bearing relaxed as he reached the bottom step. Away from the dais his step quickened like a bird spreading its wings. When he returned to his place it was with decorum and care.

5. The tablet of office is held humbly and as if heavy. Raised as if in greeting and put down as if bestowing a gift, all the while the expression serious as if in fear and trembling. When walking with shortened pace and quickened step, as if following a straight line. When receiving gifts from guests, the expression is amiable. In private meetings it is relaxed.

6. A Gentleman does not have a crimson or black border to his garments, nor does he wear garments of red or purple at home. In the summer unlined garments of coarse or fine hemp must be worn as outer clothes with an inner garment. Black clothes go with a sheepskin lined gown and white with a deerskin robe; yellow clothes go with a gown lined with fox fur; fur robes worn at home should be slightly longer but the right sleeve may be shorter. Quilts should be a length and a half of the body. Thick fox and raccoon skins may be made into cushions. Ornaments may be worn after mourning garments have been set aside. Ceremonial garments not made from cloth of the correct width must be tailored. It is not permitted to wear a sheepskin lined robe or a black official cap when paying visits of condolence.

Formal court attire is obligatory when attending court on the first of each month.

7. On days of abstinence, a cloth robe should be worn when bathing. On days of abstinence, diet should be changed, as should residence.

8. Care must be taken with foodstuffs, fish and flesh should be sliced thinly. Food stored over-long turns sour and fish and meat rot, neither can be eaten. Food that becomes discolored or changes smell should not be eaten; food that is improperly cooked should not be eaten; food that is not appropriate to the hour should not be eaten; food that is not butchered correctly should not be eaten; food that is improperly seasoned should not be eaten. At a banquet, although food may be plentiful, the amount consumed should not be excessive. There is no such limit on wine though drunkenness should be avoided. Dried meat and wine obtained from a market should not be eaten. There will be ginger after the meal but not too much should be eaten.

9. At sacrificial ceremonies sacrificial meat presented by the ruler should not be left for a second day. Generally sacrificial meat should not exceed three days, if it does it should not be eaten.

10. Do not converse while eating and do not talk while sleeping.

11. Even with coarse food or vegetable soup a portion must be set aside for sacrifice to the ancestors as solemnly as on days of abstinence.

12. When the mat is not straight, do not sit.

13. At village drinking parties, the old leave first, then you may leave.

14. When the country people performed Nuo opera to welcome the gods and banishing demons Kongzi always took the principal place on the platform clad in his court robes.

15. When asking an envoy to convey greetings to friends in other states, one salutes them twice in bidding farewell.

16. Ji Kangzi made a gift of medicinal herbs to Kongzi. The Master said: "I lack the skill, I dare not taste them."

17. The stables burned down. The Master returned from court and asked: "Was any one injured?" He did not ask about the horses.

18. When the ruler makes a gift of food, it should be tasted after being properly seated. When the ruler makes a gift of uncooked flesh it must be cooked and first offered to the ancestors. When the ruler makes a gift of livestock it must be raised. When eating with the ruler, the food must be tasted before the ruler offers prayer before the meal.

19. When ill and the ruler visits, lie with the head to the east, the body covered with the court robe and with sash extended.

20. At the summons of the ruler, do not wait for horse and carriage but proceed at once on foot.

21. Kongzi visited the Temple of Ancestors and asked about everything.

22. On the death of a friend, if there were none who could arrange the funeral, the Master would say: "Put it in my hands."

23. Unless it were an offering of sacrificial meat, Kongzi did not bow to gifts from friends, even if they were horses or carriages.

24. Do not sleep as straight as a corpse, or live as if always receiving guests.

25. When Kongzi met those in mourning his countenance became grave even when he knew them well. When he met those who wore official caps or who were blind he treated them politely even though they were familiar. When riding in a carriage and he met somebody in mourning he would lean on the crossbar and incline his head. This he would also do when he met somebody bearing official written matter. When eating at a banquet he would always rise gravely and give thanks. He would greet thunder with reverence.

26. When mounting a carriage, stand erect and mount with the

aid of the hand strap. Once in the carriage do not look around, do not talk loudly or gesticulate.

27. A flock of birds rose, stretched their wings, flew and resettled again. The Master said: "These hen pheasants on the mountain bridge, how timely, how timely." Zilu threw them some food, the birds sniffed at it and flew away.

Xian Jin XI

1. The Master said: "Those that studied ceremony and music with me early were common country people. Those that came later were Gentlemen. Were I to employ them I would prefer the former."

2. The Master said: "The disciples that were with me in the states of Chen and Cai no longer cross my threshold."

3. Of disciples of virtue there were: Yan Yuan, Min Ziqian, Boniu, and Zhonggong. Of those of eloquence there were Zai Wo and Zigong. Of those with ability to govern there were Ran You and Zilu. Of those with literary ability there were Ziyou and Zixia.

4. The Master said: "Is not Yan Yuan somebody who is there to help me? When he speaks with me there is nothing that is not a delight."

5. The Master said: "Truly filial is Min Ziqian! None disagree with the praise heaped upon him by his family."

6. Nan Rong recited the poem *The White Tablet* several times and Kongzi betrothed his elder brother's daughter to him.

7. Ji Kangzi asked: "Who amongst the disciples loves learning the most?" The Master replied: "Yan Yuan loved learning. But alas his life was short. There are none now who resemble him."

8. On the death of Yan Yuan, his father Yan Lu asked the Master to sell his carriage so that he might buy an outer coffin for his

son. The Master said: "Whether they have talent or not, I regard them all as my sons. When my son, Kong Li, died, there was an inner coffin and no outer. I cannot go on foot for the sake of an outer coffin, for I cannot follow the procession of the ministers on foot."

9. Yan Yuan died and the Master said: "Oh! Heaven has bereaved me, heaven has bereaved me!"

10. The Master wept bitterly at the death of Yan Yuan. His followers said: "The Master grieves too much!" The Master said: "If I do not grieve for him, for whom shall I grieve?"

11. Yan Yuan died and his fellow disciples wanted a grand funeral for him. The Master said: "No." The disciples continued in their wishes. The Master said: "Yan Yuan looked on me as a father, but I cannot treat him as a son. That is not my fault but of those other disciples."

12. Zilu asked about serving demons and spirits. The Master said: "When you have not yet served man, why ask about serving demons and spirits?" Zilu asked: "May I dare ask about death?" The Master said: "If you do not understand life, how can you understand death?"

13. Min Ziqian was in attendance on Kongzi, and was well spoken and respectful; Zilu was busy and active; Ran You and Zigong spoke with relaxed confidence. The Master was pleased but said: "As for Zilu, he may come to no good end."

14. The ruler of Lu was rebuilding the treasury. Min Ziqian said: "How would it be according to the old plan? Why alter it?" The Master said: "This man does not speak much, but when he does he gets to the point."

15. The Master said: "Why does Zilu have to play his harp here?" On this account the disciples had no respect for Zilu. The Master said: "Zilu may have reached the hall but he is not yet in the chamber."

16. Zigong asked: "Of Zizhang and Zixia, who is the more

worthy?" The Master said: "Zizhang is rather excessive and Zixia falls a little short." Zigong said: "Then Zizhang is better?" The Master said: "To exceed is the same as falling short."

17. Ji Kangzi was richer than the Duke of Zhou but his steward Ran You continued to amass riches for him and add to his wealth. The Master said: "He is no pupil of mine, the disciples may sound the drum and attack him."

18. Zigao was rather simple minded; Zeng Can was rather slow-witted; Zizhang was rather outspoken and Zilu was rather impulsive.

19. The Master said: "Yan Yuan excels in conduct and learning but is impoverished. Zigong is unhappy with his lot but flourishes as a merchant and always guesses the market price."

20. Zizhang asked about the behavior of people of virtue. The Master said: "They no longer follow in the footsteps of others but have not entered the chamber!"

21. The Master said: "Those who speak seriously are worthy of esteem, but are they Gentlemen? Or are they those who just appear to be serious?"

22. Zilu asked: "When one hears something, should one act immediately?" The Master said: "While father and elder brothers exist, how can one act immediately?" Ran You asked: "When one hears something, should one act immediately?" The Master said: "Act immediately!" Gongxi Hua said: "Zilu asked: 'When one hears something, should one act immediately?' and the Master replied: 'While father and elder brothers exist'; Ran You asked: 'When one hears something, should one act immediately?' and the Master replied: 'Act immediately!' I am puzzled, may I ask for clarification?" The Master said: "Ran You is hesitant, so I encouraged him, Zilu is impetuous, so I discouraged him."

23. The Master was besieged in the town of Kuang in the state of Wei and Yan Yuan was left behind. The Master said: "I thought you were dead!"Yan Yuan replied: "While the Master lives, how

could I dare to die?"

24. Ji Ziran asked: "May Zilu and Ran You be called chief ministers?" The Master said: "I thought that you were asking about others but you ask about Zilu and Ran You. A chief minister serves his ruler on the basis of the Grand Principle and if he cannot, he resigns. Zilu and Ran You may be presently regarded only as minor ministers." Ji Ziran then asked: "Are they then utterly loyal?" The Master said: "They would not commit parricide or regicide."

25. Zilu wished Zigao to become governor of the district of Fei. The Master said: "That would be to do ill to somebody's son!" Zilu said: "There are people there, there are the gods of earth and grain, why should it be that only book-learning is regarded as true learning?" The Master said: "This is the reason that I dislike those who play with words."

26. Zilu, Zeng Xi, Ran You and Gongxi Hua were sitting in attendance. The Master said: "I am older than you but do not let that prevent you from speaking. You often say 'Nobody understands me!' If people understood you, what would you then do?"

Zilu was the first to answer and said: "A nation of 1,000 chariots caught between other large states is subjected to military pressure and there is famine. Were I to deal with it, within three years I would make its people effective in warfare and understand custom." The Master smiled.

The Master then asked: "Ran You, what would you do?" Ran You replied: "Were I to govern an area of a circumference of 60 or 70, or 50 or 60 *li*, within three years there would be food and warmth for the people and as to ceremony and music, that would need to wait upon a ruler." The Master then asked: "Gongxi Hua, what would you do?" Gongxi Hua replied: "I dare not say what I would do but I would study a little more. When there were sacrifices in the temples or ceremonies of oaths of alliance taken by vassal princes, I would be willing to wear ceremonial robes and hat and be a minor master of ceremonies." The Master then asked: "Zeng Xi, what would you do?" Zeng Xi was playing the harp and was slowing to the end of a piece, he put down the harp with a "clang" and said: "My views are not the same as those of the other three!" The Master said: "What does that matter? Each must have his own say!" Zeng Xi said: "On a spring evening in the third month, I would dress in new spring clothes and then with five or six adults and six or seven children bathe in the Yi river, take the breeze on the platform of sacrifices for rain and then return home singing." Kongzi sighed and said: "I think the same as Zeng Xi!"

Zilu, Ran You and Gongxi Hua withdrew first and Zeng Xi asked Kongzi: "What did you think of the answers of those three?" The Master said: "Each described their own aspirations." Zeng Xi said: "In that case why did you laugh at Zilu?" The Master said: "A nation should be governed with Propriety, but when he spoke it was with a total lack of modesty, that is why I laughed." Zeng Xi again asked: "Then what Ran You said, was that the way to govern a state?" The Master said "How can an area of a circumference of 60 or 70, or 50 or 60 *li* not be considered a state?" Zeng Xi further asked: "Then what Gongxi Hua asked, is that the way to govern a state?" The Master said: "If sacrifices at the Temple of Ancestors and oaths of alliance taken by vassal princes are not the concerns of a ruler, then what are they? If people like Gongxi Hua can be a minor master of ceremonies, then who can take the post of principal master of ceremonies?"

Yan Yuan XII

1. Yan Yuan asked about *Ren*. The Master said: "To control

oneself and act with Propriety, that is *Ren*. Once self is controlled and Propriety is practiced then, all beneath heaven returns to *Ren*. *Ren* is of the self, how can it be obtained from others?" Yan Yuan said: "May I enquire as to its contents?" The Master said: "Do not look at that which is improper, do not listen to that which is improper, do not speak of that which is improper and do not act improperly." Yan Yuan said: "Though I am dull I shall act as you say!"

2. Zhonggong asked about *Ren*. The Master said: "Go forth as if to meet a great guest, cause people to conduct themselves as if they were preparing a great sacrifice. Do not do to others that which you would not wish done to you. Have no hatred at court, have no hatred at home." Zhonggong said: "Though I am dull I shall act as you say!"

3. Sima Niu asked about *Ren*. The Master said: "*Ren* is to be slow to speak." Sima Niu then said: "To be slow to speak may be called *Ren*?" The Master said: "It is difficult to accomplish, but can speech be without caution?"

4. Sima Niu asked what a Gentleman was. The Master said: "The Gentleman is neither anxious nor fearful." Sima Niu said: "To be without anxiety and without fear, is that to be called a Gentleman?" The Master said: "When self-reflection finds no guilt what is there to be fearful or anxious about?"

5. Sima Niu said sadly: "All have brothers, I alone lack them!" Zixia said: "I have heard it said that: 'Life and death are a matter of fate, riches and honor depend upon heaven.' If a Gentleman is prudent and without error in his conduct, and treats people with respect and Propriety, then all within the four seas become brothers and why should he be despondent at the lack of them?"

6. Zizhang asked about clarity of perception. The Master said: "If neither surreptitious calumny that soaks in like water or slander that cuts like a knife can flourish, that may be called

clarity of perception. If neither surreptitious calumny that soaks in like water or slander that cuts the skin like a knife can flourish that may be called far-sighted too."

7. Zigong asked about governance. The Master said: "Sufficient food, sufficient arms and the trust of the people." Zigong said: "If, of these three, one had to be excluded, which would be first?" The Master said: "Arms." Zigong said: "If another had to be excluded, which would be second?" The Master said: "Food. From ancient times there has always been death, but without the trust of the people the state cannot stand."

8. Ji Zicheng said: "A Gentleman merely needs to be of good character, why should he require any literary talent?" Zigong replied: "How regrettable are your remarks about Gentlemen, a team of horses could not catch them! Literary talent is character and character is literary talent. A tiger skin less its fur is the same as a dog or sheep skin less its wool."

9. Duke Ai of state Lu asked You Ruo: "There is famine this year and funds are insufficient, what is to be done?" You Ruo replied: "Why not cut taxes to one tenth?" Duke Ai said: "I have not enough with two tenths, how can I cut to a tenth?" You Ruo replied: "If the people have enough how then can the ruler not have enough? If the people have not enough how then can the ruler have enough?"

10. Zizhang asked about strengthening morality and clarifying confusion. The Master said: "Emphasize Loyalty and Integrity and follow Righteousness, that is how to strengthen morality. When you like someone you wish them to live, when you grow to dislike them, you wish them dead. So that you wish them both dead and alive, that is what confusion is! As the poem says: 'It is not to seek riches and honor but because of a change of heart!' "

11. Duke Jing of Qi asked Kongzi about governance. Kongzi replied: "Lords should be lords; ministers should be ministers;

fathers should be fathers; sons should be sons." Duke Jing said: "Excellent! Were lords not to be lords, ministers not to be ministers, fathers not to be fathers and sons not to be sons, there would be grain still but would I be able to eat it?"

12. The Master said: "There is only one man who will make a judgement after just hearing one side of a case and that is Zilu!" Zilu made no promises that could not be delivered.

13. The Master said: "In the hearing of legal cases, I am like others. What must be done is the elimination of lawsuits."

14. Zizhang asked about governance. The Master said: "Exercise it without negligence, implement it with Loyalty."

15. The Master said: "The Gentleman reads and studies widely, acts within the constraints of Propriety and thus does not stray from the path of correct principle."

16. The Master said: "The Gentleman embodies the good in man and not the evil. The rogue is the opposite."

17. Ji Kangzi asked Kongzi about governance. The Master said: "Governance is to be upright. If one is upright, who dares then not to be upright?"

18. Ji Kangzi was troubled by robbers and sought advice from Kongzi. Kongzi replied: "If you were not yourself so covetous, though robbers were to be rewarded they would not steal."

19. Ji Kangzi asked Kongzi about governance and said: "Were those without the Grand Principle to be slaughtered and those with it to be fostered, how would that be?" The Master replied: "Where is the use of slaughter in governance? If you, yourself, desire virtue then the people will be virtuous as well. The character of a ruler resembles the wind and that of the lower orders is like grass, when the wind blows the grass will bend."

20. Zizhang asked: "How may an official be called successful?" The Master said: "What is the success of which you speak?" Zizhang replied: "To be famed abroad and to be known at court." The Master said: "That is fame, not success. To be

successful is to be upright in character and to love justice, to guard one's words and gestures and to be considerate of others. This would be to be successful abroad and successful at court. What you call fame has the appearance of *Ren* but offends in action, and yet considers itself undoubtedly possessed of *Ren*. This would be to be merely famous abroad and famous at court."

21. Fan Chi was walking with the Master on the platform of sacrifices for rain and said: "Dare I ask about strengthening morality, eliminating evil and clarifying confusion?" The Master said: "Excellent! Only to ask for reward after having performed the task, is that not to strengthen morality? To criticize one's own bad habits but not the faults of others, is that not to eliminate evil? In a moment of anger to forget one's safety and to involve one's relatives, is that not confusion?"

22. Fan Chi asked about *Ren*. The Master said: "Love others." Asked about wisdom, the Master said: "It is to understand man." Fan Chi did not understand. The Master said: "To raise the upright above the unjust, may make the unjust upright." Fan Chi withdrew and said to Zixia: "I just saw the Master and asked about wisdom, the Master said: 'To raise the upright above the unjust, may make the unjust upright.' What does it mean?" Zixia replied: "A profound remark! During the rule of Shun, Gao Tao was raised from the people and those without *Ren* were put at a distance; during the rule of Tang, Yi Yin was raised from the people and those without *Ren* were also put at a distance."

23. Zigong asked about friendship. The Master said: "Advise each other out of Loyalty and lead through Virtue, draw back from that which is impermissible and do not incur shame."

24. Zeng Can said: "A Gentleman meets friends through literature and uses friendship to nurture his own *Ren*."

Zilu XIII

1. Zilu asked about governance. The Master said: "First example, then diligently encourage all." Zilu sought elucidation. The Master said: "Avoid laziness."

2. Zhonggong was to be a retainer of Ji Kangzi and asked about governance. The Master said: "Be a model for junior officials, forgive minor transgressions and raise the talented." Zhonggong further asked: "How can one know the talented so that they may be raised?" The Master said: "Raise those whom you know. Those whom you do not know, are they likely to be overlooked by others?"

3. Zilu asked: "If the ruler of Wei asked you to rule, what would you do first?" The Master said: "I would first have to correct the titles!" Zilu said: "Would you so? That would be pedantic! What titles would you correct?" The Master said: "Such insolence, Zilu! A ruler should be reticent about that which he does not know. If title and status are not correct then speech will not accord with reason, if speech does not accord with reason then matters will not be resolved and if matters are not resolved, then neither ceremonies nor music will thrive; if neither ceremonies nor music thrive then punishments will not be appropriate; if punishments are not appropriate then the people will be confused. So it is that a ruler must speak with authority. A ruler cannot be casual in what he says."

4. Fan Chi sought instruction on the sowing of crops. The Master said: "I am no old peasant." Fan Chi asked further about the planting of vegetables, the Master said: "Nor am I an old gardener." Fan Chi withdrew and the Master said: "What a rogue Fan Chi is! If those in power attach importance to rite and ceremony then the people will not dare show disrespect; if those in power have a proper regard for Righteousness then the people will not dare disobey; if those in power attach importance

to sincerity then the people will not dare to be dishonest. Were it like this, then people would flock from the four corners of the earth bearing their children on their backs to seek shelter. What need to sow oneself then?"

5. The Master said: "To have the ability to recite the 300 poems of the *Classic of Poetry*, yet to hold a post in government which one cannot manage; or to be an envoy and not to be able to conduct negotiation and conversation on one's own; what then is the use of being able to recite so many poems by heart?"

6. The Master said: "If one is upright, there is obedience without the necessity for an order; if one is not upright, though there may be an order, there is no obedience."

7. The Master said: "The politics of Lu and Wei are as close as elder and younger brothers."

8. The Master said that Jing, the minister of Duke Wei was skilled at running an estate: "When it was just established and beginning to acquire wealth, he would say: 'More or less enough.' As it became richer, he would say: 'more or less complete.' When it was really wealthy, he would say: 'More or less perfect.'"

9. The Master visited the state of Wei. Ran You drove his carriage. The Master said: "The people are many!" Ran You said: "Since the people are many what more should be done?" The Master said: "Prosper them." Ran You said: "Once prosperous, then what more?" The Master said: "Teach them."

10. The Master said: "Were I to hold an office of state, there would be results within a year and achievement within three."

11. The Master said: "'Were the virtuous to rule for 100 years, violence would be overcome and slaughter abandoned.' There is truth in this saying!"

12. The Master said: "If a ruler emerges he will come to *Ren* after a generation."

13. The Master said: "If one can correct oneself, what difficulty

lies in governance? If one cannot correct oneself how then can one correct others?"

14. Ran You returned from court. The Master said: "Why so late?" Ran You replied: "There were matters of state." The Master said: "They were merely affairs, had they been matters of state I would have known, even though I am no longer employed."

15. Duke Ding asked: "Is there a single word which may invigorate the state?" Kongzi replied: "There is probably no such word! But people say: 'It is difficult to be a ruler and not easy to be a minister.' Were one to know the difficulties of being a ruler, would that not almost be the one word that could invigorate the state?" Duke Ding asked further: "Is there a single word that can destroy the state?" Kongzi replied: "There is probably no such word! But people say: 'I find no joy in being a ruler except that none contradict me.' If he speaks with Virtue and none contradict, is that not a Virtue too? But if there is no Virtue and none contradict is that not almost the single word that can destroy the state?"

16. Duke Ye asked about governance. The Master said: "Make those that are near joyful and those that are far submit."

17. Zixia was to become an official at Jufu in the state of Lu and asked about governance. The Master said: "Do not act in haste, do not seek petty advantage. Haste does not achieve its aim and petty advantage hinders achievement."

18. Duke Ye told the Master: "In my home-town there was an honest man whose father stole a sheep and the son reported him." The Master replied: "The honest in my home-town are different: the father protects the son and the son protects the father, that is where the honesty lies."

19. Fan Chi asked about *Ren*. The Master said: "Honor at home, respect in affairs, Loyalty to others, even amongst barbarians, this is not to be abandoned."

20. Zigong asked: "How may one be a Scholar?" The Master

said: "Act with humility, in your missions abroad do not bring disgrace upon the orders of the ruler, that is to be a Scholar." Zigong said: "May I dare to ask what next?" The Master said: "To be regarded as filial within the clan and as fraternal within the village." Zigong asked further: "May I dare to ask what next?" The Master said: "To be true to one's word and for one's acts to bear fruit. Like the rattle of stones, shallow obstinacy is the mark of the rogue who can yet be a lower class of Scholar." Zigong asked: "Those who govern today, how may they be regarded?" The Master said: "Oh! As small-minded and unworthy to be considered a Scholar!"

21. The Master said: "If one cannot be with those who take the middle way must one then necessarily be with either the wild or the timid? The wild forge ahead and the timid hold back."

22. The Master said: "In the South they have a saying: 'If you will not persevere you cannot become a shaman.' That's well said! 'If you have not the perseverance to maintain Virtue it is difficult to avoid shame.'" The Master further said: "You don't need divination to work this out."

23. The Master said: "The Gentleman is in harmony with all but maintains his discrimination; the rogue does not discriminate but lacks the harmony."

24. Zigong asked: "If all the village liked him, how would that be?" The Master said: "It is hard to be certain." "If all the village hated him, how would that be?" The Master said: "It is hard to be certain. It would be better if the virtuous liked him and the bad hated him."

25. The Master said: "It is easy to serve a Gentleman but difficult to gain his praise. If service does not conform to the Grand Principle he will be displeased. In employing people the Gentleman measures them. It is difficult to serve a rogue but easy to gain his praise. If service does not conform with morality he is pleased, but in employing people the rogue

demands perfection."

26. The Master said: "The Gentleman is grand but not arrogant and the rogue is both grand and arrogant."

27. The Master said: "Strength, resolve, simplicity, and plainness of speech all approach *Ren*."

28. Zilu asked: "How may one be a Scholar?" The Master said: "Learn from and encourage each other, enjoy each other's company, that is how to be a Scholar. Encourage with friends, enjoy with brothers."

29. The Master said: "Once the people have been taught by the wise for seven years they may be called to arms."

30. The Master said: "To use untrained people in warfare may be called abandoning them."

Xian Wen XIV

1. Yuan Xian asked Kongzi about shame. The Master said: "When a state possesses the Grand Principle there are official emoluments; when a state lacks it and there are still official emoluments, that is shame." "Aggression, boasting, hatred and desire, were they not to exist would that then be *Ren*?" The Master said: "That would be difficult, whether it would be *Ren*, I do not know."

2. The Master said: "The Scholar who prefers the peaceful life is no Scholar!"

3. The Master said: "If a state possesses the Grand Principle, one can speak and act forthrightly, if it lacks it one may act forthrightly but speak with circumspection."

4. The Master said: "The virtuous must exercise speech but those that talk do not necessarily exercise Virtue. Those that possess *Ren* must possess courage; but the courageous do not necessarily possess *Ren*."

5. Nan Rong enquired of Kongzi: "Hou Yi was an archer and Ao was skilled in fighting by boat, they both came to a bad end. Yu and Ji ploughed and planted themselves and possessed the world." The Master did not answer. Nan Rong withdrew and the Master said: "Such a Gentleman! A man of such Virtue!"

6. The master said: "Are there Gentlemen without *Ren*? Amongst rogues, I have never seen any who possessed *Ren*."

7. The Master said: "Can one love and not feel concern? Can one be Loyal and yet not admonish?"

8. The Master said: "When the state of Zheng issued decrees, they were first drafted by Bi Chen, then discussed with Shi Shu, then polished by Ziyu and finally revised by Zichan."

9. Someone asked about Zichan. The Master said: "A man of great benevolence." They asked about Zixi and he said: "Oh, him! Oh, him!" They further asked about Guan Zhong and he said: "He was quite somebody, he confiscated the land of three hundred households belonging to Bo Shi at Pian Yi leaving him to eat coarse millet, and to the end of his life, Bo Shi bore no grudge."

10. The Master said: "It is difficult to be poor without complaint but easy to be rich without arrogance."

11. The Master said: "Meng Gongchuo has the qualities to be a household official in the Zhao clan or Wei clan of the state of Jin, but he could not be a minister in a small state like Teng or Xue."

12. Zilu asked about becoming the complete man. The Master said: "To have the wisdom of Zang Wuzhong, the moral continence of Meng Gongchuo, the courage of Bian Zhuangzi and the talent of Ran You, then to enrich it all with the qualities of ceremony and music, that would make a complete man." The Master also said: "Why should the complete man of today have to be like this? To see advantage but think of Righteousness, to see danger but be prepared to sacrifice one's life and to live in

poverty but not forget the promises of a lifetime, all this too, can make the complete man."

13. The Master asked Gongshu Wenzi about Gongming Jia: "Is it true? That he does not speak or smile and does not acquire wealth?" Gongming Jia said: "Whoever told you was mistaken. He speaks when the time is ripe, and people are not bored with what he says; he laughs when pleased, and people are not bored with his laughter; he acquires wealth when it is right to do so and people do not object." The Master said: "So that was the way it was. How could it have been otherwise?"

14. The Master said: "Zang Wuzhong sought to exchange the town of Fang for a title of nobility in the state of Lu for the clan of Zang. Although it is said that he did not coerce the ruler, I do not believe it."

15. The Master said: "Duke Wen of Jin was duplicitous but not upright; Duke Huan of Qi was upright but not duplicitous."

16. Zilu said: "Duke Huan of Qi killed Prince Jiu, Shao Hu thereupon committed suicide but Guan Zhong did not. Is that *Ren*?" The Master said: "Duke Huan achieved nine alliances with the vassal princes without force of arms. That was the doing of Guan Zhong. That was his *Ren*! That was his *Ren*!"

17. Zigong asked: "Can Guan Zhong be considered as possessing *Ren*? Duke Huan killed Prince Jiu, Guan Zhong did not commit suicide but instead became a minister for Duke Huan." The Master said: "Guan Zhong served as a minister to Duke Huan and achieved hegemony over the vassal states and brought order to the land, even today the people still benefit from his actions. Had it not been for Guan Zhong I would be wild-haired and with my gown opening on the left. How could he kill himself in a ditch for nothing and nobody know of it, like some ordinary person?"

18. Xun, the household official of Gongshu Wenzi, was, together with Gongshu Wenzi made a minister at court. When

the Master heard, he said: "It is possible to receive the title of 'Wen' posthumously."

19. The Master spoke of Duke Ling of Wei's lack of principle and Ji Kangzi said: "Since it is so, how is it that he has not fallen?" Kongzi said: "Zhongshu Yu receives guests from abroad, Zhu Tuo is in charge of temple sacrifices and Wangsun Jia commands the army, with such talent how can he fall?"

20. The Master said: "Shameless speech makes implementation difficult!"

21. Chen Chengzi assassinated Duke Jian of Qi. Kongzi bathed and went to court and reported to Duke Ai of Lu: "Chen Chengzi has assassinated his ruler, please send an expedition to punish him." The Duke replied: "Report this to the ministers of the three clans." Kongzi said later: "Having myself been a minister, I dared not report! The ruler then said: 'Report this to the ministers of the three clans!'" Kongzi then reported to the ministers of the three clans who did not agree that an expedition should be sent. Kongzi said: "Having myself been a minister, I dared not report!"

22. Zilu asked about serving a ruler. The Master said: "Do not deceive but one may dare to offend with forthright advice."

23. The Master said: "The Gentleman reaches for the heights, the rogue plumbs the depths."

24. The Master said: "In the past they studied for themselves, now they study to look good in the eyes of others."

25. Qu Boyu sent an emissary to Kongzi. Kongzi sat with him and asked: "What has your Master done recently?" The emissary replied: "My Master desires to diminish his faults but has not yet succeeded." The emissary left and the Master said: "Such an emissary! Such an emissary!"

26. Kongzi said: "The Master said: If you do not hold the office, do not make the policy." Zeng Can said: "The Gentleman should not think beyond his position."

27. The Master said: "A Gentleman feels shame when his speech exceeds his actions."

28. The Master said: "There are three aspects to the path of a Gentleman but I have not mastered them: those with *Ren* are not anxious, the wise are not confused and the brave do not fear." Zigong said: "The Master speaks of his own path!"

29. Zigong enjoyed talking of others. The Master said: "Zigong, are you so perfect? I lack that sort of leisure."

30. The Master said: "Fear not that others do not know you, fear only your own lack of ability."

31. The Master said: "Not always to expect to encounter deception, nor to baselessly suspect lack of sincerity, but to perceive the duplicity of others beforehand would that not be becoming of a worthy?"

32. Weisheng Mu said to Kongzi: "Why are you always so busy? Is not perhaps to show off your eloquence?" The Master said: "I dare not become a person of flowery words and fine speeches, I just hate the stubbornness of people."

33. The Master said: "One does not praise the strength of a thoroughbred horse, one praises its moral character."

34. Someone asked: "How would it be to repay hate with Virtue?" The Master said: "Then how would you repay Virtue? Repay hate with uprightness and repay Virtue with Virtue."

35. The Master said: "Nobody understands me!" Zigong said: "Why do you say that?" The Master said: "I have neither complaint against heaven, nor rebuke for man, I study the ways of the world and attain the will of heaven. Is it only heaven that understands me!"

36. Gongbo Liao brought a case against Zilu before Ji Kangzi. Zifu Jingbo told Kongzi, saying: "Although Ji Kangzi has been spellbound by Gongbo Liao, yet I still have the power to slay Gongbo Liao and display his corpse in the market place." The Master said: "If the Grand Principle is to be implemented in

the land, that is a matter for the Mandate of Heaven; if the Grand Principle is to be cast aside, that, too, is a matter for the Mandate of Heaven. What is there that Gongbo Liao can do about the Mandate of Heaven?"

37. The Master said: "The worthy avoid the tumultuous world and then the disordered state, they avoid the offensive countenance and then offensive speech. Of such worthies there are seven!"

38. Zilu stayed overnight at Shimen outside the city gate. The next morning, the gatekeeper asked him: "Where from?" Zilu replied: "From Kongzi's." The gatekeeper said: "The one who knows it can't be done but does it?"

39. While in Wei the Master played the chimes. A man with a basket on his shoulder passed by the door and said: "There is a load on your mind, it is in your playing!" He further said: "There is sadness there, in the tinkling of the chimes. Since nobody understands you, all you can do is to guard yourself. 'When the water is deep, you just have to cross with your clothes on, when it is shallow you can roll your robe up and wade across.'" The Master said: "Well said! There is nothing that you have said that may be argued with!"

40. Zizhang said: "What does the *Book of Documents* mean when it says 'King Gao Zong of Shang dynasty mourned for three years and did not speak of government'?" The Master said: "Not only King Gao Zong, all the ancients were so. When a ruler died, for three years all the officials took their instructions from the chief minister."

41. The Master said: "If those above take pleasure in Propriety then the people may be led with ease."

42. Zilu asked how to be a Gentleman. The Master said: "Cultivate oneself and act with a sense of respect." Zilu said: "Is that enough?" The Master said: "If one cultivates oneself it can bring peace and happiness to others." Zilu said: "Is that

enough?" The Master said: "Cultivating oneself can also make the people peaceful and happy. Yao and Shun were defective in bringing peace and happiness to the people through self-cultivation."

43. Yuan Rang sat with legs outstretched waiting for Kongzi. Kongzi saw him and said: "Lacking Fraternal Piety when young, no achievement worthy of praise in adulthood; now old and refusing to die, what a disaster!" And, so saying, hit him on the legs with a stick.

44. A young man in Kongzi's hometown announced guests at a banquet. Somebody asked Kongzi: "Is this a young man who will do well?" The Master said: "Seeing him sitting in the place of an adult and seeing him alongside his elders, he appears bent on success, not on doing well."

Duke Ling of Wei XV

1. Duke Ling of Wei asked Kongzi about deployment on the field of battle. Kongzi replied: "I have heard a little about the arrangement of sacrificial vessels but I have never studied military matters." He left the next day.

2. When provisions ran out in the state of Chen, his followers fell sick and none could stand. Zilu angrily asked the Master: "Do Gentlemen also become desperate in adversity?" The Master said: "Gentlemen are steadfast in the face of adversity; rogues cannot bear it."

3. The Master said: "Zigong! Do you consider me a learned man of wide knowledge?" Zigong replied: "I do, can it not be so?" The Master replied: "It is not. I merely stick to a single thing."

4. The Master said: "Zilu, there are few who understand Virtue!"

5. The Master said: "Of those who brought order to the world through non-action there is probably only Shun! What was it that he did? He just sat on the south facing throne."

6. Zizhang asked about conduct. The Master said: "Speak with Loyalty and Integrity, act steadfastly and with respect for one's calling and though you may be amongst barbarians, it will suffice. If your speech lacks Loyalty and Integrity and your actions are ungrounded and unprofessional, though you may be on your own territory, can it then suffice? See this before you as you stand; see it written on the shafts of your carriage as you travel and it will suffice you hereafter." Zizhang inscribed all this on his girdle.

7. Master said: "Shi Yu is truly upright, when a state is principled he is as straight as an arrow; when a state is unprincipled he is still as straight as an arrow. Qu Boyu is also a real Gentleman! When a state is principled he serves as an official, when it is not, you may roll him up like a scroll and hide him in your bosom."

8. The Master said: "Not to converse with those with whom one should converse is to lose a person; to converse with those with whom one should not converse is to lose conversation."

9. The Master said: "Scholars of will and those that possess *Ren* do not seek life at the expense of *Ren* but sacrifice themselves for the sake of *Ren*."

10. Zigong asked about putting *Ren* into practice. The Master said: "To do good work the craftsman must first sharpen his tools. Living within the state, work with the virtuous amongst its officials, befriend those Scholars who possess *Ren*."

11. Yan Yuan asked about rule. The Master said: "Use the calendar of the Xia, ride the chariot of the Yin. Wear the cap of the Zhou, perform the music of the Shao dance. Forbid the tunes of Zheng and distance oneself from those who flatter. The tunes of Zheng are lascivious and flatterers are dangerous."

12. The Master said: "The man without consideration of the long term, will suffer in the short term."

13. The Master said: "What a business! I have never yet met a man who loved Virtue as much as he loved beauty in women!"

14. The Master said: "Is not Zang Wenzhong one who obtained an official position by stealth? He knew of Liu Xiahui's worthiness but did not recommend him as well."

15. The Master said: "Be heavy in demands upon oneself but light in criticism of others and there will be distance from hatred."

16. The Master said: "I do not know what is to be done with those who do not say 'what is to be done.'"

17. The Master said: "To live a crowded life, never to speak of Righteousness, and to indulge in petty wit, that is difficult!"

18. The Master said: "The Gentleman takes Righteousness for his character, Propriety for his actions, modesty for his self-expression and Integrity for his achievement. That is a Gentleman!"

19. The Master said: "A Gentleman fears only his own lack of ability, not that others may not understand him."

20. The Master said: "The Gentleman grieves that after death his name may no longer be spoken of."

21. The Master said: "The Gentleman makes demands of himself but the rogue makes demands of others."

22. The Master said: "The Gentleman is reserved and does not compete, he mixes but does not form a clique."

23. The Master said: "The Gentleman does not recommend someone on their speech alone, nor does he discard all they have said on the basis of their character."

24. Zigong asked: "Is there a single word which may be acted upon throughout life?" The Master replied: "It is Thoughtfulness! Do not do to others that which you would not wish done to you."

25. The Master said: "In my dealings with people, whom have

I vilified and whom have I praised? Where there is praise, it has been given after due consideration. It is these people who enabled the Xia, Shang and Zhou dynasties to follow the right path."

26. The Master said: "I can still see the words that are missing from the histories. Like a man who has lent his horse to somebody who has ridden it off. The words existed originally but are now lost."

27. The Master said: "Fine words bring confusion to morality and failure to endure the trivial damages the major plan."

28. The Master said: "If all hate them, examine the reason; if all love them, examine the reason also."

29. The Master said: "Man may glorify the Grand Principle but the Grand Principle may not glorify man."

30. The Master said: "Failure to correct a fault is in itself a fault."

31. The Master said: "In the past I have not eaten all day and not slept all night, my thoughts in turmoil, all to no advantage, it would have been better to study."

32. The Master said: "The Gentleman strives to achieve the Grand Principle and not for food. In plowing there is hunger; in study there is salary. The Gentleman's concerns are for the Grand Principle and not for poverty."

33. The Master said: "That which is gained through wisdom and ability, if it is not preserved by *Ren,* though gained, it will be lost. That which is gained through wisdom and ability though it be preserved by *Ren* and yet does not display the dignity of government, will not earn the respect of the people. That which is gained through wisdom and skill, is preserved by *Ren*, displays the dignity of government, and yet is implemented without Propriety is imperfect."

34. The Master said: "The Gentleman does not indulge in the petty but undertakes the heavy responsibility. The rogue cannot undertake heavy responsibility but indulges in the petty."

35. The Master said: "The people are more to *Ren* than they are to fire and water. I have seen those who have died from fire and water, but never those who have died from *Ren*."

36. The Master said: "In the exercise of *Ren*, even one's teacher takes second place."

37. The Master said: "The Gentleman abides by the principle and is not caught up in the detail."

38. The Master said: "In serving a ruler, first perform his tasks and then enjoy his bounty."

39. The Master said: "In teaching there are no distinctions."

40. The Master said: "Where aspirations differ there can be no common ground."

41. The Master said: "It is enough that one's words should express their sense."

42. The musician, Master Mian, came to see Kongzi. When he reached the steps, the Master said: "These are the steps." When he reached the mat, the Master said: "This is the mat." When all had sat down, the Master told him: "So-and-so is here and so-and-so is here." Master Mian left and Zizhang asked: "Is this the way of conversing with masters of music?" The Master said: "It is indeed the way in which one should receive a teacher."

Jishi XVI

1. Ji Kangzi was about to mount a punitive expedition against Zhuan Yu. Ran You and Zilu sought out Kongzi and said: "Ji Kangzi is taking up arms against Zhuan Yu." The Master said: "Ran You, is there no mistake of yours in this? Zhuan Yu once sacrificed at Mount Dongmeng for the Zhou king and it lies within the realm of Lu, it is a minister at the court of Lu, why mount an expedition against it?" Ran You said: "Ji Kangzi desires it but we two ministers do not approve." Kongzi said: "Ran

You! Zhou Ren once said: 'Do your duty to the utmost, if you cannot, then resign.' If you cannot help in calamity or support in collapse then what is the use of you two ministers? Moreover you are mistaken. If the tiger and the rhinoceros escape their pen or the tortoise shell and jade are broken in the box, whose fault is that?" Ran You said: "Zhuan Yu's city walls are impregnable and he lies close to Fei. If it is not taken now there will be sorrow for our children and grandchildren." Kongzi said: "Ran You, a Gentleman hates those who do not say outright what they want but seek some other means of obtaining it. I have heard it said that in respect of a nation or a family, poverty is not to be feared but inequality of riches is; deficiency is not to be feared but lack of stability is. If there is equality then there are neither rich nor poor; if there is harmony then there is neither much nor little; if the state is stable then there is no danger of it being overthrown. This being so, if those afar do not submit then *Ren*, Righteousness, Propriety and music must be used to secure their submission. Those that have submitted should be allowed to live in peace. At present, Ran You and Zilu, you two ministers assist Ji Kangzi but the distant will not submit and cannot be made to, the state is divided internally and cannot be defended and yet there are plans to use force within its borders. I fear that for Ji Kangzi disaster lies not with Zhuan Yu but within his own gate."

2. The Master said: "When the Grand Principle existed under heaven, ceremony, music, and punitive expeditions all derived from the Son of Heaven; when it was absent, ceremonies, music and punitive expeditions derived from the vassal princes and after ten generations there was little that had not collapsed. When derived from ministers, there was little that had not collapsed after five generations; when derived from household retainers there was little that had not collapsed after three generations. When the Grand Principle exists under heaven,

the governance of the state is not in the hands of ministers and the commonality do not criticize."

3. The Master said: "The rulers of Lu have been out of power for five generations and the government has been in the hands of the ministers for four. In consequence, Ji, Meng, and Shusun, the descendants of Duke Huan of Lu will be weakened."

4. The Master said: "There are three kinds of good friends and three kinds of bad. The good are the upright, the sincere and the well-informed. The bad are those who flatter, those who feign friendship and those who are full of empty words."

5. The Master said: "There are three pleasures that are beneficial and three that are harmful. Those that benefit are cultivating the body and mind through ceremony and music, praising the virtue of others and engaging in friendship with the virtuous; the harmful are love of wild arrogance, love of amusement and love of banqueting."

6. The Master said: "There are three things to avoid when in the company of a Gentleman: to speak out of turn, that is impetuosity; to fail to speak when it is your turn, that is concealment; to speak before gauging the countenance, that is lack of discernment."

7. The Master said: "The Gentleman should beware of three things: in lusty youth, lechery; in vigorous manhood, brawling; in feeble old age, greed."

8. The Master said: "The Gentleman reveres three things: the Mandate of Heaven, people of standing and the sayings of the sages. The rogue has no understanding of the Mandate of Heaven and thus has no reverence. Nor does he revere people of stature and he treats the sayings of the sages with contempt."

9. The Master said: "Those who understand from birth are at the top; those who understand after study are next; those who study out of perplexity follow; those who are perplexed but do not study are, like many of the people, at the bottom."

10. The Master said: "A Gentleman has nine considerations: in looking whether or not he sees clearly; in listening whether or not he has understood; in countenance whether or not it is mild; in appearance whether or not it is modest; in speech whether or not it is sincere; in affairs whether or not he is diligent; when there are problems whether or not he should enquire; in anger whether or not there may be consequences and when there is advantage whether or not it has been secured righteously."

11. The Master said: "There are those who encounter virtuous behavior and pursue it, who encounter ill behavior and avoid it as they would avoid boiling water; I have met such people and heard such talk. There are those who live in seclusion and cultivate their aspirations, who pursue their aims with Righteousness; I have heard such talk but never met such a person."

12. Duke Jing of Qi had 4,000 horses. When he died there were none who praised him for his virtue; Boyi and Shuqi died of hunger beneath the hill of Shouyang and people praise them still. Is that the meaning?

13. Chen Kang asked the Master's son Kong Li: "Have you learned anything unusual?" Kong Li replied: "No. He was once standing in the hall as I was passing through and he asked me: 'Have you studied the *Classic of Poetry*?' I replied: 'No.' He said: 'If you do not study the *Classic of Poetry* you will not know how to converse.' So I withdrew and studied the *Classic of Poetry*. On another day he was standing there as I passed through and he asked: 'Have you studied Propriety?' I replied: 'Not yet.' He said: 'If you do not study Propriety you will not know how to stand by yourself.' I withdrew and studied Propriety. These are the two things that I have learned." Chen Kang was delighted and said: "I have received three answers for the price of one question: I have learned of the principles of the *Classic of Poetry* and of Propriety and I have also learned that a Gentleman does

not favor his son."

14. The wife of a ruler is called "Madam" (*furen*) by her spouse and a wife refers to herself as "Your child" (*xiao tong*); others address her as "Madam Ruler" (*jun furen*); in conversation with those from other states she is referred to as Madam Dowager (*gua xiaojun*) and those from other states refer to her as "Madam Ruler."

Yang Huo XVII

1. Yang Huo wished to see Kongzi but when Kongzi declined to receive him, he sent a roast suckling pig. Choosing a time when he would be absent, Kongzi paid a return visit but met him on the road. Yang Huo said: "Come! I must speak with you." Saying: "Would it be in accord with *Ren* to possess precious political ability but to allow the state to go to pot?" Kongzi said: "It would not." "Would it be called wise to possess the skill but to have allowed opportunities to escape?" Kongzi replied: "It would not." Yang Huo then said: "Time flies and waits for no one!" Kongzi said: "Then I will take office!"

2. The Master said: "Man's innate nature is common to all but becomes different through acquired experience."

3. The Master said: "Only the wisdom of the superior and the stupidity of the inferior are beyond improvement."

4. The Master visited Wucheng and listened to the sound of strings and song. The Master laughed and said: "Would you use a bullock knife to carve a chicken?" Ziyou replied: "I once heard you say: 'In studying ceremony and music the Gentleman comes to understand the love of man and the rogue becomes obedient.'" The Master said: "Disciples! Ziyou is right, I spoke in jest!"

5. Gongshan Furao occupied Fei in rebellion and called for

Kongzi who wished to go. Zilu was unwilling and said: "Why should you wish to go to Gongshan?" Kongzi said: "Can it be that calling for me is merely an empty gesture? If there are those who will employ me I will re-establish the Zhou dynasty in the East!"

6. Zizhang asked Kongzi about *Ren*. Kongzi said: "To practice these five beneath heaven, that is *Ren*." Zizhang enquired and the Master said: "Respect, magnanimity, Integrity, diligence, and compassion. Respect brings no insult, magnanimity secures support, Integrity brings appointment, diligence brings speedy achievement and compassion bestows the ability to lead others."

7. Bi Xi summoned Kongzi, and the Master intended to go. Zilu said: "In the past, I have heard you say 'The Gentleman does not visit those who themselves have done evil.' Bi Xi has rebelled and occupied the city of Zhongmou but you are going, why is this?" The Master said: "That is so, the words are mine. But is there not 'strength' that cannot be ground down or 'whiteness' that cannot be dyed black? Am I a gourd that hangs there and cannot be eaten?"

8. The Master said: "Zilu, have you heard of the Six Words and Six Ill Consequences?" "No." "Sit and I will tell you: to love *Ren* but not study has the ill consequence of stupidity; to love knowledge but not learning has the ill consequence of lack of restraint; to love Integrity but not study has the ill consequence of confusion; to love frankness but not study has the ill consequence of injurious speech; to love courage but not study, has the ill consequence of disorder; to love strength but not study has the ill consequence of wild arrogance."

9. The Master said: "Young men! Why do you not study poetry? Poetry can express your inner feelings, can show you all in nature's world, can join you with others and can express your grief. It can serve your parents at home and your ruler abroad

and teach you the names of birds, beasts, plants and trees."

10. The Master said to his son Kong Li: "Do you know the "Zhou Nan" and the "Shao Nan," if people do not know these two, isn't it like standing facing a wall?"

11. The Master said: "Propriety! Propriety! Is it just jade and silk? Music! Music! Is it just bells and drums?"

12. The Master said: "Tough on the outside and weak inside, when compared with a rogue, would that be like a thief who bores a hole through a wall?"

13. The Master said: "The outwardly amiable who lack a sense of right and wrong are the ruin of Virtue!"

14. The Master said: "To listen to street gossip and spread it is an abandonment of morality!"

15. The Master said: "How should one serve a ruler with colleagues of base character? Having not yet gained it, fearful of not gaining; having gained it, then fearful of losing. Once they fear loss, they are capable of anything."

16. The Master said: "The people of the past had three defects, today they are different. In the past madness was merely wild, now it is licentious; in the past the proud were merely aloof now they are arrogant; in the past a fool was merely stupid, now he is crafty."

17. The Master said: "Honeyed words and a fine appearance, where is the *Ren* in that!"

18. The Master said; "I loathe the fact that purple has replaced red, that the decadent sounds of the Zheng state have disturbed the elegance of music and I loathe those that use facile eloquence to subvert the state."

19. The Master said: "I desire not to speak." Zigong said: "If you do not speak, then what may your disciples pass on?" The Master said: "Must heaven needs speak? Yet the four seasons proceed and all things grow. Must heaven needs speak?"

20. Ru Bei wished to call on Kongzi, but Kongzi declined to

receive him on the grounds of illness. As the messenger came out of the gate, Kongzi took up his harp and sang to it so that Ru Bei could hear.

21. Zai Wo asked: "Three years mourning is a long time! If a Gentleman does not perform ceremonies for three years, the ceremonies will collapse; if he does not practice music for three years, music will be abandoned. For the old grain to be exhausted and the new grain to reach market and for the fire-drill to need replacing a year is enough." The Master said: "Would you be easy in your mind eating new rice and wearing brocade?" Zai Wo said: "I would." The Master said: "That being so, then do it! When the Gentleman observes mourning he eats but tastes nothing, takes no joy in music, lives in leisure but feels no comfort and so does not do as you would. Since you now feel as you do, then do it!" Zai Wo withdrew. The Master said: "Zai Wo is without *Ren!* A child does not leave the embrace of its mother and father until the age of three. Three years of mourning is observed everywhere. Did not Zai Wo receive three years of love from his mother and father?"

22. The Master said: "To eat well each day, to have nothing to occupy the mind, that is difficult! A game of chess would be worthy!"

23. Zilu said: "Does a Gentleman esteem courage?" The Master said: "The Gentleman puts Righteousness first. For a Gentleman to possess courage but not Righteousness would be disorder. A rogue with courage but not Righteousness would be a robber."

24. Zigong said: "Master, are there things that you hate?" The Master said: "Indeed there are: I hate those who speak evil of others, I hate those who mock their betters, I hate those who are courageous but are without Propriety, and I hate those who are resolute but obstinate and inflexible." The

Master then asked: "Zigong, are there things that you hate?" Zigong said: "I hate those who appropriate the work of others as their own, I hate those who regard lack of modesty as courage and I hate those who attack others but regard themselves as upright."

25. The master said: "Only women and rogues are difficult to train! Near and they show you no respect, far and they complain."

26. The Master said: "To be loathed at 40, that really is the end!"

Weizi XVIII

1. Weizi was forced to flee and Jizi became a slave, Bigan remonstrated and was killed. Kongzi said: "There were three possessed of *Ren* in the Yin dynasty!"

2. Liu Xiahui was a prison official and was dismissed three times. Someone said: "Why do you not leave the state of Lu?" He replied: "If one serves a ruler properly, where might one go and not be dismissed thrice? If one is to serve a ruler unjustly, why must one needs leave the state of Lu?"

3. Duke Jing of Qi sought to keep Kongzi in his employ and said: "I cannot treat you like Jishi in the state of Lu but I can treat you as if you were between a senior and a junior minister." Later he said: "I am old and can use you no longer." Kongzi departed.

4. The state of Qi made a gift of dancing girls to the state of Lu. Ji Huanzi accepted them and did not attend court for three days. Kongzi left.

5. In the state of Chu, a madman Jieyu met his carriage and passed Kongzi singing: "Phoenix! Oh. Phoenix! Why so downcast on this day of virtuous fate? The past is beyond repair but the future gives time to repent. Enough! Enough! Those in

power are in peril!" Kongzi dismounted seeking to talk to him but he escaped and Kongzi was unable to speak with him.

6. Chang Ju and Jie Ni were plowing a field together, when Kongzi passed by and told Zilu to ask the way to the ford. Chang Ju said: "Who is it that is holding the reins?" Zilu said: "It is Kong Qiu." "Kong Qiu of Lu?"asked Chang Ju. Zilu said: "It is." "Then he should know the way to the ford!" said Chang Ju. Zilu then asked Jie Ni. Jie Ni said: "And who might you be?" Zilu replied: "I am Zilu." "The pupil of Kong Qiu?" asked Jie Ni. "I am." replied Zilu. Jie Ni then said: "The world rains disaster and who will change it? Rather than follow one who wishes to escape evil people, would it not be better to be as carefree as those who flee society?" So saying, he carried on plowing. Zilu returned and told Kongzi who said in disappointment: "Man cannot live with birds and beasts, if one cannot live with people with whom may one be? Heaven has its principle and I cannot change it."

7. Zilu fell behind and met an old man carrying a bamboo weeding tool suspended from a pole over his shoulder. Zilu asked: "Have you seen the Master?" The old man replied: "My limbs are heavy and I cannot tell one crop from another, tell me, who is the Master?" So saying, he stuck his pole in the ground and began weeding. Zilu stood there and saluted him. The old man took Zilu home, killed a chicken to eat with millet and introduced his two sons. The next day Zilu took to the road and told Kongzi. The Master said: "He was a hermit." He told Zilu to go back and see him. Zilu returned but the old man had left. Zilu said: "It is not right not to be an official. The manners between young and old should not be abandoned, how can the relationship between ruler and minister be of no concern? To be concerned just with the purity of self throws human relationships into chaos. The Gentleman becomes an official so as to practice Righteousness. As to the difficulty of implementing the Grand

Principle, that has been known all along."

8. Those worthies have become scattered amongst the people are: Boyi, Shuqi, Yuzhong, Yiyi, Zhuzhang. Liu Xiahui and Shaolian. The Master said: "Those who did not compromise their ideals nor bring shame upon themselves were, perhaps, Boyi and Shuqi?" As to Liu Xiahui and Shaolian, he said: "They compromised their ideals and brought shame upon themselves but they spoke in accordance with the law and acted after consideration, that was the way it was!" Of Yuzhong and Yiyi, he said: "Living as a hermit and speaking at will and yet to retain purity and self respect is to abandon the petty shifts of life. I am not the same, there is nothing that I may venture, and nothing that I may not venture."

9. The Master of Music Zhi fled to the state of Qi, Gan, the director of the second banquet ensemble fled to the state of Chu, Liao, the director of the third ensemble fled to the state of Cai, Que, the director of the fourth ensemble fled to the state of Qin. The master drummer Fang Shu reached the Yellow river and Wu, the drummer of the small drums reached the Han river. The deputy master of music Yang and Xiang, the master of the chimes reached the sea.

10. Duke Zhou said to Duke Lu: "A ruler does not neglect his relatives nor cause ministers to complain at lack of trust. Provided that old friends are without blame they should not be discarded. One should not put one's faith in one man alone."

11. In the Zhou dynasty there were eight worthy of the title of Scholar: Boda, Boshi, Botu, Zhonghu, Shuye, Shuxia, Jisui and Jigua.

Zizhang XIX

1. Zizhang said: "The Scholar will offer his life in the face of

danger; will consider morality when he encounters advantage; will consider decorum at sacrificial ceremonies and grief in mourning. This is appropriate."

2. Zizhang said: "To possess Virtue yet not to promote it, to believe in the Grand Principle yet not to be steadfast in it, can this be morality? Can this be steadfastness?"

3. A disciple of Zixia asked Zizhang about friendship. Zizhang said: "What does Zixia say?" The disciple replied: "He said: 'One can be friends with those with whom one may and reject those with whom one may not.'" Zizhang said: "This is not the same as I have heard. The Gentleman respects the worthy and tolerates all, praises the virtuous and pities the incapable. Were I to be worthy, what would there be that others could not tolerate and were I to be unworthy and people rejected me, how then could I reject others?"

4. Zixia said: "Though there may be something to be gained from minor skills they are of little account in the long run and for this reason the Gentleman does not employ them."

5. Zixia said: "To learn each day that which one did not know, every month to remember that which has been learnt, that may be called love of learning."

6. Zixia said: "There is *Ren* in broad study and a steadfast will, in careful questioning and deep thought."

7. Zixia said: "The craftsman works in a workshop in order to learn his trade, the Gentleman studies to realize the Grand Principle."

8. Zixia said: "The rogue will always conceal his mistakes."

9. Zixia said: "There are three changes in aspect for a Gentleman: he appears dignified when viewed from a distance, he may appear warm and approachable when close up and serious in speech when giving instruction."

10. Zixia said: "The ruler must first gain the trust of the people, then he can demand their labor; otherwise they will feel

oppressed. He must gain their trust before admonishing them; otherwise they will feel ill used."

11. Zixia said: "In the large, the limits of morality may not be crossed, in the small one may to and fro."

12. Ziyou said: "Zixia's disciples are very good at sweeping up and can manage replies to questions and greeting and seeing off visitors. But these are minor details, the basis is not there, what is to be done?" Zixia heard and said: "Ha! Ziyou speaks in error! The principles of the Master, how they should be transmitted and how strengthened, are like the distinction between grass and trees. How can the principles of the Master be distorted at will? Only a sage can teach them from beginning to end!"

13. Zixia said: "In office if there is effort to spare, then study, in study if there is effort to spare, then seek office."

14. Ziyou said: "Mourn until grief is exhausted."

15. Ziyou said: "My friend Zizhang has rare ability but he does not achieve *Ren*."

16. Zeng Can said: "Zizhang is very grand in appearance but a difficult man with whom to seek *Ren*."

17. Zeng Can said: "I heard the Master say: 'People rarely unburden their feelings, should they do so, it must be at the death of mother and father!'"

18. Zeng Xi said: "I heard the Master say that the Filial Piety of Meng Zhuangzi could be emulated by others but it was difficult for them to attain the way in which he did not alter the rules and precepts of his father and older ministers."

19. Meng Yizi appointed Yang Fu director of prisons and Yang Fu sought guidance from Zeng Can. Zeng Can said: "If those in power depart from the correct way, then the spirit of the people is lost. To know true reality is to feel pity rather than joy."

20. Zigong said: "The wickedness of Zhou was not as bad as recounted. Consequently a ruler does not place himself in a degrading position lest evil repute should engulf him."

21. Zigong said: "The mistakes of a Gentleman are like an eclipse of the sun or moon. Everybody sees them but when they are corrected, all admire."

22. Gongsun Chao of Wei asked Zigong: "How did Kongzi acquire his learning?" Zigong said: "The teachings of King Wen and King Wu are with us still and have not been lost. The worthy know them in the main and the unworthy know them a little and these teachings of the kings are everywhere. How could the Master not have acquired learning? There is no set teacher who instructs."

23. Shusun Wushu said to the ministers at court: "Zigong is more worthy than Kongzi." Zifu Jingbo told Zigong of this. Zigong said: "It's rather like the wall round a house, my wall is shoulder height and you can look in and readily see the fine appearance of the house; the Master's wall is higher by several measures, unless you can find the door and enter, you cannot see the splendor of the temple or the beauty of the buildings. There are few that can find the door and enter. Is it not natural that Shusun Wushu speaks as he does?"

24. Shusun Wushu vilified Kongzi. Zigong said: "This cannot be done! Kongzi is not to be slandered. The virtues of others resemble a range of hills that can be crossed; those of Kongzi are like the sun and the moon and are insurmountable. What harm can befall the sun and the moon if people do not wish to see them? It merely shows how they overestimate their own abilities!"

25. Ziqin of the stae of Chen said to Zigong: "You are a man of respect and modesty, how can it be that Kongzi exceeds you in virtue?" Zigong said: "The Gentleman could show his wisdom in a single word and his ignorance in a single word. Speech must always be cautious! The unattainability of Kongzi resembles an ascent to heaven without stairs. If the Master secured appointments under the vassal princes and ministers

it was like the saying: 'If there is establishment then the system that is established will succeed, if there is leadership then the people will follow, if there is pacification then the peoples at a distance will submit; if there is mobilization then people will respond. In life, glory. In death, grief.' This being so, how could I possibly attain his level?"

Yao Yue XX

1. Yao said: "Oh, Shun! The Mandate of Heaven has fallen upon you. Justly exercise impartiality! Should those within the four seas suffer, then heaven's bounty will be withdrawn from you forever." When Shun yielded his throne to Yu he passed this mandate to him. (Shang Tang) said: "I, King Lü of Shang, sacrifice a black bull and promise the Emperor of Heaven that I will not, of my own accord, dare pardon the guilty nor dare conceal the crimes of officials. All is known to the heart of the Emperor of Heaven. If I offend, do not visit it upon the people, if the people offend then the guilt is mine." (King Wu of Zhou) said: "The House of Zhou bestows great gifts upon its vassals and the virtuous are honored. Though there is a royal family, it is better to employ those with *Ren*. If the people offend, it is upon my head." Carefully institute a system of measures, set up laws and statutes, reform official posts and the writ of government will run throughout the land. Raise the nations that have fallen, continue the clans that have been destroyed, use the talents of the people that have been scattered and all the peoples under heaven will obey. Pay attention to the people, to supplies of food, to funeral ceremonies, and to sacrifices. Magnanimity will secure the support of the people. Integrity will secure their trust. Diligence will secure achievement and fairness will bring joy.

2. Zizhang asked Kongzi: "How may government be administered?" The Master said: "Respect the five good principles and reject the four evils, thus can government be administered." Zizhang said: "What are the five good principles?" The Master said: "That the ruler should be benevolent but not wasteful, he should cause the people to labor without hatred, that they should not be avaricious in their desires, that splendor should not be accompanied by arrogance, and that majesty should not be cruel." Zizhang said: "What is benevolent but not wasteful?" The Master said: "To cause the people to profit from their own interests, is that not benevolence without waste? To choose labor that can be undertaken at the right season, who may hate that? To desire *Ren* and to achieve it, what more may be desired? That the ruler, no matter in the many or the few, in the large or the small, should not be neglectful, is this not splendor without arrogance? That a ruler should be careful in his dress and comport himself with gravity so that people hold his dignity in awe, is this not majesty without cruelty?" Zizhang said: "What are the four evils?" The Master said: "To slaughter without civilizing is called cruelty: to demand success without warning is called violence; to demand completion without supervision is called disaster, to be stingy in disbursements is called pettiness."

3. The Master said: "Not to understand the Mandate of Heaven is to be unable to become a Gentleman; not to understand Propriety is to be unable to stand by oneself; not to divine the speech of others is to be unable to understand people."

INDEX OF PERSONALITIES

Bi Chen A minister of the state of Zheng.

Bigan An uncle of King Zhou who forcefully argued with him and was killed by the king in a fit of fury.

Bi Xi Household minister of Zhao Jianzi who held the territory of Zhongmu.

Bian Zhuangzi Minister of the state of Lu who resided in the town of Bian.

Boniu Ran Geng, surname Ran, given name Geng, style name Boniu. Inhabitant of the state of Lu and a disciple of Kongzi's early period.

Bo Shi A minister of the state of Qi.

Boyi, Shuqi Two brothers, ancient worthies who each gave way to the other without ascending the throne. In the end, because of their opposition to King Wu of Zhou's punitive expedition against King Zhou and rather than "Eat the grain of Zhou" they perished of starvation in the mountains of Shouyang.

Chang Ju Hermit and person of talent whom Kongzi met on his peregrination through the states.

Chen Chengzi Surname Chen, given name Heng, minister of the state of Qi. He assassinated Duke Jian of Qi and seized power.

Chen Kang Style name Ziqin, disciple of Kongzi's later period, frequent questioner of Kongzi on matters of learning.

Chen Wenzi Given name Xuwu, minister of the state of Chen.

Cui Zhu Minister of the state of Qi and assassin of Duke Zhuang of Qi.

Duke Ai Duke Ai of Lu, surname Ji, given name Jiang, ruler of the state of Lu. "Ai" was his posthumous title. On the throne when Kongzi returned to Lu in his old age.

Duke Chu of Wei Given name Zhe, Duke Ling of Wei's grandson. His father had been banished for plotting the assassination of Nanzi, Duke Ling's wife. Zhe became ruler on the death of Duke Ling.

Duke Ding Surname Ji, given name Song, ruler of the state of Lu, "Ding" was his posthumous title. He appointed Kongzi minister of justice and concurrently prime minister.

Duke Huan of Qi Surname Jiang, given name Xiaobai, ruler of the state of Qi. One of the hegemonic rulers of the Spring and Autumn period.

Duke Jian of Qi Surname Jiang, given name Ren. Ruler of the state of Qi.

Duke Jing of Qi Given name Chujiu. Ruler of the state of Qi. He sought, unsuccessfully, to employ Kongzi when the latter was in Qi.

Duke Ling of Wei Surname Ji, given name Yuan. Ruler of the state of Wei.

Duke Lu Refers to Boqin the son of Duke Zhou who succeeded his father as ruler of Lu.

Duke Wen of Jin Surname Ji, given name Zhong'er, ruler of the state of Jin. One of the hegemonic rulers of the Spring and Autumn period.

Duke Ye Surname Shen, given name Zhuliang, style name Zigao. Minister of the state of Chu, known as Duke Ye because he had been granted the fief of Ye.

Duke Zhao Ruler of the state of Lu, given name Chou, "Zhao" was his posthumous title.

Duke Zhou Surname Ji, given name Dan, son of King Wen of Zhou and younger brother of King Wu of Zhou, founder of the state of Lu and initiator of the Western Zhou system of ceremony and music.

Fan Chi Surname Fan, given name Xu, style name Zichi. Inhabitant of the state of Lu. A young disciple of Kongzi's early period.

Gongbo Liao Style name Zizhou, a disciple of Kongzi, somewhat lacking in moral character.

Gongming Jia Surname Gong, given name Zijia. A minister of the state of Wei.

Gongshan Furao Also known as Gongshan Buniu, household

minister of Ji Kangzi. See Ji Kangzi.

Gongshu Wenzi Surname Gongsun, given name Ba, a minister of the state of Wei.

Gongsun Chao Surname Gongsun, given name Chao, a minister of the state of Wei.

Gongxi Hua Surname Gongxi, given name Chi, style name Zihua, son of a wealthy family, inhabitant of the state of Lu and a comparatively young disciple of Kongzi's early period.

Gongye Chang Surname Gongye, given name Chang, style name Zichang, inhabitant of the state of Qi and an early disciple of Kongzi.

Guan Zhong Surname Guan, given name Yiwu, style name Zhong. Well known minister of the state of Qi who helped Duke Huan of Qi become hegemonic ruler of the vassal princes. See also Prince Jiu and Duke Huan of Qi.

Huan Tui Minister of war in the state of Song.

Jie Ni Hermit and person of talent whom Kongzi met on his peregrination through the states.

Jieyu A madman of the state of Chu.

Ji Huanzi Surname Jisun, given name Si, power-holder of the state of Lu.

Ji Kangzi Surname Jisun, given name Fei, also called Jishi. Minister of the state of Lu, "Kang" was his posthumous title.

When in power he called Kongzi back from his travels but, in the end, could not employ him.

Ji Wenzi Surname Jisun, given name Xingfu, Duke Cheng of Lu's most senior minister. "Wen" was his posthumous title.

Jizi Uncle of King Zhou who remonstrated with him without success, feigned madness, and was finally enslaved.

Ji Zicheng Minister of the state of Wei.

Ji Ziran A member of Jishi's clan in the state of Lu and also believed to be one of Kongzi's disciples.

Jing Surname Ji, given name Jing, style name Nanchu, son of the duke of Wei.

King Gao Zong of the Shang dynasty The Shang king Wu Zong, also known as Wu Ding.

King Wen of Zhou Surname Ji, given name Chang, father of King Wu of Zhou, the founder of the Zhou dynasty.

King Wu of Zhou Surname Ji, given name Fa, founder of the Zhou dynasty.

Kong Li Kongzi's son. Surname Kong, given name Li, style name Boyu.

Kong Wenzi Surname Zhongshu, given name Yu. A minister of the state of Wei. "Wen" was his posthumous title.

Lao Said to have been a disciple of Kongzi.

Lao Peng Unclear, possibly a worthy of the Yin or Shang dynasties.

Lin Fang Style name Ziqiu, an inhabitant of the state of Lu. Reputed to have been a disciple of Kongzi.

Liu Xiahui Surname Zhan, given name Huo. Style name Qin. His fiefdom was known as "Under the Willows." Hui was his personal posthumous style so he was called "Hui Under the Willows." One of the worthies of the state of Lu.

Meng Gongchuo A minister of the state of Lu. A worthy whom Kongzi respected.

Meng Jingzi Surname Mengsun, given name Jie. A minister of the state of Lu.

Meng Wubo Surname Zhongsun, given name Zhi. A minister of the state of Lu and son of Meng Yizi, his posthumous title was "Wu."

Meng Yizi Surname Zhongsun, given name Heji. "Yi" was his posthumous title. A Lu aristocrat and member of the Mengsun clan. An early disciple of Kongzi. His father, on his deathbed, urged him to study Propriety under Kongzi.

Meng Zhifan A minister of the state of Lu.

Meng Zhuangzi Surname Mengsun, given name Su. A minister of the state of Lu.

Min Ziqian Surname Min, given name Sun, style name Ziqian. Inhabitant of the state of Lu and early disciple of Kongzi with a reputation for Filial Piety.

Nan Rong Surname Nangong, given name Kuo, style name Zirong. Inhabitant of the state of Lu and early disciple of Kongzi.

Nanzi The wife of Duke Ling of Wei, renowned for her beauty. Actual political control of the state of Wei lay in her hands.

Ning Wuzi Surname Ning, given name Yu. A minister of the state of Lu. "Wu" was his posthumous title.

Prince Jiu Crown Prince of the state of Qi and elder brother of Duke Huan of Qi with whom he competed for the throne. Eventually assassinated. Guan Zhong was one of his household ministers.

Qidiao Kai Surname Qidiao, given name Kai. Style name Zikai. Inhabitant of the state of Lu and early disciple of Kongzi.

Qu Boyu A minister of the state of Wei. Kongzi stayed with him when in Wei.

Ran You Surname Ran, given name Qiu, style name Ziyou. An early disciple of Kongzi.

Ru Bei Inhabitant of the state of Lu. Little is known of his life but it is said that Duke Ai of Lu sent him to study Propriety with Kongzi.

Shao Hu Like Guan Zhong, one of Prince Jiu's household ministers. See also under Prince Jiu.

Shen Cheng Also with given name Dang and style name Zhou. Inhabitant of the state of Lu and disciple of Kongzi.

Shi Shu Surname You, given name Ji. A minister of the state of Zheng.

Shi Yu Given name Qiu, style name Ziyu. A minister of the state of Wei.

Shun The sage king who succeeded Yao.

Shusun Wushu Given name Zhouqiu. A minister of the state of Lu.

Sima Niu Surname Sima, given name Geng, style name Ziniu. Inhabitant of the state of Song and a younger disciple of Kongzi's early period.

Song Zhao Crown prince of the state of Song and reputedly good-looking.

Taibo Eldest son of Gugong Danfu, first ancestor of the Zhou dynasty. Knowing that his father intended to pass the throne to his third youngest brother Jili (the father of King Wen), he and his second youngest brother left the territories of Wu.

Tantai Mieming Style name Ziyu. Inhabitant of the state of Lu and disciple of Kongzi's later period.

Wangsun Jia Minister to Duke Ling of Wei.

Weisheng Gao Surname Weisheng, given name Gao. An inhabitant of Lu with a reputation for straightforwardness.

Weisheng Mu Inhabitant of the state of Lu. A somewhat reclusive figure of whom little is known.

Weizi Half-brother to King Zhou of the Yin dynasty who unsuccessfully remonstrated with him a number of times and finally left.

Wuma Qi One of Kongzi's disciples. Surname Wuma, given name Shi, style name Ziqi.

Wu Mengzi Wife of Duke Zhao of Lu.

Xun A household official of Gongshu Wenzi.

Yan Lu Surname Yan, given name Wuyou, style name Lu. Inhabitant of the state of Lu, early disciple of Kongzi and father of Yan Yuan.

Yan Pingzhong Yanzi, Surname Yan, given name Ying, style name Pingzhong. Well known minister of the state of Qi with a reputation as a worthy.

Yan Yuan Surname Yan, given name Hui, style name Yuan. Inhabitant of the state of Lu. One of the most important disciples of Kongzi's early period. His understanding of Kongzi's thought was the most profound. He was the disciple of whom Kongzi was the most fond but unfortunately he died early.

Yang Fu Disciple of Zeng Can. See under Zeng Can.

Yang Huo A comptroller for the Ji family who once held power in the state of Lu.

Yao The most famous of China's ancient mythological kings.

You Ruo Style name Ziyou. Inhabitant of the state of Lu and a disciple of Kongzi's later period.

Yu Mythological king who succeeded Shun and first ruler of the Xia dynasty.

Yuan Rang Inhabitant of the state of Lu and possibly fellow countryman of Kongzi.

Yuan Xian Style name Zisi. Inhabitant of the state of Lu and comparatively young disciple of Kongzi's early period.

Zai Wo Surname Zai, given name Yu, style name Ziwo. Inhabitant of the state of Lu and disciple of Kongzi's early period who held unorthodox and rebellious views and attitudes and enjoyed challenging the theories of his teacher.

Zang Wenzhong Surname Zangsun, given name Chen. Inhabitant of the state of Lu. His posthumous title was "Wen."

Zang Wuzhong Surname Zangsun, given name Ge. Inhabitant of the state of Lu.

Zeng Can Style name Ziyu. Inhabitant of the state of Lu and an important disciple of Kongzi's late period.

Zeng Xi Surname Zeng, given name Dian, style name Zixi. Inhabitant of the state of Lu. Early disciple of Kongzi and father of Zeng Can.

Zhi Music master of the state of Lu.

Zhonggong Surname Ran, given name Yong, style name Zhonggong. Inhabitant of the state of Lu, a comparatively young disciple of Kongzi's early period.

Zhongshu Yu See under Kong Wenzi.

Zhu Tuo Style name Ziyu. Minister of the state of Wei, reputed to have been skilled in argument.

Zichan Surname Gongsun, given name Qiao, style name Zichan. Worthy and minister of the state of Zheng who was in power and ruled the state for over 20 years.

Zifu Jingbo A minister of the state of Lu, posthumous title Jing.

Zigao Surname Gao, given name Chai, style name Zigao. Inhabitant of the state of Wei and comparatively young disciple of Kongzi's early years.

Zigong Surname Duanmu, given name Ci, style name Zigong. Inhabitant of the state of Wei and one of the most important disciples of Kongzi's early period. Skilled in both government and commerce. After the death of Kongzi he built a hut by his grave and kept vigil there alone for six years.

Zijian Surname Fu, given name Buqi, style name Zijian. Inhabitant of the state of Lu and comparatively young disciple of Kongzi's early years.

Zilu Surname Zhong, given name You, style names Zilu and Jilu. Inhabitant of the state of Lu and one of the most important disciples of Kongzi's early years. He was renowned for Loyalty and courage. He was always at Kongzi's side but finally perished in a *coup d'etat* in the state of Wei.

Ziqin See Chen Kang.

Zisang Bozi Also called Sanghu, Zisanghu. A hermetic figure of whose life little is known. A man who esteemed brevity and simplicity.

Ziwen Famous prime minister of the state of Chu. Surname Dou, given name Gou, style name Yutu.

Zixi Should refer to Gongsun Xia, brother of Zichan and in power after Zichan.

Zixia Surname Bu, given name Shang, style name Zixia. Inhabitant of the state of Jin and important pupil of Kongzi's later years.

Ziyou Surname Yan, given name Yan, style name Ziyou. Inhabitant of the state of Wu. An important disciple of Kongzi's later period.

Ziyu Surname Gongsun, given name Hui, style name Ziyu. A minister of the state of Zheng.

Zizhang Surname Zhuansun, given name Shi, style name Zizhang. Inhabitant of the state of Chen, an important pupil of Kongzi's later period.

Zuoqiu Ming Surname Zuoqiu, given name Ming. Inhabitant of the state of Lu. A worthy.

This book is edited and designed by the Editorial Committee of *Cultural China* series

Compiled by Qian Ning
Translated by Tony Blishen
Cover Image by Quanjing
Designed by Diane Davies, Wang Wei

Editor: Zhang Yicong
Editorial Director: Zhang Yicong

Senior Consultants: Sun Yong, Wu Ying, Yang Xinci
Managing Director: Wang Youbu

ISBN: 978-1-60220-146-0

Address any comments about *The New Analects: Confucius Reconstructed* to:

Better Link Press
99 Park Ave
New York, NY 10016
USA

or

Shanghai Press and Publishing Development Company
F 7 Donghu Road, Shanghai, China (200031)
Email: comments_betterlinkpress@hotmail.com

Printed in China by Shenzhen Donnelley Printing Co., Ltd.

1 3 5 7 9 10 8 6 4 2